Building
Knowledge Cultures

Critical Education Policy and Politics
Series Editor: Michael A. Peters

This series focuses on current issues in education. Books will explore the development of the new educational policies and practices that are changing the structure and functions of educational institutions—primary, secondary, and higher—both here and abroad. In the United States, the new federal involvement in primary and secondary education, most conspicuously in passage of the No Child Left Behind legislation, has brought a new era of testing and accountability while raising questions about the role of schools in promoting social inclusion and providing basic training for the new "information" economy. Books will explore such hot topics as charter schools, testing, vouchers and tax deductions for education, teacher education and the teaching profession, and public private competition, to name a few.

Titles in the Series:

Building Knowledge Cultures

Education and Development in the Age of Knowledge Capitalism

Michael A. Peters with A.C. (Tina) Besley

ROWMAN & LITTLEFIELD PUBLISHERS, INC.
Lanham • Boulder • New York • Toronto • Oxford

ROWMAN & LITTLEFIELD PUBLISHERS, INC.

Published in the United States of America
by Rowman & Littlefield Publishers, Inc.
A wholly owned subsidary of The Rowman & Littlefield Publishing Group, Inc.
4501 Forbes Boulevard, Suite 200, Lanham, Maryland 20706
www.rowmanlittlefield.com

PO Box 317
Oxford
OX2 9RU, UK

British Library Cataloguing in Publication Information Available

Library of Congress Cataloging-in-Publication Data

Peters, Michael A.
  Building knowledge cultures : education and development in the age of
knowledge capitalism / Michael A. Peters with A.C. (Tina) Besley.
    p. cm. — (Critical education policy and politics)
  Includes bibliographical references and index.
  ISBN-10: 0-7425-1790-X (cloth : alk. paper)
  ISBN-10: 0-7425-1791-8 (pbk. : alk. paper)
  ISBN-13: 978-0-7425-1790-5 (cloth : alk. paper)
  ISBN-13: 978-0-7425-1791-2 (pbk. : alk. paper)
  1. Education—Economic aspects. 2. Knowledge management—Economic
aspects. 3. Knowledge, Sociology of. 4. Postmodernism and education.
I. Besley, Tina, 1950– II. Title. III. Series.
  LC65.P47 2006
  338.4'737—dc22   2005032025

Printed in the United States of America

∞ ™ The paper used in this publication meets the minimum requirements of
American National Standard for Information Sciences—Permanence of Paper
for Printed Library Materials, ANSI/NISO Z39.48-1992.

Contents

List of Tables

Preface and
Acknowledgments

First, I would like to take this opportunity to acknowledge and thank my coauthor, Tina Besley, who discussed most of the ideas in this book with me and wrote substantial chunks of text and most of the chapter entitled "The Theater of Fast Knowledge: Performative Epistemologies," which she presented at the Oxford University conference of the Philosophy of Education Society of Great Britain in 2004. Tina has been my constant intellectual companion, and I am indebted to her beyond words. She brings a critical realism to our joint deliberations, together with a wealth of experience and scholarship.

I would also like to acknowledge the research committee of the Faculty of Education at the University of Glasgow, which in its wisdom decided to grant me a small internal research grant to advance this project. While my research has been supported by the faculty at the University of Glasgow under the RAE (Research Assessment Exercise) imperative, the decision makers are more interested in counting my publications than in reading them. At the same time, I have been told by those in authority with engineering and science backgrounds that my work is too scholarly, too abstract and obtuse, and not sufficiently grounded in "useful knowledge." ("What on earth is the *use* of Foucault to education?" I have been asked on more than one occasion). I guess I have to be prepared to wear these charges and let readers judge for themselves. And yet I am deeply suspicious of a knowledge culture that is driven by the ideology of "useful knowledge," a shallow and ultimately misleading kind of pragmatism of "what works" based on the value of research grants rather than the value of ideas, and one that is more symptomatic of an industrial model of research and education than one designed for the creative knowledge economy. For those who come to the field of education imbued with the scientific spirit based on an outdated logical empiricism, wanting to discover "laws" or incontrovertible evidence that such and such is the case, I encourage them to read some of the original members of the Vienna Circle, who were never so unsophisticated and foolish as those who parade their ideas, sometimes implicitly and unknowingly.

Finally, I would like to thank Dean Birkenkamp, who commissioned the contract for this book now some considerable period ago when he was still acquisitions editor at Rowman & Littlefield, and Alan McClare who took over from Dean to help bring the project to fruition.

Some chapters have seen the light of day as published papers. A version of chapter 3 appears as "Education Policy in the Age of Knowledge Capitalism" in *Policy Futures in Education*, vol. 1, no. 2, pp. 361–80; a version of chapter 4 appears in *Journal of Educational Inquiry*, vol. 2, no. 1, pp. 1–22; a version of chapter 5 appears as "Classical Political Economy and the Role of University in the New Knowledge Society" in *Globalisation, Societies and Education*, vol. 1, no. 2, pp. 153–68; a version of chapter 6 appears as "The Theatre of Fast Knowledge: Performative Epistemologies in Higher Education" in *The Review of Education, Pedagogy and Cultural Studies*, vol. 27, no. 2, pp. 111–26; a version of chapter 8 appears in P. Smeyers and M. Depaepe, eds., *Beyond Empiricism: On Criteria for Educational Research*; and a version of chapter 10 appears in *Journal of Future Studies*, vol. 8, no. 1, pp. 39–52.

Michael A. Peters
San Francisco
April 2004

Introduction: Building Knowledge Cultures

Some books are written with great ease at a lightning pace. Some books are written in fits and starts, almost episodically. And some books resist their form and fight all the way. This is such a book. It has taken us much longer than we anticipated from when we first thought of composing a book on the knowledge economy and the role of education within it. We first entertained the idea for this book back in the late 1990s, when we started publishing on the topic in academic journals. These early efforts represented the unusual combination of our joint interests in contemporary public policy, French philosophy, and, in particular, the development of poststructuralist views in relation to education policy in the knowledge economy. To us, education policy is the critical area in relation to the development of what we call *knowledge cultures*, for achieving the ambitions of the knowledge economy, and also for mitigating its worst inequalities. To be able to think imaginatively about the role, form, provision, funding, and mode of education in all its aspects will define the society we inhabit in the next millennium.

In 2001, Michael Peters wrote a book entitled *Poststructuralism, Marxism and Neoliberalism: Between Politics and Theory* (Peters 2001c), which encapsulated his critical arguments against the megaparadigm of neoliberal economics and its steady extension into all forms of life and human endeavor as the means of understanding the way we behave. Using poststructuralist arguments concerning the "philosophy of the subject"—the human subject, or "rational agent," as is demanded by economics—Peters attempted to demonstrate the critique of the main underlying assumptions governing *Homo economicus*. These assumptions, and particularly

1

the rationality assumption, have been subject to scathing treatment by Vivian Walsh (1996) in his *Rationality, Allocation and Reproduction*. He showed how neoclassical economics that prided itself on its neutrality and its avoidance of all metaphysical assumptions was merely adopting one of its latest forms, the metaphysics of logical positivism. The distinguished Harvard philosopher Hilary Putnam (2002) has recently reviewed the history and collapse of the fact-value distinction at the heart of positivist science and economics to argue that science itself presupposes values, albeit epistemic ones, that fall into the same boat as ethical ones when it comes to questions of "objectivity." He also effectively critiques the "completeness" assumption of rational choice theory. Philosophy and ethics are thus closer to economics than most mainstream economists would admit.

The assumptions of individuality, rationality, and self-interest all seemed to us to be strictly limited in conception and application, and philosophically impoverished when compared to the rich and complex developments of contemporary French philosophy and its critique of the subject in its Cartesian-Kantian, Hegelian, and phenomenological forms. By contrast to the rationalism and abstract individualism of neoclassical economics, the trajectory of French philosophy in the postwar period questioned all scientific pretensions to universal constructions while at the same time historicized questions of ontology (Foucault) to emphasize the subject in all its sociohistorical complexity. One of the aims of *Poststructuralism, Marxism and Neoliberalism* was also to demonstrate that poststructuralism is not anti-Marxist. Indeed, the book tried to show how the legacy of Marx's thinking still looms in the background and informs much of the theorizing we are now accustomed to in the work of thinkers like Deleuze, Foucault, and Derrida.

In this book, we have left the field of philosophy pretty well alone, at least in any explicit sense. Of course, it is not possible to write about the knowledge economy without presupposing concepts that stand in need of philosophical explication—"time," "space," "information," "knowledge," "freedom," "communication," "control." Part of the difficulty of writing such a book is due to a number of factors. First is the need to learn the language of economics, especially those fields closely related to the knowledge economy, including the economics of knowledge, information, science, and education. Second is the necessity of reading both the classics and the new works in these fields, not only Hayek, Becker, Stigler, and Stiglitz, but also advocates of endogenous growth theory and proponents of the new economy like Quah and Alcaly, among others. Third, there is the requirement in writing a book of this nature to traverse literatures in quite diverse disciplines—economics, certainly, and also sociology, public policy, epistemology, information science, education, and so on. Much of what is most exciting in this area is border territory among the disciplines and is dependent on ongoing developments in international law concerning emerging property rights regimes, the development of new trade protocols, telecommunications policies in comparative perspective, and network analysis in its various forms.

When we first started writing this book, the claims for the "new economy" had not yet been punctured by the collapse of the dot-com market in 2002, nor had corporate capitalism been scandalized by the corruption and fraud characterizing the collapse of Enron, WorldCom, or Parmalat. We started writing also before September 11, 2001, when the extremist terrorism of radical Islam struck at the heart of corporate capitalist America with its demolition of the Twin Towers and for the first time threatened the easy globalization of neoliberalism. And yet while talk of the new economy has subsided and no one now holds to the end of the business cycle, most commentators agree with Solow (1956) and Abramovitz (1956) that new technologies and innovations have fueled long-term productivity growth. While there is disagreement over the job-creation capacities of the new economy, its form and replicability outside the United States, and its distributed social benefits, the acceleration of sustained productivity growth appears undisputed. It seems clear that there is a strong though not invariant relationship between the new information and communication technologies on the one hand and innovation and productivity growth on the other. The adoption of the new technologies goes hand in hand with changed business practices and new ways of working. We are less concerned with examining the evidence of these claims than with exploring the consequences for education and development if they are taken as true. There are better minds than ours, more experienced and well placed, to review this evidence. We are more concerned with understanding what is involved in accepting claims about the new economy, what constitutes the knowledge economy, and what its consequences are for education policy.

In this endeavor, we are struck by a central paradox of the pervasiveness and increasing abstractness of information as the ultimate stuff of the universe, if we are to believe the likes of Hans Christian von Baeyer (2004), and its embodiment in rich, complex social relationships called *networks*, if we are to believe the likes of John Seely Brown and Paul Duguid (2002). Von Baeyer writes of "in-formation" as "the communication of relationships," and he speculates on the status of the "qubit" in quantum information. Brown and Duguid, by contrast, point to the social life of information and its development in "communities of practice." This brings us to emphasize our own conception of *knowledge cultures* as a central notion underwriting the thesis of this book. It is a view that resonates with a number of recent emphases in the literature: *The Future of Ideas* and the need to protect the freedom of the intellectual commons (Laurence Lessig 2002); *The Rise of the Creative Class* (Richard Florida 2002); and

Culture Matters: How Values Shape Human Progress (Lawrence E. Harrison and Samuel P. Huntington 2000). We shall take the opportunity of this introduction to briefly comment on these three books because they set the tone of so much that comes after. *The Future of Ideas* is a passionate defense of the intellectual commons which provides a model of development in terms of the model of a networked communication system with its layered complexity—physical infrastructure, code, and content—and discusses forthcoming culture wars at each level in terms of the metavalues of freedom and control. The case of Microsoft and how it fares in the EU is an instructive case study. The battle for the control of intellectual property is a policy issue both for the creation, generation, and development of knowledge, and for its use, transmission, storage, and retrieval. In order to progress this discussion, we need to know a great deal more about the production of academic knowledge and its uses, inevitably an issue that returns to its fundamental historical, economic, and cultural questions concerning a "work" and its "authorship." These questions in turn cannot evade the history of intellectual property and its modes of regulation and regimes emerging though the concepts of copyright, patent, and trade secrets. Insofar as the formation of the intellectual is closely tied to the development of literature as a public institution and to a reading public, the future of the intellectual will be determined by the ways in which questions of the authorship and ownership of knowledge are determined by the neoliberal university (see McSherry 2001).

In *The Rise of the Creative Class*, Richard Florida (2002, xiii) suggests that "human creativity is the ultimate economic resource." We are sure that Afghanistanis, Rwandans, or Ugandans will be pleased to hear this. Creativity or innovation in itself is no panacea. Historically, much of the "creativity" of the West, especially in the region of aesthetics, has come from other cultures, often regarded as primitive. These have acted as sources of cultural renewal. We are thinking of the history of modern art and literature in its search for the "primitive," the "exotic," and the "authentic"; its development as works and movements in the Western canon; and its translation and commodification as fashion and design goods. Florida's theory of the creative economy is based on an analysis that is Americentric: he plots the central importance of *place* as the key economic and social organizing unit of our time, as the ecosystem that harnesses human creativity and turns it into economic value. He also describes the emergence of a new social class as the fundamental source of innovation and economic growth. He charts the dimensions and new institutions of the creative economy, arguing that not only will it transform work, leisure, community, and everyday life, but that it is both possible and desirable to build the creative community. Florida suggests that it is possible to build a creative community by creating appropriate working conditions, by managing creativity, by encouraging the shift from social to creative capital, and by developing the city and university as creative hubs. While Florida's work is unabashedly utopian, we take from it both the geographical imperative and the notion that with appropriate investment and policies, it is possible to build what we prefer to call *knowledge cultures*, from whence creativity can flow.

This brings us to the final book and the last conceptual point we want to foreshadow in this introduction, focusing on the word *culture*, which in its various theoretical incarnations has resisted any easy definition. Lawrence E. Harrison and Samuel P. Huntington (2000) indicate how cultures count, how when social scientists try to explain "modernization, political democratization, military strategy, the behavior of ethnic groups, and the alignments and antagonisms among countries," they turn to cultural factors (xiv). Together they substitute the cultural paradigm, developed out of the Harvard academic symposium "The Cultural Values and Human Progress," as the basis for explaining both the successes and failures of economic development. While we are happily prepared to accept this obvious set of linkages, we are less happy to accept the link between values and progress, or the link between progress and the universality of values that Harrison and Huntington hold to. The concepts of "progress," "development," and the "universality of values" require a lot of philosophical work before we can even understand what precisely is being claimed, let alone its empirical testability. The implicit dangers of talking of "unproductive" or "uncreative" cultures also become an anthropological and political minefield. The question of knowledge cultures can be examined from the micro, meso-, or macro level, yet we are inclined to think that the question is best pursued in relation to the nature of institutions, rather than ethnic or even national cultures, although we have to recognize how policies of the "creative nation" or the "clever country" now encourage the process of cultural reconstruction in ways previously unthought of—not only the "creative nation," often a deliberate refashioning and renarrativizing of the past to serve present political purposes, but also the strategy to establish a new entrepreneurialism, a culture of innovation, and thereby move away from the so-called culture of dependency. "Culture" has become now as important as science, and cultural policy is no longer seen as separate and divorced from science policy, competing for the same limited public purse, but rather complementary and overlapping in its interests. Yet we must remain skeptical of these policy constructions that very often have few organic roots in communities and serve limited short-term political objectives.

"Culture" also has its explanatory force in relation to organizations and in defining organizational strategies and processes for collective learning. In its specialized sociological sense at the level of the "subculture," it is of inestimable help in understanding the sociology of youth and the processes of self-formation and identity development, and thus contributes to the outstanding problem in educational theory—the problem of the knowledge of other minds, as Jerome Bruner expresses it, that is, the problem of *intersubjectivity*, which is integral to both communication and any form of educational transaction.

1

Cultural Knowledge Economy: Education, the New Economy, and the Communicative Turn

THE COMMUNICATIVE TURN: DIGITALIZATION, SPEED, AND COMPRESSION

Increasingly the world is a global interconnected space of communication, or collections of such communicative spaces. This fundamental fact, with its multiple facets and consequences, has redefined economic development for countries of both the North and the South, and for both developing or transitional economies and those of advanced liberal capitalist states, and it will influence the direction of the global economy in the future. At the center of this development has been a set of cultural forces and intellectual movements that have been in train since the early twentieth century. First, the movement of European formalism, operating across disciplines of logic, mathematics, architecture, physics, economics, philosophy, linguistics, literature, aesthetics, and art, defined a new set of analytical tools and interdisciplinary applications that quickly impacted the technologies and infrastructures of communication and information. One aspect of this broad movement was the Vienna Circle and the rise of logical empiricism that developed out of the logicism of Frege and Russell and involved most of the prominent analytic philosophers of the twentieth century: Schlick, Reichenbach, Feigle, Ayer, Wittgenstein, Popper, and Quine. Many of these philosophers left Austria and Germany prior to World War II to escape the German invasion and settled in American or British philosophy departments. Philosophy flourished as a form of epistemology or philosophy of science, and Quine, echoing the thoughts of many philosophers, including Ludwig Wittgenstein and Martin Heidegger, coined the term *semantic ascent* as a means of resolving first-order problems.

Richard Rorty (1967) was later to popularize this move in philosophy as the "linguistic turn" of twentieth-century philosophy.

The linguistic turn received an impetus from another source that sprang from the science of linguistics itself and coalesced in the notion of culture as a symbolic system open to analysis in terms of its structure, its codings, and the transmission of its motivating values. From the turn of the century, in separate locations of Moscow, St. Petersburg, and Geneva, the linguists Roman Jakobson and Fernand de Saussure, and later the semiotician Charles Sanders Pierce, began to develop formal methods for understanding and analyzing language as a system or structure. Structuralism—the word itself was coined by Jakobson in 1939—developed first in linguistics and quickly spread to other disciplines such as poetics, art, literature, the structural anthropology of Claude Lévi-Strauss, who applied new methodologies to "primitive" culture; the genetic epistemology of Jean Piaget, who turned to the study of children's thinking; Roland Barthes, who turned to texts and popular culture; the structural Marxism of Louis Althusser; and the Bachelardian neostructuralism of Michel Foucault's histories.

Another aspect was the development of mathematical theory and its applications to communication. Claude Shannon wrote "A Mathematical Theory of Communication," which was published in two parts in the July and October editions of the *Bell System Technical Journal* in 1948. Shannon clearly is one of the founders of the so-called Information Age, and his ideas form the basis for the field of information theory. By defining the critical relationships among the main elements of a communication system—power at the source of a signal, the bandwidth or frequency range of a channel through which the signal travels, the noise or static of the channel, and the receiver that decodes the signal—he at once defined *information*, mathematically stated the principles of data compression, and demonstrated how we could transmit information over noisy channels. Shannon's information theory indicated that all communication involves coding a message at its source, transmitting the message through a channel, and decoding the message at its destination. Thus the message is first encoded into a symbolic representation (words, notes, equations, or bits) before it is transmitted (by voice, letter, telephone, broadcast media, or e-mail) and decoded at the destination. Shannon's mathematical model of information enabled him to encode and compress the source output into a sequence of bits that concentrated on the unpredictable, leaving out the unpredictable symbols, as in the sentence "only infrmatn essentil to undestandn mst b tranmitd." When Shannon announced his theory in 1948, the largest cable carried 1,800 voice conversations; twenty-five years later, the capacity had increased to 230,000 simultaneous conversations. Today, a single strand of optical fiber can carry more than 6.4 million conversations.[1]

A simultaneous development occurred in the field of economics, which underwent a formalization and mathematization of its methodology between the 1940s and 1970s, when mainstream neoclassical economic theory became expressed more and more in formal models, with the exception of development economics, which did not make the transition (see Krugman 2004). Mathematical modeling of the economy in the emergent field of the economics of knowledge and information also borrowed heavily from Shannon's work. For instance, Kenneth J. Arrow (1952), who worked at Columbia University and the Cowles Commission for Research in Economics at the University of Chicago in the late 1940s under the spell of the econometricians Tjalling Koopmans and Jacob Marschak, argued strongly for the use of mathematical models in the social sciences and won a Nobel Prize for his work in 1972. Arrow drew on the von Neumann-Morgenstern theory of games to provide a theory of social interaction based on games of strategy as they would be played by fully rational individuals under conditions of risk. He advocated the use of theoretical models of inductive inference. Jacob Marschak (1960) helped to shape the field of the economics of information by using formal notation to clarify the cost and value of information.

When Norbert Wiener (1948) wrote his *Cybernetics*, he initiated the systematic study of communication as a feature common to physiology, modern servomechanisms, and human society, inspiring researchers to focus on the use of technology to extend human capacities. Wiener completed his PhD on mathematical logic at Harvard and went to study with Bertrand Russell at Cambridge. He returned to the United States after studying with David Hilbert, to a job as a mathematics instructor at MIT, where his first mathematical work led him to examine Brownian motion. His engineering friends at MIT forced him to generalize his work on Brownian motion to more general stochastic processes.

During World War II, he worked on antiaircraft gunfire control, which is credited with giving him the idea of considering the human operator as part of the steering mechanism and of applying to him the notions of feedback and stability originally devised for mechanical systems. Wiener was convinced that the behavior of man, animals, and machines could be explained by making use of cybernetic principles, principally communication, control, and learning by means of feedback. In *Cybernetics: Or Control and Communication in the Animal and the Machine*, he writes,

It is the thesis of this book that society can only be understood through a study of the messages and the communication facilities which belong to it; and that in the future development of these messages and communication facilities, messages between man and machines, between machines and man, and between machine and machine, are destined to play an ever increasing part. (16)

At the same time, Wiener was pessimistic about applying cybernetics to social systems because in the social sciences, "observer dependence" is hardest to minimize. Yet he emphasized the significance of learning and the survival value for human communities of learning through social feedback. He also stressed that much of learning takes place through language, and he focused his interest on coding and decoding, the necessary preconditions for effective communication. He proposed that human communities were limited in size, scope, and complexity by their communication systems (from oral transmission, through the written word, to modern media).

In the postwar period, a number of noted intellectuals, including John von Neumann, Warren McCulloch, Claude Shannon, Heinz von Foerster, Gregory Bateson, and Margaret Mead, clustered around Wiener, a group that became known as the Cybernetics Group by the Josiah Macy Jr. Foundation, which staged Macy Conferences on Cybernetics. Cybernetics was thought to cohere with the school of general systems theory (GST) founded at about the same time by Ludwig von Bertalanffy, and the whole enterprise was aimed at building a unified science by uncovering the common principles that govern open, evolving systems (Heims 1991).

The combination of the linguistic turn in philosophy with cybernetics, general systems theory, and applied mathematics helped to distill a theory of communication, which operated on linguistic metaphors and the engineered processes of encoding, transmission, and decoding. These metaphors have been powerful in suggesting lines of research aimed at unraveling the genetic code, and the concept of feedback in communication that Gregory Bateson used in anthropology to define a kind of learning and to diagnose the "double-bind" characteristic of schizophrenia has been adapted in family therapy and organizational learning.

Following World War II, advances in related areas of ballistics, encryption, and computing culminated in the development of the modern digital computer based on the use of binary code—sequences of 0s and 1s—to accomplish tasks of communication and computation at a speed close to the speeds of sound and then light. The digital theory of communication had come to fruition, and new forms of digital media multiplied. We had entered into the first stage of the digitalization of culture and knowledge. Vannevar Bush, who died in 1974 before the creation of the World Wide Web, is the grandfather of hypertext research. As dean of the MIT department of electrical engineering, he worked on optical and photocomposition devices as well as on machines for rapid microfilm selection. As director of the Office of Scientific Research and Development, he worked on radar antennae and was first to propose the development of an analog computer. Bush published an article, "As We May Think," in the July issue of the *Atlantic Monthly* in 1948, which profiled his "memex," a thinking machine. He wrote,

Consider a future device for individual use, which is a sort of mechanized private file and library. It needs a name, and to coin one at random, "memex" will do. A memex is a device in which an individual stores all his books, records, and communications, and which is mechanized so that it may be consulted with exceeding speed and flexibility. It is an enlarged intimate supplement to his memory. It consists of a desk, and while it can presumably be operated from a distance, it is primarily the piece of furniture at which he works. On the top are slanting translucent screens, on which material can be projected for convenient reading. There is a keyboard, and sets of buttons and levers. Otherwise it looks like an ordinary desk.

Under President Dwight Eisenhower's imperative, Bush established the U.S. military-university research partnership that later developed the ARPANET (Advanced Research Projects Agency Network). The program was motivated by catch-up strategies with the Soviet Union after they launched their first satellite in 1957. The ARPANET, employing the technology of package switching developed by Paul Baran at RAND Corporation, went live in 1969. New networking protocols were invented, and the TCP/IP protocol developed by Bob Kahn and others became the most widely used. Universities were first linked in North America, and then to research facilities in Europe. The use of the Internet exploded after 1990, with large numbers of people logging on and its commercialization in the late 1990s.[2]

In the 1990s, the economics of networks were used theoretically to explain global changes in the economy effected by information technology. The world telecommunications industry increasingly moved toward liberalization, and economists increasingly talked of "techno-economic paradigms," prompting policy makers to invent new terms such as the *knowledge economy* and the *new economy*, linking the shift strongly to economic development. Now the terms *information economy* and *knowledge economy* are well ensconced in the literature, and the discourse now examines "network economics" or "economics of the Internet," as well as "information goods," "intellectual property," "e-commerce," and "e-publishing."[3]

The Internet economy is becoming an integral part of the global economy, creating jobs, increasing productivity, and transforming companies and institutions. Employment in the Internet economy is growing faster than in the traditional economy. In the U.S. economy alone, the Internet generated an estimated $830 billion in revenues in 2000, which represented a 58 percent increase over 1989.[4]

Communication is at the heart of learning and the creation, transmission, and production of knowledge. It is also at the heart of culture and language. Advances in information technologies and communications technologies have created new tools and a changed ethos of innovation. Digitalization, speed, and compression are the forces at work that have transformed the global economy and have now begun to affect every aspect of knowledge production—its organization, its storage, its retrieval, and its transmission. The knowledge economy has certainly arrived, although this does not signal the end of the business cycle, as many early pundits singing the praises of the new economy maintained. But it does signal structural shifts and new sources of growth in some Western economies (e.g., the United States, Finland) that have witnessed both low unemployment and low inflation due to increased productivity. While it is clear that ICT (information and communications technology) investment and ICT-driven productivity increases have led to a higher growth path, there is a risk of exaggerating the expansion potential due solely to ICT investment. Yet, as a recent OECD (Organisation for Economic Cooperation and Development) report, *The New Economy: Beyond the Hype* (2001), put it,

> It would be wrong to conclude that there was nothing exceptional about the recent US experience, that the new economy was in fact a myth. Some of the arguments posited by new economy sceptics are of course true: the effect of ICT may be no greater than other important inventions of the past, like electricity generation and the internal combustion engine. Moreover, far greater productivity surges were recorded in previous decades, not least in the period before the 1970s. (10)

Nevertheless, the evidence suggests that something new is taking place in the structure of OECD economies. The report continues by maintaining that ICT has facilitated

> productivity enhancing changes in the firm, in both new and traditional industries, but only when accompanied with greater skills and changes in the organisation of work. Consequently, policies that engage ICT, human capital, innovation and entrepreneurship in the growth process, alongside fundamental policies to control inflation and instil competition, while controlling public finances are likely to bear the most fruit over the longer term. (10)

Crucially, the report investigates and recommends a set of relationships and policies that harness ICT, human capital, innovation, and business creation, focusing on the wider diffusion of ICT and the role of education and training policies in meeting today's skill requirements.

In *Business at the Speed of Thought*, Bill Gates (2000) puts the emphasis on the transformation of business brought about by the increased velocity of information flows. He writes, "If the 1980s were about quality and the 1990s were about reengineering, then the 2000s will be about velocity" (xv). The "Web workstyle" is changing the practices of business, and the "Web lifestyle" is changing the lives of consumers. Gates articulates twelve key steps to making digital flow an intrinsic part of a company, focusing on knowledge work, business operations, and commerce. For instance, he suggests the following for knowledge work:

1. Insist that communication flow through the organization over e-mail so that you can act on news with reflexlike speed.
2. Study data online to find patterns and share insights easily. Understand overall trends and personalize service for individual customers.
3. Use PCs for business analysis, and shift knowledge workers into a high-level thinking work about products, services, and profitability.
4. Use digital tools to create cross-departmental virtual teams that can share knowledge and build on each other's ideas in real time, world wide. Use digital systems to capture corporate history for use by anyone.
5. Convert every paper process to a digital process, eliminating administrative bottlenecks and freeing knowledge workers for more important tasks.

Shorn of their preoccupation with profits and efficiency, it is interesting to think of a public-service application of his ideas. How well do universities approximate the Gates ideal? Do learning institutions possess their own digital nervous systems, and to what extent do they self-consciously employ principles of organizational learning?

Gates's penultimate chapter is entitled "Create Connected Learning Communities," and it begins, "PCs can empower teachers and students more than any other group of knowledge workers" (431). He goes on to repeat the connectivity mantra—of teachers with students via distance learning, of teachers with each other via e-mail, and of schools with parents and the community via websites. Gates claims that the school infrastructure can lift the skills of all citizens and that a PC for every student can offer a variety of ways to learn. This is the way to prepare for the digital future, Gates informs us, a future where business and education, where electronically mediated communication and culture, come together in new ways to foster and promote development and well-being. This may be so, although Gates's vision is techno-optimistic, apolitical, and naive. The underlying assumption of the book, that "communication at the speed of light" equals "thought or knowledge at the speed of light," is questionable in the extreme. For obvious reasons, Gates's book does not broach questions of the monopolistic, anticompetitive behavior of Microsoft or of the antitrust case it faced soon after it launched its Internet Explorer 4.0 in 1997. In that year, the U.S. Justice Department sued Microsoft, alleging that it had violated its 1994 consent decree, which forced computer makers to sell Microsoft's Internet browser as a condition for selling its popular Windows software. In May 1998, the United States and twenty state attorneys general sued Microsoft, alleging that it had violated the Sherman Antitrust Act by unlawfully maintaining its monopoly in the market for Intel-compatible PC operating systems (OSs) and by unlawfully attempting to monopolize the market for Internet browsers. The United States also argued that Microsoft had violated Section 1 of the act by illegally tying its Windows OS to its Internet Explorer browser. The court ordered Microsoft to submit a plan of divestiture that would split the company into an OS business and an applications business. After protracted legal proceedings, the Justice Department announced in 2001 that it would no longer seek a breakup of Microsoft, and the Court approved a settlement order.[5] The browser wars continue, and across the Atlantic, the Competition Commission of the European Union is already focusing on the allegation that Microsoft used its dominance in desktop operating systems to gain unfair advantage in the market for server software.

United States of America v. Microsoft Corporation demonstrates in part the legal stakes in international law that centrally involve questions of intellectual property—that is, copyright, patent, trademark, and trade-secret law. In the symbolic economy, the protection of intellectual property and digital goods becomes paramount if knowledge capitalism is to harness, exchange, and profit from knowledge transactions. It was less than three hundred years ago, in 1710, that the Statute of Anne passed into law in Britain, providing for copyright in books and other writings, which gained protection under an act of parliament. Since then, and especially in the twentieth century, there has been a dramatic expansion of intellectual property rights. The law, it could be argued, has evolved to suit the changing needs of the American economy, from a "pirating" nation in the nineteenth century, to a net producer of intellectual property in the twentieth. This issue demonstrates how important is the "culturalization" of economic knowledge and, indeed, the significance of what we called a "cultural knowledge economy," a term we explore below.

THE NEW ECONOMY?

J. Bradford DeLong, former deputy assistant secretary for economic policy in the U.S. Department of the Treasury, begins his as yet uncompleted *Economic History of the Twentieth Century* (see http://econ161.berkeley .edu/TCEH/Slouch_title.html) with the assertion that the last one hundred years is above all a history determined and driven by economics and by the unrivalled events of the Depression and the end of the command economy of Soviet Russia, which imploded and allowed neoconservatives to herald the close fit between long-term economic modernization and democracy. Paul Krugman (1995), largely in sympathy with DeLong's analysis, nevertheless traces the rise of neoconservative economics to the attack on Keynes, taxes, and "big government" and to the emergence of the supply siders during the late 1970s and early 1980s. Once in power under Ronald Reagan, the supply siders and "policy entrepreneurs" flourished, and neoliberalism was king. But by the mid-1980s, as Krugman writes,

> New theories of industrial organization, international trade, economic growth, and the business cycle emerge: all these theories suggest that markets are less perfect, and the role of government less malign, than the now reigning political orthodoxy would have it. (17)

By the 1990s, new Keynesian economics (see, e.g., Mankiw, Romer, and Weil 1992) had replaced monetarism. The new economics, unheralded by the press, not only abandoned laissez-faire principles but adopted a realist view of the business cycle, indicating that governments *can* successfully intervene to correct recessions. The so-called new economy kicked in during the 1990s and lasted, as part of a decade-long upswing of the U.S. economy, until the dot-com bubble burst in May 2000. Yet its ongoing legacy, especially the sustained growth rates of productivity in the United States, survived and continued after May 2000.

If the history of the twentieth century is primarily economic, as DeLong maintains, then the history of twentieth-century education, especially in its postwar years, is also economic. DeLong also depicts the new economy as one of both knowledge and innovation, where clusters of innovation, based on new technologies and new business models, succeed each other in a procession that is likely to continue for an extended time with pervasive consequences. He provides an analytical overview of the digital economy, conveying how different it is from the market economy of orthodox economics. He likens the digital economy to the enclosure of the common lands in early modern Britain, which paved the way for the agricultural and industrial revolutions. Digital commodities, he maintains, do not behave like the standard goods and services of economic theory; rather, they are nonrivalrous, barely excludable, and not transparent. The supply of music track is not diminished when one downloads a track from the Internet, it is difficult if not impossible to restrict the distribution of goods that can be reproduced with little or no cost, and a consumer does not know how good a particular software package is before purchase or indeed how its successor versions will perform in the future.

Yet this general picture of the knowledge economy needs to be refined. Kevin Smith (2002) suggests that the term *knowledge-based economy* has been used in a superficial and uncritical way and that there is no coherent definition, let alone a coherent theoretical concept. He criticizes, for instance, the OECD (1996a, 7) definition of *knowledge economies* as "those which are directly based on the production, distribution and use of knowledge and information." Smith (7) argues that the OECD's definition covers everything and nothing, and he suggests that definitional problems in the literature stem from a reluctance to "consider what knowledge is in epistemological or cognitive terms." He distinguishes four basic views about the changed significance of knowledge:

1. knowledge as an input is quantitatively and qualitatively more important than capital (e.g., OECD, Drucker 1998);
2. knowledge as a product is more important than before, and hence the rise of new forms of trading activity of knowledge products;
3. codified (as opposed to tacit) knowledge is more important than before as a component of the basis for the organisation and conduct of economic activities (Abramowitz and David 1996);
4. the knowledge economy rests on technological changes in ICT (e.g., Lundvall and Foray 1996).

Smith concludes that there is no evidence to support the first claim and that the separability of knowledge and capital is difficult to sustain conceptually. There is some evidence to support the second claim, but business services remain relatively small as an activity. While there is clear evidence for an extension of formal education and a rising number of patents, "it is not clear that they are either new, or that they represent some new role for knowledge" (Smith 2002, 11). Smith agrees with Lundvall and Foray that ICT plays a new role in knowledge production and distribution, but it does not "justify talking about a new mode of economic or social functioning" (12).

It is important to recognize that the knowledge economy is both classical and new. Danny Quah of the London School of Economics indicates that the economic importance of knowledge can be found in examples where the deployment of machines boosted economic performance, such as the Industrial Revolution. By contrast, he talks of the "weightless economy," where "the economic significance of knowledge achieves its greatest contemporary resonance," and suggests that it comprises four main elements:

1. Information and communications technology (ICT), the Internet.
2. Intellectual assets: Not only patents and copyrights but also, more broadly, namebrands, trademarks, advertising, financial and consulting services, and education.
3. Electronic libraries and databases: Including new media, video entertainment, and broadcasting.
4. Biotechnology: Carbon-based libraries and databases, pharmaceuticals. (Quah 2003b)

Elsewhere, he argues,

Digital goods are bitstrings, sequences of 0s and 1s, that have economic value. They are distinguished from other goods by five characteristics: digi-

tal goods are nonrival, infinitely expansible, discrete, aspatial, and recombi-
nant. (Quah 2003a)

Quah (2001) also has been influential in suggesting that knowledge con-
centrations spontaneously emerge in space, even when physical distance
and transportation costs are irrelevant. The dynamics of spatial distribu-
tions manifest themselves in convergent clusters. This is an important feature, especially given the development of the "e-conomy" first in Silicon
Valley.

In *Getting the Measure of the New Economy*, Diane Coyle and Danny
Quah (2002), while noting the 11 percent productivity gap between the
United Kingdom and Germany, and the 45 percent productivity gap with
the United States (1999 base year), at the same time note the considerable
impact of ICT on the economy. They demonstrate on the basis of evidence
from the United States that those businesses responding the quickest to
ICT developments are driving the rest of the economy forward, although
at the same time Coyle and Quah maintain that technology takes time to
filter through and set up the cascade effects that become evident in changing organizational and business practices. They acknowledge that after
the dot-com bubble burst, confidence in the new economy waned, yet
they remain optimistic about long-term technology-led economic growth
based on the processing power of the microchip, which encompasses
well-known developments like the Internet as well as developments in information and communications technologies with advancements in gene
technology, nanotechnology, robotics, and advanced materials.

Zysman (1999) pits the "single e-conomy" view against the alternative
"plural e-conomies" view. The first, the Silicon Valley view of the economy, maintains a center-periphery model, with development spreading
out from the West Coast, south of Palo Alto, and forcing the development
of a single international market dominated by American multinationals.
By contrast, the plural view suggests that leading-edge Internet use and
e-commerce centers are beginning to emerge in Europe and Asia, and as
new technologies emerge—along with different uses, business models,
and legal frameworks—they will challenge the early dominance of American policy and the international market. If there are different local configurations of market demand, distinct trajectories of development, and
separate national e-conomies, then they are most likely to emerge around
fundamental empirical criteria such as distinct technologies and applications, locally differentiated market structures, different business models,
perhaps distinct structures of comparative advantage, and culturally different legal and policy frameworks. In one major respect, these differences
will also be related to local patterns of use. For example, the Finns have
made a huge commitment to the development of cellular and digital technology, which is manifest in their collective belief that the development of

technology is a matter of priority for economic policy and corporate strategy. Thus the Finns' strategic focus on technology manifested itself in an early commitment to digital applications and in their endeavor to maintain an open and competitive telecommunications market since the 1980s.

MODERNIZATION, INFORMATIZATION, AND ILLUSIONS OF DEVELOPMENT

Modernization theory has passed through various phases since the growth of development economics as a separate field but poor cousin to mainstream economic theory because of its lack of formal methods and rigorous methodologies. During the 1950s, development economics rested on an acceptance of dualistic development based on the belief that a modern commercial sector could develop alongside a labor-intensive sector with marginal rates of productivity. It also looked to an industrialization strategy that could overcome backwardness through massive investment in industrial projects where there were expected economies of scale. Developmentalism has followed modernization theory in its being founded on Enlightenment beliefs concerning change for the better and amelioration of the human condition through scientific strategies of rational planning that lead to social and economic progress. To this extent, it has echoed the main beliefs, stages, and tropes of modernism and the history of modernity insofar as this history is Western in essence.

While sociological modernization theory differed from its economic counterpart, both shared similar assumptions about the shift from traditional to modern society and a conception committed to historical stages of development. Thus, for instance, the transformation was hypothesized to involve an increase in societal differentiation, greater economic specialization reflected in the growth of occupational differences, the development of modern markets, greater urbanization, and also the move toward democracy. Education was also seen as a key element in effecting this shift. It was theorized as one of the main mechanisms for the transformation of tribal or traditional cultures with ascribed roles based on traditional hierarchies into a modern culture based on merit and national group identification. This kind of theory was captured, perhaps, most influentially by Rostow's (1960) *Stages of Economic Growth*, which proposed a theory in opposition to Marx, postulating five historical stages: transitional societies, preconditions for takeoff, takeoff, the drive toward maturity, and the final stage of high mass consumption. These were conceived as universal stages constituting an invariant sequence that followed or recapitulated the historical experience of the development of the West.

The major challenge to mainstream modernization theory came from Marxist and neo-Marxist theories of development that grew in the first instance from a materialist and embedded understanding of the mode of production as a system of social relations, combined with a critique of capitalism as a form of development that was based on the extraction of surplus from workers. In the postwar period and during the 1960s, various perspectives emerged that analyzed the class relations of industrial capitalism in relation to the expansionist development and acquisition of territory that took place with colonialism. Dependency theory, originating in the Latin American experience and popularized by Andre Gunder Frank (1969), and world systems theory, originating from the Annales school and developed by Immanuel Wallerstein (1979), provided alternatives to the functionalism of Rostow and other development economists. These challenges to mainstream development theories, largely informed by Marxist categories, have also included theories of Fordism and post-Fordism, such as the Regulation school.

The 1980s was dominated by the rise of neoconservative economics and neoliberalism with its emphasis on structural adjustment policies, its strategies of privatization, and its commitment to rolling back the state. Neoliberalism is still the dominant policy paradigm and is characteristic of the IMF (International Monetary Fund) and a number of national governments, including the Bush administration in the United States. When he was chief economist at the World Bank, Joseph Stiglitz (1998a) argued,

> The neoliberal model accords the government a minimal role, essentially one of ensuring macroeconomic stability, with an emphasis on price stability, while getting out of the way to allow trade liberalization, privatization, and getting the prices right. Many of these policies are necessary for markets to work well and contribute to economic success, but they are far from sufficient. Some aspects of the neoliberal model might not even be necessary conditions for strong growth, and if undertaken without accompanying measures, say to ensure competition in relevant areas of the economy, they may not bring many gains and could even lead to setbacks. Some countries have closely followed the dictates of the neoliberal model, but have not seen especially strong economic performance. Other countries have ignored many of the dictates—at least with respect to the crucial details of sequencing—and have experienced among the highest rates of sustained growth the world has ever seen.

In the neoliberal model, strongest under the combined forces of the Thatcher-Reagan alliance, private-sector education is strengthened, and the market is substituted for the state at every level. The major change in human capital theory is that the onus and responsibility has been shifted away from the state and to private individuals for investment in themselves. This shift has been particularly obvious at the level of tertiary education, where continued expansion and increased participation are increasingly seen to depend upon students' investing in themselves, thus

subsidizing state funding and provision. The structural adjustment policies of neoliberalism have been disastrous for the Third World.

During the 1980s, and in tandem with the dominant neoliberal policy
paradigm, poststructuralist and postcolonialist models of development
theory came to the fore based on critiques of Marxist structuralist models
and articulations of modes of production. To a large extent, Marxist and
neo-Marxist models experienced a strong backlash from the collapse of
actually existing communism and the breakup of the Soviet system, with
its emphasis on state planning. Poststructuralist and postcolonialist theories based on the works of Foucault and Edward Said tied truth and
knowledge to power, providing an analysis that historically enabled critiques of Eurocentrism and logocentrism and allowed developmentalism
as a discursive assemblage of these Western logics of rationality. Poststructuralism, itself vulnerable to forms of Eurocentric critique, when
wedded to the postcolonial theory developed in the writing of Homi
Bhabha, Gayatri Spivak, and others, began to question modernization
theory and development studies as a discourse, elaborating its historical
linkage to the Cold War and to American hegemony. According to Arturo
Escobar (1995), for instance, "Development can be described as an apparatus . . . that links forms of knowledge about the Third World with the
deployment of forms of power and intervention." For Escobar (1995, 44),

> Development was—and continues to be for the most part—a top-down, eth-
> nocentric, and technocratic approach, which treated people and cultures as
> abstract concepts, statistical figures to be moved up and down in the charts
> of "progress."

Escobar attempts to link the critique of development with social movements, and a number of scholars now tend to talk of alternatives *to* development in a discourse of postdevelopment rather than of the search for
alternative development paradigms.

In their book *Empire*, Michael Hardt and Antonio Negri (2001) express
the dominant view of development as one of three successive paradigms
based on agriculture, manufacturing, and services:

> It has now become common to view the succession of economic paradigms
> since the Middle Ages in three distinct moments, each defined by the domi-
> nant sector of the economy: a first paradigm in which agriculture and the ex-
> traction of raw materials dominated the economy, a second in which indus-
> try and the manufacture of durable goods occupied the privileged position,
> and a third and current paradigm in which providing services and manipu-
> lating information are at the heart of economic production. The dominant po-
> sition has thus passed from primary to secondary to tertiary production. Eco-
> nomic modernization involves the passage from the first paradigm to the
> second, from the dominance of agriculture to that of industry. Modernization
> means industrialization. We might call the passage from the second para-

digm to the third, from the domination of industry to that of services and information, a process of economic postmodernization, or better, informatization. (280)

Hardt and Negri question the discourse of economic development as something "imposed under U.S. hegemony in coordination with the New Deal model in the postwar period" (282), and they go on to argue that "modernization has come to an end," meaning that "industrial production is no longer expanding its dominance over other economic forms and social phenomena" (285). Quantitative changes have taken place in employment: where modernization implied a massive migration from agriculture to industry, informatization implies a massive shift from industry to service jobs. These services cover a wide range of activities and are characterized by a demand for flexibility and mobility. "More important," they argue, "they are characterized in general by the central role played by *knowledge, information, affect, and communication*. In this sense many call the postindustrial economy an informational economy" (285, our emphasis). And yet Hardt and Negri argue that postmodernization of informatization does not mean a process of substitution or a replacement of services for industry. Informatization will transform both agriculture and industry, making them both more productive, although not necessarily all countries will follow the same model. Drawing on Manuel Castells and Yoko Aoyama's work, they postulate two basic models: the service economy model (the United States, the United Kingdom, and Canada), characterized by a rise in service-sector jobs (especially financial services) and a corresponding decline in industrial jobs, and the info-industrial model (Japan and Germany), where the "process of informatization is closely integrated into and serves to reinforce the strength of existing industrial production" (286).

Perhaps most importantly for our purposes, Hardt and Negri propose a sociology of immaterial labor in which information and communication play key roles in the production process, denoted by the shift from Fordism to Toyotism, where the latter relies on a feedback circuit from consumption to production, allowing for instantaneous changes according to a changing market. They continue,

> The service sectors of the economy present a richer model of productive communication. Most services indeed are based on the continual exchange of information and knowledges. Since the production of services results in no material and durable good, we define the labor involved in this production as *immaterial labor*—that is, labor that produces an immaterial good, such as a service, a cultural product, knowledge, or communication. (290)

They push the analogy with computers. In the industrial age, humans and human activity were seen in terms of the machine; today, it is understood in terms of the computer: "Today we increasingly think like computers while communication technologies and their model of interaction are becoming more and more central to laboring activities" (291). Interactivity, continual communication, and networking now characterize a huge range of contemporary productive activities. As Hardt and Negri express the point,

> The computer and communication revolution of production has transformed laboring practices in such a way that they all tend toward the model of information and communication technologies. Interactive and cybernetic machines become a new prosthesis integrated into our bodies and minds and a lens through which to redefine our bodies and minds themselves. The anthropology of cyberspace is really a recognition of the new human condition. (291)

Hardt and Negri distinguish three types of immaterial labor that drive the service sector at the top of the informational economy: industrial production that has been informationalized; the immaterial labor of analytical and symbolic tasks identified by Robert Reich, which divides into "creative and intelligent manipulation on one hand and routine symbolic tasks on the other" (293); and "the production and manipulation of affects," which virtual or actual requires human contact (293). They also suggest that the network has replaced the assembly line as the organizational model of production, deterritorializing and decentralizing production. Thus informatization policies are crucial points of transformation, as the structure, control, and ownership of communication networks are the essential infrastructure for production in the informational economy.

Hardt and Negri distinguish two different models of network systems: an oligopolistic model that is characterized by broadcast systems and a democratic model that is completely horizontal and deterritorialized. The former, in the Deleuzo-Guattarian discourse, is a tree structure "that subordinates all of the branches to the central root" (300), while the latter is a rhizome-like "nonhierarchical and noncentered network structure" (299). They argue, "The networks of the new information infrastructure are a hybrid of these two models" (300). "The new communication technologies," they add, "which hold out the promise of a new democracy and a new social equality, have in fact created new lines of inequality and exclusion," and they invoke the notion of a new "intellectual commons"—"the incarnation, the production, and the liberation of the multitude" (303)—as *a more radical and profound commonality than has ever been experienced in the history of capitalism*" (302, emphasis in original). They conclude,

> *The fact is that we participate in a productive world made up of communication and social networks, interactive services, and common languages. Our economic and so-*

cial reality is defined less by the material objects that are made and consumed than by co-produced services and relationships. Producing increasingly means construct-ing cooperative and communicative commonalities. (302, emphasis in original)

It is also the case that postmodernization of production may offer leapfrog strategies for traditional societies; new possibilities and new de-velopment strategies and models are now possible that tend to displace old hegemonic development narratives based on one-path industrializa-tion, and for the Third World they are supposed to recapitulate the entire Western history of development in an accelerated form.

Escobar (2003), in a recent paper presented at the World Social Forum in Porto Alegre, Brazil, also, it seems, renounces something of his postde-velopment discourse to pick up on the promise of a new cyberspatial in-ternational that can provide for the democratic development of social and economic life:

What we want is the full development of cyberspatial practices ("cybercultures") that fulfill the novel promises of digital technologies while contributing to, and pro-viding a new model for, the pluralization and democratization of social, economic, and ecological life. In is [sic] utopian conception—and to some extent in actual practice—cyberspace builds on a decentralized, non-hierarchical logic of self-organization. This logic can also be seen at play in many instances of complexity in biological and social life; at their best, this complexity fosters the emergence of unex-pected cultures and forms of life. We want social movements and social actors to build on this logic in order to create unheard of forms of collective intelligence—subaltern "intelligent communities" capable of re-imagining the world and of in-venting alternative processes of world-making. Meshworks of social movements are the best hope to achieve this goal at present, although net artists and others are also making valuable contributions. The result could be a type of world-scale networking based on internationalist principles (a Fifth International? The Cyber-spatial inter-national). (Escobar 2003, emphasis in original)

THE NEW EDUCATION?

It is not hard to make the leap from informatization and the postmodern-ization of production to an understanding of the implications for higher education or, indeed, schooling per se. In this context, we can easily talk of the informatization of knowledge production. We can recognize, as have many national governments, the significance of higher education in the knowledge economy, and the role of research in bolstering productiv-ity. Many of the strategies concerning technology transfer have been cen-tered on universities, with an emphasis on partnerships with business and the development of new start-up and spin-off companies. Govern-ments have also tried to encourage the "clustering" of universities as a means of regional development. There has been a general reorientation of university curricula toward more practical and vocational knowledge, and university teachers and lecturers are increasingly encouraged to engage in e-learning and to prepare their lectures as part of online courses. In this context, the questions of immaterial labor, intellectual property, and the culturalization of economic knowledge become leading policy issues.

The World Bank recognizes the importance of tertiary education systems for developing and transitional economies, which face significant new trends regarding the convergent impacts of globalization, the information and communication revolutions, and the increasing importance of knowledge as a main driver of growth. The bank now argues that the role of tertiary education in the construction of knowledge economies and democratic societies is more influential than ever and that tertiary education is central to knowledge creation and production. At the same time, there is the danger of a growing digital divide both between strata within developing countries and between North and South.

In a major report, *Constructing Knowledge Societies: New Challenges for Tertiary Education*, the World Bank (2002) describes how tertiary education contributes to building up a country's capacity for participating in an increasingly knowledge-based world economy. It also investigates policy options for tertiary education that have the potential to enhance economic growth and reduce poverty. In some ways, the report indicates new directions. While it expands on *Higher Education: The Lessons of Experience* (World Bank 1994), it also emphasizes new trends, particularly the emerging role of knowledge as a major driver of economic development, and greater competition from nontraditional providers in a "borderless education" environment. The report recognizes that modes of delivery and organizational structures will become transformed as a result of the communications revolution. It comments on the rise of market forces in tertiary education and the emergence of a global market for advanced human capital.

Fundamental to the World Bank report is the recognition of how social and economic progress is dependent upon the advancement and application of knowledge. While the bank maintains that tertiary education is necessary for the effective creation, dissemination, and application of knowledge, it also observes that developing and transitional countries are at risk of being further marginalized in a highly competitive world economy if they cannot promote the creation and use of knowledge through tertiary education. In this new environment, the bank indicates a strong role for the state—a noticeable departure from principles of neoliberalism—to develop "an enabling framework" that will help tertiary institutions be more innovative and more responsive, not only to the needs of a globally competitive knowledge economy, but also to the changing labor-market requirements for advanced human capital.[6] The World Bank's view, then, reflects an emerging consensus that development in the Third World crucially depends upon developing a knowledge economy in which tertiary education has a double role to play: in the creation of knowledge and its translation for local conditions and also in the development of knowledge as human, social, and intellectual capital. The form of development education advocated by the bank for the third world does not differ greatly from knowledge development strategies adopted by the developed world.

Cunningham and his colleagues (2000), for instance, in a report called *The Business of Borderless Education* submitted to the Australian government, usefully identify eight change-driving trends in modes of higher education provision (see table 1.1).

In response to these trends, Cunningham and his colleagues suggest that new forms of higher-education provision are beginning to emerge in the United States to serve the needs of corporations or to exploit market opportunities, where the overwhelming emphasis is on the working adult who requires vocational, practical, and relevant qualifications. In this new

Table 1.1. Borderless Education

- Globalization, and the need to deliver appropriate courses worldwide, as well as to develop cross-cultural competencies at the management level.
- New information and communication technologies (ICTs) and the need to continually upgrade skills in how to use ICTs throughout the organization as the "half-life" of knowledge falls dramatically.
- The knowledge economy, and the need to reduce the cycle time between developing and executing new ideas, as well as to make knowledge portable and transferable through sharing best practices.
- The need to create a learning organization, which promotes learning agility, an orientation to change, and a commitment to lifelong learning throughout the organization—the major issue is no longer seen as the acquisition of skills, but how to teach behaviors, which are primarily learned through challenging experiences.
- The growth of user-pays higher education and closer attention on the part of corporations to the "bottom line" of externally provided training, as well as the decline in public funding to universities.
- Use of ICTs to distribute knowledge through the organization at lower costs, through the Internet and corporate intranets, in order to lever competitive advantage through the sharing of intellectual capital.
- The growing demand for education and training with "credential creep" in the labor market and the professions, and the need for formal certification to ensure "lifetime employability," leading to the emergence of the "learner-earner" and "earner-learner" education markets.
- Shortages of skilled personnel, particularly in the booming U.S. economy (until the 2000 recession after the World Trade Center attack), and the expectation of new employees (so-called Generation Xers) that continuous training opportunities will be provided, and that a corporate university is a marker of that commitment and hence an "employer of choice."

Source: Cunningham et al. (2000).

Table 1.2.   Education in the "Old Economy" and the "New Economy"

Old Economy	New Economy
Four-year degree	Forty-year degree
Training as cost center advantage	Training as no. 1 source of competitive
Learner mobility	Content mobility
Distance education	Distributed learning
Correspondence and video	High-tech media centers
One size fits all	Tailored programs
Geographic institutions	Brand-name universities and celebrity professors
Just-in-case	Just-in-time
Isolated	Virtual learning communities

mixed mode, traditional campus-based learning activity is supplemented and sometimes replaced by a virtualization of the university.

Cunningham and colleagues (2000) also draw upon analyses of the new economy by corporate analysts such as Merrill Lynch and the Gartner Group, who identified the implications of these trends for postsecondary education, as described in table 1.2. Of course, this simple division does not do justice to the continuities and overlaps between paradigms, nor to the deeper structural policy issues that fall out of the new political economy of global knowledge production, but it does raise the issues, if only in an ideal-typical way, and it does demonstrate more than ever before in human history the centrality of education to economic and social "progress."

CULTURAL KNOWLEDGE ECONOMY

We have invented this term *cultural knowledge economy* as a composite term trading on notions of "cultural knowledge," "knowledge as culture," and "knowledge cultures," as well as the now-accepted term "knowledge economy" and the idea of "cultural economy," employed as an approach similar to political economy. Knowledge is now the dominant feature of the *social* transformations associated with globalization as the worldwide integration of economic activity. What this statement registers is the argument that knowledge and the value of knowledge are rooted in social relations—a position that is common to philosophies of *practice*, including Marxian, Heideggerian (or phenomenological), and Wittgensteinian philosophies.

This book employs the concept of practice that has become the new desideratum for education and the social sciences, as we argue in more detail in chapter 8. The term, now widely employed in social theory, has taken on a kind of ontological status in the postfoundationalist and post-positivistic social sciences, substituting for *truth* and *validity* (Turner 1994). The term also features unproblematically in a characterization of the "new pedagogy" (Cullen et al. 2002) that investigates social constructionism and postmodern theory as its basis. It has been taken up by those who champion "culture," especially in relation to organizations and firms, with a strong emphasis on the associated concept of the "practitioner" and practitioner knowledge—a trend that dates from the work of Schön (1987, 1995) and Argyris (1999). More recently, Wenger (1998) has popularized the term *communities of practice*, emphasizing learning as a social system defined as a joint enterprise that is continually negotiated by its members; a form of mutual engagement that binds its members; and a shared repertoire of routines, sensibilities, artifacts, and vocabularies (see www.co-i-l.com/coil/knowledge-garden/cop/lss.shtml).

In this context, the concept of practice signifies the privileging of practical knowledge over theoretical knowledge and registers the full force of the phenomenological arguments of Wittgenstein and Heidegger, among others, on the priority of already being in the world, and of thinkers such as Merleau-Ponty, who in addition emphasizes the body. Thus Gibbons and his colleagues (1994), for instance, stress a distinction between Mode 1 and Mode 2 knowledge in a way that highlights applied knowledge and contexts of use.

The contemporary turn to practices results in part from the theoretical tendency in linguistics and cognitive science to emphasize engagement with the practical world, from a materialist social ontology that focuses on embodied knowledge and rationalities, and also from accounts of learning and knowledge in terms of practices.

While we recognize, with Marx (and Wittgenstein), that knowledge and education are fundamentally social activities developed through language and communication within cultures, we jettison the old Marxist dualism of economic structure and an epiphenomenal cultural superstructure that is determined by the former. Today, more than at any time in the past, the cultural has become the economic, and the economic the cultural. This is the basic insight of the knowledge economy, which is based on a facility with signs, symbolic analysis, and manipulation. The new economy, then, rests on the production and use of knowledge and innovation and on communication through electronic networks that have become the global medium of social exchange. In this new configuration, the production of new meanings is central to the knowledge process, and media or communication cultures once centered on literacy and printing are now increasingly centered on the screen or image and on the radical and dynamic concordance of image, text, and sound.

Paul du Gay and Michael Pryke (2002, 1) use the term *cultural economy* to denote the cultural turn—for example, the shift in organizational theory that acknowledges (1) that "culture" structures "the way people think, act and feel in organizations"; (2) its importance in structuring knowledge practices and activities; and (3) the way that "markets" and "economies" belong to the discourse of those economics that form related sets of representational and technological practices that constitute "the spaces within which economic action is formatted and framed" (2). They note the inseparability of production and consumption in interactive service and certain kinds of retail work. In these activities, they suggest, it is difficult to separate cultural from economic categories, especially when it comes to marketing and advertising. They go on to note the ways in which the finance industry can be viewed as primarily a cultural industry dependent not only on global streams of information but also on matters of cultural style in negotiation, presentation, and framing.

Cultural economy is also meant to carry the connotation that "we are living through an era in which economic and organizational life has become increasingly 'culturalized'" (Gay and Pryke 2002, 6). They cite Scott Lash and John Urry's *The Economies of Signs and Space*:

> Economic and symbolic processes are more than ever interlaced and interarticulated; that is . . . the economy is increasingly culturally inflected and . . . culture is more and more culturally inflected. (1994, 64)

The culturalization of the economy is clearly evident in a number of related developments: the creation, development, distribution, and production of both hardware and software as part of the information infrastructure for other knowledge and cultural industries; the growth of a highly stylized consumer culture where ordinary products are increasingly aestheticized and imbued with cultural meaning in relation to questions of lifestyle and the "fashioning" of personal identity; the convergence of telecommunications with entertainment and edutainment media cultures based on radio, film, TV, Internet, and mobile phones, with their assorted mixed media; and the importance accorded to signifying and other cultural practices in the actual organizational life of firms as well as in the production, design, and marketing of products. This culturalization of economic knowledge and markets is also reflected in the dominance of the appropriation of the drama-related notion of "performance" that now serves as the primary social model for evaluating and assessing human and technical behavior (see also Thrift 2002). John Allen (2002, 40) argues for a symbolic basis for *all* forms of economic knowledge while acknowledging that "expressive or affective forms of knowledge are often unintentionally marginalized in favour of cognitive reason" in today's cultural-coded economies. He draws on Ernst Cassirer's exposition of three symbolic functions of expression, representation, and signification as a means of demonstrating that each operates under specific epistemological conditions not reducible to either science or habit. Allen is at pains to point out that knowing through codes depends upon shared cultural meanings. Thus the emphasis falls on codifiable knowledges and tends to overlook cultural modes of knowing such as "knowing through affect," which have close affinities with embodied or experiential forms of knowing that are nonrepresentational.

Drawing on poststructuralist theory, the present book explicitly develops the notion of "knowledge cultures" as a basis for avoiding the dualism of present debates on the "knowledge economy" and the "knowledge society," where the first term points to the economics of knowledge and information, and the second to the concepts and rights of knowledge workers as citizens in the new economy, focusing on the subordination of economic means to social ends. The knowledge society–knowledge economy dualism tends to echo the traditional disciplinary distinction between economy and society and therefore tends to be conceptually blinded to the radical interpenetration of these spheres: both the economization of society and the culturalization of economics. The notion of "knowledge cultures," then, points to the cultural preconditions that must be established before economies or societies based on knowledge can operate successfully as genuine democratic cultures. Knowledge cultures are based on *shared practices*—they embody culturally preferred ways of doing things, often developed over many generations. They point to the culture boundedness of symbolic functions and also to the ways in which cultures have different repertoires of representational and nonrepresentational forms of knowing. Simplified in the extreme, the argument is that knowledge creation, production, and dissemination requires the cultural exchange of ideas, and such exchanges, in turn, depend upon certain cultural conditions, including trust; reciprocal rights and responsibilities between different knowledge partners; and institutional routines, regimes, and strategies. There is no one prescription or formula that fits all learners, institutions, societies, or knowledge traditions. The term *knowledge cultures* has the advantage of helping to focus upon *learning per se*—learning styles, processes, economies, and systems. *Knowledge cultures* also implies that the economics of knowledge ultimately depend upon philosophical and cultural concepts and analyses. This book focuses on the relationships between education, knowledge, and economy, and it proposes a theory for the development of knowledge cultures that is designed to provide an alternative to mainstream neoliberal accounts and is aimed at the recognition of plural institutional knowledge cultures and their enhancement.

NOTES

1. For this paragraph, we have drawn on "The Significance of Shannon's Work" at cm.bell-labs.com/cm/ms/what/shannonday/work.html. See also his original paper at cm.bell-labs.com/cm/ms/what/shannonday/paper.html.

2. For histories of the Internet, see www.isoc.org/internet/history. See also the Next Generation Internet, http://playground.sun.com/pub/ipng/html/ipng-main .html. In President Bill Clinton's 1998 State of the Union Address, he asked Congress to step up support for building the next-generation Internet, emphasizing that it will operate at speeds up to a thousand times faster than today.

3. See the e-resources compiled by Hal R. Varian under the head "The Information Economy" at www.sims.berkeley.edu/resources/infoecon.

4. For the Web Indicators Portal, see www.webindicators.org.

5. For the full hearing, see "Antitrust Case Filings, Antitrust Division, United States v. Microsoft: Current Case" at www.usdoj.gov/atr/cases/ms_index.htm.

6. For the full report, see www1.worldbank.org/education/pdf/Constructing %20Knowledge%20Societies.pdf.

2

The Politics of Postmodernity and the Promise of Education

INTRODUCTION: NEOLIBERALISM, THE THIRD WAY, AND THE DECLINE OF WELFARE

In this chapter, we want to argue that postmodernity can be pursued broadly as the *question of value*, which involves both the reexamination of our traditional sources and orientations of normativity and the search for new ethical and political directions for our major institutions and our social and economic policies. In the Western world since in the early 1980s (with the election of the Reagan and Thatcher governments), postmodernity and the question of value have been dominated by contemporary forms of neoliberalism, which have cleverly colonized the future with a view of the market and globalization as a political project of world economic integration based on the ideology of "free trade." Neoliberalism, which has its immediate roots in debates that took place in the 1920s and 1930s over the efficiency of the market, the role of the state, and government failure, is undeniably still the ruling ideology, though it has transmuted in form a number of times since its rearticulation by the Chicago school in the early 1960s. We think there is a different view of postmodernity that runs against the standard neoliberal model of the future and its Third Way adaptation.

During the 1980s, a distinctive strand of neoliberalism emerged as the dominant paradigm of public policy in the West and continues to exert influence: citizens were redefined as individual consumers of newly competitive public services, with the consequence that "welfare rights" have become commodified as consumer rights; the public sector itself underwent considerable "downsizing" as governments pursued an agenda of commercialization, corporatization, and incremental privatization; and management of public services, following principles of "new public management" and emulating private-sector styles, was often delegated rather than genuinely devolved, while executive power became concentrated even more at the center.

Nowhere was this shift more evident than in the related areas of education and social policy. In many OECD countries, there has been a clear shift away from universality to a "modest safety net." The old welfare goals of participation and belonging that prevailed in countries committed to principles of social democracy were abolished. User charges for social services and education were introduced across the board. Sometimes these changes were accompanied, especially at the height of the New Right ascendancy, by substantial cuts in benefits and other forms of income support and eligibility criteria, for all forms of welfare have been tightened up under the guise of "accountability." Targeting social assistance became the new ethos of social philosophy, and in addition there was greater policing of the welfare economy aimed at reducing benefit fraud. The stated goal of neoliberals has been to free people from dependence on state welfare, and some commentators have talked of the shift from welfare to workfare, where stable employment is now taken as the basis for participation in society. The old welfare policies allegedly discouraged effort and self-reliance and, in the eyes of neoliberals, can be held responsible for *producing* young illiterates, juvenile delinquents, alcoholics, substance abusers, school truants, "dysfunctional" families, and drug addicts.

Liberalism, considered as both a political tradition and an economic doctrine, has been the dominant metanarrative in economic and social policy in the West. Since the early 1980s, a particularly narrow variant—neoliberalism—has become the dominant metanarrative, to use Jean-François Lyotard's terminology. This particular variant, which revitalizes the master discourse of neoclassical economic liberalism, has been remarkably successful in advancing a *foundationalist* and *universalist* reason as a basis for a radical global reconstruction of all aspects of society and economy. A form of economic reason encapsulated in the notion of *Homo economicus*, with its abstract and universalist assumptions of individuality, rationality, and self-interest, has captured the policy agendas of most Western countries. Part of its innovation has been the way in which the neoliberal master narrative has successfully extended the principle of self-interest into the status of a paradigm for understanding politics itself and, in fact, not merely market but *all* behavior and human action. Consequently, in the realm of education policy, especially in the United States and the OECD countries, but also in developing countries, at every opportunity the market has been substituted for the state: citizens are now "customers," and public servants are "providers." In education, the notion of vouchers is suggested as a universal panacea to problems of funding and quality, and the teaching-learning relation has been reduced to an implicit contract between buyer and seller. As Lyotard argued prophetically in *The Postmodern Condition*, not only has knowledge and research become commodified, but so have the relations of the production of knowledge in a new logic of *performativity*.

Assessments of the global force of neoliberalism differ. Thus, for instance, David Henderson (1999, 1), previously head of the Economics and Statistics Department for the OECD, comments on the way economic policies across the world have changed their character, with the effect of "making their economies freer, more open and less regulated." In a book titled *The Changing Fortunes of Economic Liberalism*, Henderson suggests that it is a mistake to interpret these developments as a victory for conservatism:

> More justly, the recent evolution of economic policies can be seen as the latest chapter in a continuing story which goes back at any rate to the mid-18th century, the hero of which is economic liberalism. Recent events have involved a shift, not from left to right, but in the balance between liberalism and interventionism in economic systems. (1999, 2)

Here, he is using the term *liberalism* in the European sense of "the realisation, enlargement and defence of individual freedom" (4), and he argues, "The extension and exercise of economic freedoms make for closer *economic integration*, both within and across national boundaries" (5). He states, "Liberalism is individualist, in that it defines the interests of national states, and the scope and purposes of government, with reference to individuals who are subject to them" (7). Liberalism, which for Henderson implies restricting the power and functions of governments so as to give full scope for individuals and enterprises, after a hundred years of decline, has regained ground in the economics profession, especially after the period from the 1930s to the 1970s. The economic policies enacted by a variety of world governments on the basis of principles of economic liberalization emphasize a "strong association between political and economic freedoms" (46). He reviews "economic freedom ratings" over the period from 1975 to 1995 in order to map the geography of reform, purportedly demonstrating that core OECD countries are all "reforming" governments, and while he examines overlapping areas of policy (financial markets, international transactions, privatization, energy, agricultural, labor, and public spending), he is unable to draw any conclusions concerning so-called reforming policies (i.e., greater economic liberalization) and increased levels of national prosperity.

Henderson (1999), following Milton and Rose Friedman (1962), who also provide the foreword for his book, indicates that while *the battle of ideas has been won* insofar as both economists and governments hold to the revival of economic liberalism (i.e., neoliberalism), its victory has so far been disappointing, and its chronic weakness lies in the fact that it has *"no solid basis of general support"* (58). It is in this context that he comments on what he calls antiliberal ideas and their increasing support, which he lists in relation to three related developments: opposition to greater freedom of international trade and capital flows; the "excessive drive to equality" (the phrase is taken from the Friedmans); and the spread of "cultural studies" in the universities. He is worth quoting on the last of these developments:

> Economists have given little attention to this trend, probably because their own subject has so far escaped the ravages of "deconstruction," "post-modernism" and related tendencies, while these movements in turn have not developed a systematic economic orientation or philosophy of their own which has claims to be taken seriously. (65)

He continues,

> Both post-modernism in its different guises and the more recent forms of egalitarianism characteristically share a vision of the world in which past history and present-day market-based economic systems are viewed in terms of patterns of oppression and abuses of power. Free markets and capitalism are seen as embodying and furthering male dominance, class oppression, racial intolerance, imperialist coercion and colonialist exploitation. The appeal of this anti-liberal way of thinking seems to have been little affected by the collapse of communism. (65)

What is interesting is that Henderson, as an economist, should directly perceive the threat to economic liberalism in terms of "postmodernism," even though he does not really engage with its multiple strands or show any sign of understanding its philosophical roots in Nietzsche, Heidegger, and contemporary French philosophy, or its diverse engagements with classical liberal thought. These engagements—for instance, Derrida and Foucault on Kant, or more directly, Foucault's governmentality studies—are considerably more sophisticated than Henderson's own brief historical foray. To be sure, there are antiliberal (and antimodernist) elements in Nietzsche's and Heidegger's thinking, and there are strong evaluative critiques of liberalism in both poststructuralism and postmodernism, but this should not be taken to mean that poststructuralists and postmodernist thinkers stand against political freedom. Such a simplistic reduction defies the complexity of the range of philosophical positions that have developed over the last fifty years.

While Henderson believes that neoliberalism has won the battle of ideas and is now the dominant policy story, others have taken up oppositional views. Jan Nederveen Pieterse (2000) maintains,

As an ideology, neoliberalism is probably past its peak. The trust in the "magic of the marketplace" that characterized the era of Ronald Reagan and Margaret Thatcher has run its course. The criticisms of "the market rules OK," common and widespread, are gradually crystallizing into an alternative perspective. (8)

Although he concedes,

Institutionally, in the WTO and IMF, neoliberalism remains the conventional wisdom. In development politics, it prevails through the remnants of the "Washington consensus." In NAFTA, it prevails in principle. In Euroland, it prevails through the European Monetary Union. (9)

He suggests that this is a reflection of the hegemony of finance capital and that the global future of a borderless world for capital is a self-fulfilling prophecy achieved through structural reform policies of the IMF and the World Bank. At the same time, he notes that "neoliberal futures are being contested on many grounds—labour, the right to development, the environment, local interests, and cultural diversity" (10).

Pieterse (2000) wants to develop a critical approach to global futures that seeks to be inclusive of interests excluded by the mainstream managerial approach based on forecasting and risk analysis, yet seeks to inform futures in utopian and postmodern ways. While we see considerable value in this approach, unlike Pieterse, we are less convinced that neoliberalism is exhausted and past its peak. As a long-term historical tendency, it will ebb and flow. There are, we think, good grounds to believe that the Bush administration will provide a reversal of the attempted current alignment of neoliberalism and social democracy in Third Way politics back to a neoconservative alignment.

Robert Cox (1997), longtime chief of the International Labor Organization's (ILO) Program and Planning Division, and later of Columbia and Toronto universities, describes the latest thrust toward globalization in terms of the internationalization of production and the internationalization of the state, with the emphasis changing from domestic welfare to the adaptation of domestic economies to the world economy. He also mentions the new international division of labor, which is creating a new pattern of uneven development, and, in this regard, he talks about the emergence of a Fourth World, seemingly outside the new developments that characterize the advent of the global economy. He offers his prognosis in the following terms:

The continuing residue of the Cold War contributes to the progressive decay of the old world order. The outlines of a new world order are yet to be perceived. Two factors may, in the longer run, be formative of a new order. One is the rivalry among different forms of what Polanyi called "substantive economies," i.e., the different ways in which production and distribution are organized. The struggle between rival forms of capitalism (hyperliberalism versus social market) in Europe may be critical in determining the balance of social and economic power in the global economy. At stake are the prospects of subordinating the economy to social purpose, and the prospects of redesigning production and consumption so as to be compatible with a sustainable biosphere. (34)

It is clear that neoliberalism, both as a political philosophy and as a policy mix, had taken deep root by the early 1980s as the world's dominant economic and development metanarrative. During that decade, many governments around the world supported the modernizing-reforms thrust of neoliberalism, particularly the exposure of the state sector to competition and the opportunity to pay off large and accumulating national debts. By contrast, many developing countries had structural adjustment policies imposed on them as loan conditions from the IMF and the World Bank. The reforming zeal soon ideologized the public sector per se and ended by damaging key national services (including health and education). By the midnineties, the wheel had turned again—this time toward a realization that the dogmatism of the neoliberal right had become a serious treat to social justice, national cohesion, and democracy itself. Large sections of populations had become structurally disadvantaged from working and living on the margins of the labor market; rapidly growing social inequalities had become more evident as the rich had become richer and the poor poorer; companies were failing and underperforming; public services had been "stripped down" and were unable to deliver even the most basic of services; many communities had become split and were endangered by the rise of racism, crime, unemployment, and social exclusion. Governments throughout the world looked to a new philosophy and policy mix—one that preserved some of the efficiency and competition gains but did not result in the forms of nation splitting and social exclusion.

One model advocated by the current British prime minister, Tony Blair, and the immediate past U.S. president, Bill Clinton, called the "Third Way," aims to revitalize the concern for social justice and democracy while moving away from traditional policies of redistribution to define freedom in terms of autonomy of action, demanding the involvement and participation of the wider social community. Some commentators see nothing new in the Third Way, regarding it as a return to the ethical socialism of "old Labor." Other critics see it as a cover for the wholesale adoption of conservative policies of privatization and the continued dismantling of the welfare state. Still others suggest that the Third Way is nothing more than a spin-doctoring exercise designed to brand a political product as different from what went before. Sloganized as "market economy but not market society," advocates of the Third Way see it as uniting the two streams of left-of-center thought—democratic socialism and classical liberalism—where the former is said to promote social justice, with the state as its main agent, and the latter to assert the primacy of individual liberty in the market economy. Understood in this light, the Third Way might be construed as a continuance of classical liberalism, born of the same political strategy of integrating two streams as with the New Right (neoliberalism and neoconservatism), but this time the "other" stream is social democracy rather than conservatism.

Critics have pointed out that the Third Way is an amorphous political project that fails to sustain the traditional values of the Left and that accepts the basic framework of neoliberalism, thus demonstrating that it has no distinctive economic policy. Finally, critics also raise the question of tacit acceptance of globalization and the implicit rules of the global marketplace, implying that Third Way politics, with its emphasis on modernization of social democracy, theoretically cannot control or come to terms with the damaging ecological consequences of world economic development. Anthony Giddens (2000, 163), in reply to his critics, suggests that the Third Way is not an attempt to occupy the middle ground; rather it is "concerned with restructuring social democratic doctrines to respond to the twin revolutions of globalization and the knowledge economy." Yet, as Ramesh Mishra (1999) has argued and amply demonstrated, the relationship between globalization and social policy tends to be a destructive one that undermines the ideology of welfare as a non–market mediated public good and weakens solidarity and social democratic politics (see table 2.1).

What we find particularly problematic in Giddens's defense is the lack of attention to alternative ways of conceptualizing education and the role that it can play in moderating the worst national and individual effects of globalization. Giddens (2000, 73–74) acknowledges the importance of education as "the key force in human capital development." He writes, "It is the main public investment that can foster both economic efficiency and civic cohesion. Education isn't a static input into the knowledge economy, but is itself becoming transformed by it" (73). But having acknowledged its importance, he simply emphasizes that "education needs to be redefined to focus on capabilities that individuals will be able to develop through life" (74) as opposed to the traditional idea of acquiring qualifications for adulthood. The underlying concept of education is a conceptual weakness in Third Way politics. While the Third Way professes a commitment to "education, education, education," to quote Tony Blair's manifesto, it has not yet attempted to rework the concept of education as the basis for economic and social participation, citizenship, and access in the knowledge economy beyond paying lip service to the OECD notion of "lifelong education." In order to succeed, the Left must customize or indigenize the concept of education for social democratic politics. To do

Table 2.1. Social Policy and the "Logic" of Globalization

1. Globalization undermines the ability of national governments to pursue the objectives of full employment and economic growth through reflationary policies. "Keynesianism in one country" ceases to be a viable option.
2. Globalization results in an increasing inequality in wages and working conditions through greater labor-market flexibility, a differentiated "post-Fordist" workforce, and decentralized collective bargaining. Global competition and mobility of capital result in "social dumping" and a downward shift in wages and working conditions.
3. Globalization exerts a downward pressure on systems of social protection and social expenditure by prioritizing the reduction of deficits, debt, and taxation as key objectives of state policy.
4. Globalization weakens the ideological underpinnings of social protection, especially that of a national minimum, by undermining national solidarity and legitimating an inequality of rewards.
5. Globalization weakens the basis of social partnership and tripartism by shifting the balance of power away from labor and the state and toward capital.
6. Globalization constrains the policy options of nations by virtually excluding left-of-center approaches. In this sense, it spells the "end of ideology" as far as welfare-state policies are concerned.
7. The logic of globalization comes into conflict with the "logic" of the national community and democratic politics. Social policy emerges as a major issue of contention between global capitalism and the democratic nation state.

Source: Ramesh Mishra (1999, 15–16).

this, we must return to the history of education rights in the early documents of human rights and renew its ethos as a basis for the new society. We must investigate the links between education, knowledge, and learning processes, especially metacognitive abilities. We must also look to establishing the means for fostering what we call "knowledge cultures." Above all, we must reestablish education as a minimum welfare right and global public good.

The continuing thread of our argument implicit in this chapter and running through this book as a whole concerns establishing the *value* of education in postmodernity. Education in the global knowledge economy, to quote from political party manifestos, is more than ever the passport to a relatively secure job and income, and also to active participation in society as a knowledge worker and as a citizen. Education in the so-called new knowledge economy more than ever before is intimately tied up with welfare and with democracy. In the next section, we begin by talking in broad philosophical terms about the concept of postmodernity, about which there is much confusion and fiercely held views. We want to provide a clearer understanding of this term, especially in relation to the question of value and its sibling concept of "modernity."

POSTMODERNITY AND THE QUESTION OF VALUE

We adopt a perspective to the challenge of postmodernity by drawing upon the philosophy of Nietzsche and Heidegger, for these philosophers were the first to open up the reflective space of postmodernity. We want to argue that postmodernity can be pursued as the *question of value* after the event that Nietzsche called the "death of God," which, as we stated above, involves a reexamination of our traditional moral orientations and a search for new ethical and political directions.

Accounts of the concept of "postmodernity" and so-called postmodern philosophy that attribute its source and power of inspiration to Nietzsche typically begin with Nietzsche's revelation that "God is dead." Often on the basis of a rudimentary understanding of this remark, commentators falsely attribute a form of nihilism to Nietzsche (and to postmodern philosophy), as though Nietzsche was actively advocating nihilism. Nihilism, from the Latin *nihil*, meaning "nothing" or "that which does not exist," is the belief that there is no legitimate foundation to values or, more simply, that the world is meaningless. Nihilistic themes have dominated twentieth-century art, literature, and philosophy. It is evidenced as a kind of existential despair in the work of Albert Camus and Jean-Paul Sartre, who suggested in *Existentialism and Humanism* that "man is condemned to be free"—meaning that in a world of pure contingency, we have no choice but to make choices, however terrible the options might be. Nihilism surfaces in contemporary themes of the destruction of the earth, identity crisis, cosmological purposelessness, and the desperate search for meaning and identity.

Yet to attribute this intensely skeptical doctrine to Nietzsche is wrongheaded—nothing could be further from Nietzsche's purpose. While it is true for Nietzsche that nihilism proceeds as a consequence from the fact that "God is dead," it is also the starting point for a philosophy of the future that promotes the *revaluation of all values*, "to pursue the problem of the total health of a people, time, race or of humanity," aimed at "growth, power, life" (1974, 35). It is also the case that those who follow Nietzsche, particularly Martin Heidegger, but also those contemporary French philosophers we (sometimes falsely) call "postmodern," sympathetically understand Nietzsche's philosophy as a basis to overcome the desire to substitute any surrogate or replacement for God as the transcendental truth, center, or eternal guarantee for morality and self-certainty. And this is so, whether that replacement be reason, science, or—perhaps the greatest temptation of all—man or humankind.

In the final volume of his *Nietzsche*, Heidegger traces the philosophical use of the word *nihilism* to Friedrich Jacobi and later to Turgenev, Jean Paul, and Dostoyevsky. Against these early uses, Heidegger claims,

Nietzsche uses nihilism as the name for the historical movement that he was the first to recognize and that already governed the previous century while defining the century to come, the movement whose essential interpretation he concentrates in the terse sentence: "God is dead." That is to say, "the Christian God" has lost His power over beings and over the determination of man. "Christian God" also stands for the "transcendent" in general in its various meanings—for "ideals" and "norms," "principles" and "rules," "ends" and "values," which are set "above" the being, in order to give being as a whole a purpose, and order, and—as it is succinctly expressed—"meaning." (1991, 4:4)

For Heidegger, drawing heavily on fragments of *The Will to Power*, Nietzsche's sense of nihilism is interpreted in terms of the historical process completing the modern era and culminating in the "end of metaphysics" and a "revaluation [that] thinks Being for the first time as value" (4:6).

Some would argue that it is the Christian reactive response to the all-too-human origin of our values by declaring existence or life meaningless that is the real source of nihilism. That is, once the transcendental guarantees of (Christian) morality and the grand expectations based upon them have collapsed or been exposed for what they really are, an active nihilism ensues. And yet the same genealogical critique, the loss of faith in the categories of reason, can also inspire a revolutionary demand for things to be different. One can tell the story of contemporary Continental philosophy by emphasizing the importance of central notions of practice, a critique of the present, the production of crisis (especially in relation to modernity), and antiscientism (as a modernist metanarrative) in defining a tradition that recognizes the essential historicity of philosophy and therefore also the radical finitude of the human subject and the contingent character of human experience. We might argue that post-Nietzschean philosophy not only provides a critique of the rational, autonomous (Christian-liberal) subject but also redirects our attention to historical sources of normativity that are embedded in cultures. It provides, in other words, a path for moral reconstruction after the so-called death of God—a way forward and a positive response to the question of nihilism that demands the revaluation of values. In doing so, it belongs to the counter-Enlightenment tradition of thought that asserts the historicity of human reason and experience on the basis of a radical questioning of the transcendental guarantee and moral authority of God, and of all possible substitutes for God (humanity, reason, science, or the transcendental signifier).

Gianni Vattimo (1991), the Italian philosopher, begins his book *The End of Modernity* by emphasizing the theoretical links between Nietzsche and Heidegger in relation to the question of postmodernity. He takes Nietzsche's analysis of nihilism and Heidegger's critique of humanism "as 'positive' moments for a philosophical reconstruction, and not merely as symptoms and declarations of decadence" (Vattimo 1991, 1). Vattimo goes on to suggest that such an interpretation is possible "only if I have the courage . . . to listen attentively to the various discourses concerning postmodernity and its specific traits that are at present being developed in the arts, literary criticism, and sociology" (1–2). For Vattimo, the vital link between Nietzsche and Heidegger is that together they call the heritage of European thought into question *without* proposing the means for a critical "overcoming." For both Nietzsche and Heidegger, despite their differences, Vattimo argues,

> Modernity is in fact dominated by the idea that the history of thought is a progressive "enlightenment" which develops though an ever more complete appropriation and reappropriation of its own "foundations." These are often also understood to be "origins," so that the theoretical and practical revolutions of Western history are presented and legitimated for the most part as "recoveries," rebirths, or returns. The idea of "overcoming," which is so important in all modern philosophy, understands the course of thought as being a progressive development in which the new is identified with value through the mediation of the recovery and appropriation of the foundation-origin. (2)

As Vattimo goes on to explain, both Nietzsche and Heidegger take up a critical attitude toward European and Enlightenment thought insofar as its represents, in one way or another, *forms of foundational thinking*; the difficulty is that they do so but *not* in the name of another, truer, more real, or more enlightened foundation. It is this feature, Vattimo claims, that distinguishes Nietzsche and Heidegger as philosophers of postmodernity. If we may quote Vattimo one last time in connection with this reading,

> The "post-" in the term "post-modernity" indicates in fact a taking leave of modernity. In its search to free itself from the logic of development inherent in modernity—namely the idea of a critical "overcoming" directed toward a new foundation—post-modernity seeks exactly what Nietzsche and Heidegger seek in their own peculiar "critical" relationship with Western thought. (3)

We find Vattimo's observation here particularly helpful in distinguishing the critical attitude and ethos between neoliberalism, considered as a distinct Anglo-American continuation, mutation, or reinvention of the tradition of European liberal thought, and poststructuralism, precisely as a critique of that same tradition (and, more broadly, the culture of modernity to which it belongs), but not one that criticizes in the name of a better, truer, or more "real" foundation.

Postmodern philosophy can be characterized as seeking a positive answer to nihilism—a way forward that suggests, while there may be no foundation for values or for knowledge, that this does not mean that knowledge is not possible or that the creation of new value is denied. Jean-François Lyotard (1984), the French philosopher, defines postmodernism as an "incredulity toward metanarratives," that is, a skepticism of those "big stories" that purport to ground our cultural practices and to legitimate our institutions—narratives on which we have relied to make sense of the world and our place in it.

In *The Postmodern Condition*, Jean-François Lyotard was concerned with metanarratives that had grown out of the Enlightenment and had come to mark modernity. In *The Postmodern Explained to Children*, Lyotard (1992, 29) mentions

> the progressive emancipation of reason and freedom, the progressive or catastrophic emancipation of labour . . . , the enrichment of all through the progress of capitalist technoscience, and even . . . the salvation of creatures through the conversion of souls to the Christian narrative of martyred love.

These metanarratives, which have the goal of legitimating our institutions and our practices all, have centrally involved education. Indeed, education is not merely one of the institutions that have been shaped or legitimated by the dominant metanarratives; at the lower levels, it has been instrumentally involved with their systematic reproduction, elucidation, and preservation, and at the higher levels, it has been concerned with their ideological production, dissemination, and refinement.

Postmodernity, then, can be understood at a philosophical level. But it is also a cultural, political, and socioeconomic phenomenon that emphasizes not only the break with traditionally modern ways of understanding the world but also the transformations of the dominant mode of economic organization, including changes in the mode of production as well as changes in the organization of work, the labor market, and patterns of work. In the economic domain, postmodernity is sometimes referred to as "late capitalism," "multinational capitalism," "post-Fordism," or "flexible specialization." Together these descriptions emphasize a new techno-information and communications infrastructure that supports the globally networked knowledge economy. While the internationalization of the new economy is itself not a novel feature, there is no doubt that the technological infrastructure, which permits complex economic transactions to be completed at an unprecedented speed, certainly is new. As Manuel Castells (2000a, 52) argues,

> Productivity and competitiveness are, by and large, a function of knowledge generation and information processing; firms and territories are organised in networks of production, management, and distribution; the core economic activities are global—that is, they have the capacity to work as a unit in real time, or chosen time, on a planetary scale.

This new techno-infrastructure and the info-capitalism based upon it, together with the new technologies, has already transformed both our institutions and our subjectivities. As a working basis for outlining the concept of postmodernity, we argue for the concept as a complex or multilayered one involving three elements: socioeconomic postmodernization, cultural transformation, and the emergence of new political forms (see table 2.2).

Table 2.2. Sociology of Postmodernity

1. Socioeconomic postmodernization
   Variously described as "post-industrial," "post-Fordist," "information society," "flexible specialization," "late capitalism" (Mandel, Jameson), "reflexive modernization" (Giddens), "knowledge economy."
   - Globalization as a market-driven and political project of world economic integration
     Abolition of capital controls, fixed exchange rates, and growth of world financial markets and neoliberal (Anglo-American) capitalism—world influence of G8, IMF, OECD, WB, and WTO
   - Emergence of truly "stateless" transnational corporations (MNCs) and NGOs
   - Development of world infrastructure of information and (tele)communications technologies
   - Substitution of capital for labor in the industrial economy
     Full automation of primary, secondary, and tertiary industries
   - Collapse of base/superstructure distinction
     "Culture as knowledge" and "knowledge as economy"; rise of "sign" or "symbolic" economy based on intellectual capital
2. Cultural differentiation and homogeneity
   Hyperdifferentiation, commodification, and rationalization
   Differentiation of "culture" internal to the nation-state described in terms of the growth of postwar youth cultures, subcultures, and "lifestyles"; national cultures, cultural reconstruction, and enterprise culture; and external to the nation-state described in terms of postcolonialism, ethnic nationalism, national independence, diasporas, immigration flows, the growth of refugee and asylum seekers, extranational unions and regional blocs, and the emergence of global cultures.
   - Decentering of the West and growth of non-Western postmodernisms
   - Commodification and aesethicization of everyday life
   - Capitalization of all forms of knowledge and the self
   - Collapse of high and popular culture; growth of media cultures
   - Cultural globalization—emergence of American global consumer style
   - Social individualization and growth of "risk society"
   - Linguistic turn and increased significance of language
   - Different cultural experience and expression of time
3. Emergence of new political forms
   - Collapse of the socialist alternative leaving capitalism now almost self-legitimating
     Globalization curtails classical social democratic strategy of full employment, high levels of public expenditure, and progressive taxation.
   - Emergence of neoliberalism and "Third Way" politics
   - Growth of "new social movements"
   - Relative decline of the nation-state vis à vis global capital
     Globalisation has weakened influence of national politics on social policy growth of extranational economic associations (e.g., EU, NAFTA).

These world-historical transformations represent the challenge for education and culture, and, as you can see, they are central elements in the shift from an industrial to a knowledge economy. They are also central ingredients in our overall argument, for the conception of the relationship between education and culture is critical in the transition to the knowledge economy, particularly when we speak of the development of education as knowledge cultures. And in this formulation, we must also acknowledge and make good the warrant for picturing postmodernity in terms of a closer relationship between education and knowledge, and not only in terms of a transformed economic relationship—that is, education in the knowledge economy as a defining feature of postmodernity—but also in terms of how the question of value is part of this overall equation.

In this complex, then, we are strongly influenced by Nietzsche, Heidegger, and Wittgenstein—those philosophers whom we call prophets of postmodernity. In each case, they provide us with a way through. Two books published recently that raise the question of value in relation to knowledge also particularly strike us and offer a brief means of considering the question: Frederick Ferré's (1998) *Knowing and Value: Toward a Constructive Postmodern Epistemology* and Barry Allen's (2004) *Knowledge and Civilization*. Both men have difficulties with the term *postmodern* and yet both also, though in different ways, focus on the value commitments of knowing and of traditional epistemology. Ferré (1998, 16) clearly states, "My thesis is that epistemology, no less than metaphysics, is deeply rooted in judgements of value, explicit and implicit." His task is to show, first, how the epistemological gap between the knower and the known came about and how it was first discovered; second, the coping strategies that philosophers develop for reducing, webbing, and leaping the gap; and, third, how we might deconstruct the gap and come to know the world. He explains the inextricability of knowing and valuing in these terms:

> From its humblest origins to its highest aspirations, knowing is mingled with value. Experience arrives in a flood of affective tone; its earliest glimmerings, rising from preconscious states, are already selective, busy with affirmations and negations. Praxis is motivated by the urge to learn methods for the sake of survival and for the flourishing of life. Sign cognition depends on intuitions of importance among discriminated regularities in experience and on normative judgements that memory is reliable, that sign tokens fall within the accepted range of sign types, and that associations are fruitful. Concept formation rests on what is deemed worthy of noticing and naming. (Ferré 1998, 372)

And so he goes on to talk of the valuing implicit in observation, theory construction, and theory justification. His strategy, then, is to reveal the epistemological gap as a grand modern myth and to deconstruct it, "lay-ing bare the preferences, assumptions, and commitments behind the seeming discovery" (267). Ferré, by contrast, wants to invoke an alternative view that offers an account of experience, thinking, and knowing as natural parts of an "ecological worldview," inspired by Alfred Whitehead's process philosophy and the "bellwether of modern science" (268). This he takes to be the "postmodern turn" in science, which can be grounded in ecology as a kind of "relational ontology" that emphasizes continuities and connectedness in experience.

Where Ferré's attempt is an explicit attempt to build a constructive postmodern epistemology, Allen's is less self-consciously postmodern and is yet remarkably consonant with Ferré's project. Allen describes his book as "a contribution to the rehabilitation of philosophy from the rationalist bias of its origin, at the origin of Western rationalism . . . toward an ecological philosophy of technology and civilization" (Allen 2004, 3). Both approaches are especially pertinent to knowledge economy and the economy of knowledge. Allen begins with what he calls "the epistemological bias":

> Partiality for the proposition, and especially its truth, is such a bias. Knowledge—or the philosophically most important knowledge—has to be true. Since a proposition, as logic understands it, is simply whatever admits of evaluation as true or false, knowledge . . . has to be propositional—knowing *that* such-and-such *is true*. On my argument, knowledge embraces more than propositions, more than discursive knowledge of justified statements, more than anything language can say. Knowledge runs the range of artefacts, its domain no less than technical culture in its widest sense. (3)

Knowledge for Allen is an artifact, and knowing is artifactual performance. He also begins with the question "What was epistemology?" to consider the art of knowledge as artifact or a characteristic product of human activity, from the Latin *arte*, meaning "skill," and *factum*, meaning "doing." He argues, "An *arte-factum* is a skilled doing (a performance), and its effect (a work or product)" (63). Knowing as artifact involves the transformation of a given raw material, which is a form of creation and fabrication. Allen's theory of knowing is thus very close to creating a product. Knowledge is effective performance in the sense that it is consequential, "engaged with artefacts, environment, and agents, in a way that no mere representation can be," which leads him to distinguish between learning and knowing. "Learning is the accomplishment of an individual, whereas knowledge is the accomplishment of an artefact" (71). Allen also embraces an ecological view in the sense that he argues that knowing is tied to human evolution—"civilization"—clearly evidenced in the growth of cities and "the urbanization of knowledge." On his model, the evolution of knowledge is "the contingent and cultivation of aesthetic preference" (88), but the conditions under which knowledge exists change with the development of civilization, and to this extent, when "the density of artefactual mediation rises sharply . . . knowledge tends to become technological" (89). He also considers postmodern philosophers—Nietzsche, Foucault, and Rorty—to conclude that in philosophy we should recognize "of language games, history or politics but artefact and ecology as the ultimate context for understanding knowledge" (4).

Allen's and Ferré's theses fit nicely with our own on knowledge cultures, for together they recognize the deficiencies of standard epistemologies; of knowledge as justified belief; and of the paradigm of theoretical knowledge, based as it is on *theoria* and the ideal of contemplation over practical engagement with the world. Together they emphasize the hidden biases and implicit values of philosophy as epistemology, and going beyond "the end of epistemology" and Western rationalism, they overcome the epistemological gap with ecological models that recognize the value of practice—an implicit commitment to contingency, human evolution, and civilization. The ethos of an economy of knowledge is thus written into "artefactual performance" and technology, although not necessarily also into specific historical and political formations of technology.

If we differ from both Ferré and Allen, it is because we are historicists who want to privilege questions of the politics and ethics of knowledge, to read knowledge as technology against deliberate strategies and policies that create economies of knowledge. Only in this way can we understand the Cold War regime of science organization and funding in the United States and chart its shift to the privatization funding regime that followed the end of the Cold War. Curiously, Allen's knowledge as cultural technologies seems oblivious to different political and economic readings that might give the emergence of a new techno-infrastructure under capitalism. Allen (2004, 272) does record,

> The commercialisation of scientific research ("intellectual property") is the presently dominant source of new business opportunities in the world, and techno-scientific products contribute the principal source of added value and competitive advantage.

And he is skeptical about corporate capitalism in relation to the promotion of innovation. What really is at stake, he says, is "the *control* of innovation, even at the price of subverting it." He continues,

> Seriously new alternatives are not something that can be managed or made predictable without compromising the very quality (performance) that makes knowledge valuable. . . . The market is not and cannot be the primary economy of life; instead, the so-called free market and its presumptions—its short-term thinking and brutal abstraction—undermine what is primary.

But then this observation seems to clash with Allen's thesis of human evolution and knowledge as civilization, for contemporary civilization—

life in cities—takes place within the larger framework of globalization. If one accepts an artifactual technology of knowledge that in terms of human evolution cashed itself out in "civilization"—that is, in cities and urbanism—then to be self-consistent, it is necessary to examine the latter and contemporary episodes of this development, including globalization and the development of the Internet and the World Wide Web, which together imply the informatization of knowledge, the time-space compression of its products, and the decentralization of its effects.

3

Education Policy in the Age of Knowledge Capitalism[1]

INTRODUCTION

Martin Carnoy and Diana Rhoten (2002) have recently argued that "linking economic and social change to changes in how societies transmit knowledge is a relatively new approach to studying education." Beginning in the 1960s and 1970s, historical studies challenged the old view of comparative education that focused on the philosophical and cultural origins of national systems of education by situating educational reform in economic and social change. Carnoy and Rhoten write,

> Some of them went further, using approaches based in political economy, world systems theory, and theories of neo-colonialism and underdevelopment to show that economic imperatives on a global scale were a major force in shaping education worldwide.

They recognize how globalization provides both a new empirical challenge and a theoretical framework for comparative education, arguing,

> Globalization is a force reorganizing the world's economy, and the main resources for that economy are increasingly knowledge and information. If knowledge and information, usually transmitted and shaped by national and local institutions, are fundamental to the development of the global economy, and the global economy, in turn, shapes the nature of educational opportunities and institutions, how should we draw the directional arrows in our analysis?

They go on to argue that "if knowledge is fundamental to globalization, globalization should also have a profound impact on the transmission of knowledge," yet while the decentralization of educational administration and finance has proceeded apace, there has been little apparent change at the level of the classroom.[2] Carnoy and Rhoten also analyze the relationship between the nation-state and the globalized political economy as one that involves, on the one hand, processes that may diminish the power of the state through growth promotion and enhancement of national competitiveness based on attracting multinational capital flows at the expense of domestic education policy, and on the other, processes that may shift and enhance specific powers of the state to control the territorial and temporal spaces for capital investment, especially in the new complexity of layered world and regional governance. Elsewhere, Carnoy (2000) argues that globalization is impacting education in terms of finance (reduction of public spending and the search for other founding sources); the labor market (providing a ready supply of skilled labor as a basis to attract foreign capital); the quality of national educational systems (through international comparison, testing, and standards); and the adoption of information technology (to expand quantity of education at low cost). In this regard, he suggests that "globalized information networks mean transformation of world culture," which is increasingly contested by new global movements (see also Peters 2002a). Prophetically, he remarks, "This constitutes a new kind of struggle over the meaning and value of knowledge," yet he acknowledges that these educational changes, while sharing certain characteristics, also vary greatly across regions and nations.

It is clear that accounts of globalization differ considerably. *Globalization* is a contested term, and different forms of globalization (economic, cultural, ecological, technological) can be understood as parallel and differential processes that proceed differently and affect countries in varied ways. Yet what we might call "the neoliberal project of globalization"—an outcome of the Washington consensus and modeled by world policy agencies such as the IMF and the World Bank—has predominated in world policy forums at the expense of alternative accounts of globalization.[3] It is an account that universalizes policies and obscures country and regional differences. It also denies the capacity of local traditions, institutions, and cultural values to mediate, negotiate, reinterpret, and transmute the dominant model of globalization and the emergent form of knowledge capitalism on which it is based. Yet voices of criticism, even from mainstream economists, have been raised against this monolithic and homogenizing model of globalization.

For example, Joseph Stiglitz (2002), as former chief economist of the World Bank, has recently criticized the policy decisions of the IMF as "a curious blend of ideology and bad economics." In particular, he argues that the IMF's structural adjustment policies imposed on developing countries have led to hunger and riots in many countries and have precipitated crises that have led to greater poverty and international inequalities. Elsewhere, Stiglitz (1999a) identifies the new global knowledge economy as one that differs from the traditional industrial economy in terms of the scarcity-defying characteristics of ideas. He argues that the reality of the knowledge economy requires a rethinking of economics because knowledge behaves differently from other commodities such that its sharing may add to its value. He maintains that knowledge also shares many of the properties of a *global* public good, implying the necessity of government intervention in the protection of intellectual property rights in a global economy, especially where the tendency to natural monopolies is even greater than in the industrial economy, marked by a greater potential for monopolies than under industrial capitalism (see also Peters 2001b, 2002b, 2002f, 2002g).

Yet at the heart of Stiglitz's (2002) analysis of globalization and its discontents is an approach based on the economics of information—in particular, *asymmetries of information*—and its role in challenging standard economic models of the market that assumed perfect information. Information economics provide better foundations for theories of labor and financial markets. His work on the role of information in economics evolved into an analysis of the role of information in political institutions, where he emphasized

> the necessity for increased transparency, improving the information that citizens have about what these institutions do, allowing those who are affected by the policies to have a greater say in their formulation. (Stiglitz 2002, xii)

The transformation of knowledge production and its legitimation, as both Stiglitz and Carnoy indicate, are central to an understanding of globalization and its effects on education policy. If transformations in knowledge production entail a rethinking of economic fundamentals, the shift to a knowledge economy also requires a profound rethinking of education as emerging forms of knowledge capitalism involving knowledge creation, acquisition, transmission, and organization. This chapter is an essay on the new political economy of knowledge and information. It adopts the concepts of "knowledge capitalism" and "knowledge economy" as overarching and master concepts that denote a sea change in the nature of capitalism, and it seeks to understand this change by reference to economic theories of knowledge and information. Comparativists in education, while alert to the forthcoming struggles of the meaning and value of knowledge, must also come to understand the driving economic theories, in part responsible for influential characterizations of knowledge capitalism and the knowledge economy, as a first stage in sensitizing themselves to regional and cultural differences in the way educational policies are formulated and implemented.

The term *knowledge capitalism* emerged only recently to describe the transition to the so-called knowledge economy, which we characterize in terms of the economics of abundance, the annihilation of distance, the deterritorialization of the state, and investment in human capital (see table 3.1).

As the business development and policy advocate Burton-Jones (1999, vi) puts it, "Knowledge is fast becoming the most important form of global capital—hence 'knowledge capitalism.'" He views it as a new *generic* form of capitalism as opposed to simply another regional model or variation. For Burton-Jones and analysts of world policy agencies such as the World Bank and OECD, the shift to a knowledge economy involves a fundamental rethinking of the traditional relationships between education, learning, and work, focusing on the need for a new coalition between education and industry. *Knowledge capitalism* and *knowledge economy* are twin terms that can be traced at the level of public policy to a series of reports that emerged in the late 1990s by the OECD (1996b) and the World Bank (1998) before they were taken up as a policy template by world governments in the late 1990s (see, e.g., Peters 2001b). In terms of these reports, education is reconfigured as a massively undervalued form of knowledge capital that will determine the future of work, the organization of knowledge institutions, and the shape of society in the years to come.

This chapter, then, focuses on the twin notions of "knowledge capitalism" and the "knowledge economy" as a comparative context for formu-

Table 3.1. Characteristics of the Knowledge Economy

The knowledge economy differs from the traditional economy in several key respects:

1. The economics is not of scarcity but rather of abundance. Unlike most resources that deplete when used, information and knowledge can be shared and may actually grow through application.
2. The effect of location is diminished. Using appropriate technology and methods, virtual marketplaces and virtual organizations can be created that offer benefits of speed and agility, round-the-clock operation, and global reach.
3. Laws, barriers, and taxes are difficult to apply on solely a national basis. Knowledge and information "leak" to where demand is highest and barriers are lowest.
4. Knowledge-enhanced products or services can command price premiums over comparable products with low embedded knowledge or knowledge intensity.
5. Pricing and value depend heavily on context. Thus the same information or knowledge can have vastly different value to different people at different times.
6. Knowledge when locked into systems or processes has higher inherent value than when it can "walk out of the door" in people's heads.
7. Human capital—competencies—are a key component of value in a knowledge-based company, yet few companies report competency levels in annual reports. In contrast, downsizing is often seen as a positive "cost-cutting" measure.

Source: David Skyrme Associates, www.skyrme.com/insights/21gke.htm.

lating education policy. First, it briefly analyzes recent documents of world policy agencies concerning these two concepts, focusing on the OECD's emphasis on "new growth theory"; second, it examines the World Bank's *Knowledge for Development*; and, third, it briefly discusses the notion of knowledge capitalism as it appears in the recent work of Alan Burton-Jones (1999). These examples serve as three accounts of knowledge capitalism, or, better, of contemporary capitalism, that explain its advanced development from the single perspective of the economic importance of knowledge and information. In the concluding note, the chapter raises a series of issues for comparative education and entertains a concept of knowledge socialism as an alternative organizing concept underlying knowledge creation, production, and development.

THE KNOWLEDGE ECONOMY:
THE OECD AND NEW GROWTH THEORY

The OECD report *The Knowledge-Based Economy* (1996b) begins with the following statement:

> OECD analysis is increasingly directed to understanding the dynamics of the knowledge-based economy and its relationship to traditional economics, as reflected in *"new growth theory."* The growing codification of knowledge and its transmission through communications and computer networks has led to the emerging *"information society."* The need for workers to acquire a range of skills and to continuously adapt these skills underlies the *"learning economy."* The importance of knowledge and technology diffusion requires better understanding of knowledge networks and *"national innovation systems."*

The report is divided into three sections, focusing on trends and implications of the knowledge-based economy; the role of the science system in the knowledge-based economy; and indicators, essentially a section dealing with the question of measurement (see also OECD 1996a, 1996c, 1997; Foray and Lundvall 1996). In the summary, the OECD report discusses knowledge distribution (as well as knowledge investments) through formal and informal networks as being essential to economic performance and hypothesizes the increasing codification of knowledge in the emerging "information society." In the knowledge-based economy, "innovation is driven by the interaction of producers and users in the exchange of both codified and tacit knowledge." The report points to an interactive model of innovation (replacing the old linear model), which consists of knowledge flows and relationships among industry, government, and academia in the development of science and technology. With increasing demand for more highly skilled knowledge workers, the OECD indicates,

Governments will need more stress on upgrading human capital through promoting access to a range of skills, and especially the capacity to learn; enhancing the *knowledge distribution power* of the economy through collaborative networks and the diffusion of technology; and providing the enabling conditions for organisational change at the firm level to maximise the benefits of technology for productivity. (7)

The science system—public research laboratories and institutions of higher education—is seen as one of the key components of the knowledge economy, and the report identifies the major challenge as one of reconciling its traditional functions of knowledge production and the training of scientists with its newer role of collaborating with industry in the transfer of knowledge and technology.

In an analysis of the knowledge-based economy in one of the earliest reports to use the concept, the OECD observes that economies are more strongly dependent on knowledge production, distribution, and use than ever before and that knowledge-intensive service sectors (especially education, communications, and information) are the fastest growing parts of Western economies, which, in turn, are attracting high levels of public and private investment (spending on research reached an average of 2.3 percent, and education accounts for 12 percent, of GDP in the early 1990s). The report indicates how knowledge and technology have always been considered external influences on production and that now new approaches are being developed so that knowledge can be included more directly. (The report mentions Friedrich List on knowledge infrastructure and institutions; Schumpeter, Galbraith, Goodwin, and Hirschman on innovation; and Romer and Grossman on new growth theory). New growth theory, in particular, demonstrates that investment in knowledge is characterized by increasing rather than decreasing returns, a finding that modifies the neoclassical production function, which argues that returns diminish as more capital is added to the economy. Knowledge also has spillover functions from one industry or firm to another, yet types of knowledge vary: some kinds can be easily reproduced and distributed at low cost, while others cannot be easily transferred from one organization to another or between individuals. Thus, knowledge (as a much broader concept than information) can be considered in terms of "know-what" and "know-why," broadly what philosophers call propositional knowledge ("knowledge that"), embracing both factual knowledge and scientific knowledge, both of which come closest to being market commodities or economic resources that can be fitted into production functions. Other types of knowledge, what the OECD identifies as "know-how" and "know-who," are forms of tacit knowledge (after Polanyi 1967; see also Polanyi 1958) that are more difficult to codify and measure. The OECD report indicates that "*Tacit knowledge* in the form of skills needed to handle codified knowledge is more important than ever in labour markets" (1996b, 13, emphasis in original) and reason that "education will be the centre of the knowledge-based economy, and learning the tool of individual and organisational advancement" (14), where *"learning-by-doing"* is paramount.[4]

THE WORLD BANK:
STIGLITZ'S KNOWLEDGE FOR DEVELOPMENT

In 1998 the World Bank released its influential *World Development Report: Knowledge for Development* (World Bank 1998), which indicated a major shift in the development paradigm away from its status as a bank that provided infrastructure finance to one that resembles a "knowledge bank," with a greater emphasis on the role of knowledge, learning, and innovation in development (see chapter 9).

Knowledge for Development tends to separate knowledge about technology from knowledge about attributes, or what is traditionally called human capital formation. The aim is to reduce "knowledge gaps" and to foster knowledge creation and acquisition. In this changed picture of development, education takes on a central role in terms not only of basic education but also of lifelong education (see chapter 9).

Let us briefly note the importance of education to this development recipe. Acquiring knowledge not only involves using and adapting knowledge available elsewhere in the world—best acquired, so the report argues, through an open trading regime, foreign investment, and licensing agreements—but also local knowledge creation through research and development and building upon indigenous knowledge. Absorbing knowledge is the set of national policies that centrally concerns education, including universal basic education (with special emphasis on extending girls' education and that of other disadvantaged groups); creating opportunities for lifelong learning; and supporting tertiary education, especially science and engineering. Communicating knowledge involves taking advantage of new information and communications technology, as the report would have it, through increased competition, private-sector provision, and appropriate regulation. Arguably, without delving further into this substantial report, the World Bank maintains its neoliberal orientation with an emphasis on open trade and privatization, although it is recast in terms of the perspective of knowledge.

Stiglitz, perhaps, deviates more from the Washington consensus. In a series of related papers delivered in his role as chief economist for the World Bank, he (1999c) argues that knowledge is a public good because it is nonrivalrous—that is, knowledge once discovered and made public operates expansively to defy the normal "law" of scarcity that governs most commodity markets.[5] Knowledge in its immaterial or conceptual forms—ideas, information, concepts, functions, and abstract objects of thought—is purely nonrivalrous such that there are essentially no marginal costs to adding more users. Yet once materially embodied or encoded, such as in learning or in applications or processes, knowledge becomes costly in time and resources. The pure nonrivalrousness of knowledge can be differentiated from the low cost of its dissemination resulting from improvements in electronic media and technology, although there may be congestion effects and waiting time (e.g., to reserve a book or download from the Internet). Stiglitz (1999c) delivered his influential paper "Public Policy for a Knowledge Economy" to the United Kingdom's Department for Trade and Industry and Center for Economic Policy Research on the eve of the release of the UK white paper *Our Competitive Future: Building the Knowledge Driven Economy* (www.dti.gov.uk/comp/competitive/main.htm), which subsequently became a template for education policy in England and Scotland (see Peters 2001b). Stiglitz's paper also provides a useful guide for understanding some of the analytics of the knowledge economy (see table 3.2).

Table 3.2.   Analytics of the Knowledge Economy

It is argued that the knowledge economy is different from the traditional industrial economy because knowledge is fundamentally different from other commodities, and these differences, consequently, have fundamental implications both for public policy and for the mode of organization of a knowledge economy.

The Scarcity-defying characteristics of ideas
   1. Nonrivalry
   2. Conceptual vs. Material Knowledge
Intellectual property rights
   1. Excludability
   2. Externalities
   3. Competition
Organizational dimensions of knowledge
   1. Knowledge markets
   2. Knowledge transactions within firms
   3. Openness and knowledge transfer
   4. Experimentation
The marketplace of ideas
   1. Pluralism in project selection
   2. Robustness
   3. The failure of central planning
   4. Decentralization and participation within firms
   5. Openness in the political process

Source: Adapted from Joseph Stiglitz (1999c).

While nonrivalrous, knowledge can be *excluded* (the other property of a pure public good) from certain users. The private provision of knowledge normally requires some form of legal protection, because otherwise firms would have no incentive to produce it. Yet knowledge is not an ordinary property right. Typically, basic ideas, such as mathematical theorems, on which other research depends, are not patentable, and hence a strong intellectual property rights regime might actually inhibit the pace of innovation. Even though knowledge is not a pure public good, there are extensive externalities (spillovers) associated with innovations. As Stiglitz notes, the full benefits of the transistor, microchip, and laser did not accrue to those who contributed to those innovations.

While competition is necessary for a successful knowledge economy, Stiglitz maintains that knowledge gives rise to a form of increasing returns of scale, which may undermine competition, for with large network externalities, forms of monopoly knowledge capitalism (e.g., Microsoft) become a possible danger at the international level. New technologies provide greater scope for the suppression of competition, and, if creativity is essential for the knowledge economy, then small enterprises may provide a better base for innovation than large bureaucracies. Significantly, Stiglitz provides some grounds for government funding of universities as competitive knowledge corporations within the knowledge economy and for government regulation of knowledge or information monopolies, especially those multinational companies that provide the so-called information infrastructure.

On the basis of this analysis, Stiglitz provides a number of pertinent observations on the organizational dimensions of knowledge. He maintains that just as knowledge differs from other commodities, so too do knowledge markets differ from other markets. If each piece of information differs from every other piece, then information cannot satisfy the essential market property of *homogeneity*. Knowledge market transactions for nonpatented knowledge require that we disclose something and thus risk losing property. Thus, in practice, markets for knowledge and information depend critically on reputation, on repeated interactions, and also, significantly, on trust.

On the supply side, knowledge transactions within firms and organizations require trust and reciprocity if knowledge workers are to share knowledge and codify their tacit knowledge. Hoarding creates a vicious circle of knowledge restriction, whereas trust and reciprocity can create a culture based on a virtuous circle of knowledge sharing. On the demand side, *learning cultures* (my construction) artificially limit demand for knowledge if they denigrate any request for knowledge as an admission of ignorance.

Stiglitz argues that these knowledge principles carry over to knowledge institutions and countries as a whole. If basic intellectual property rights are routinely violated, the supply of knowledge will be diminished. Where trust relationships have been flagrantly violated, learning opportunities will vanish. Experimentation is another type of openness, which cannot take place in closed societies or in institutions hostile to change. Finally, he argues that changes in economic institutions have counterparts in the political sphere, demanding the institutions of an open society, such as a free press, a transparent government, pluralism, checks and balances, toleration, freedom of thought, and open public debate. This political openness is essential for the success of the transformation toward a knowledge economy.

KNOWLEDGE CAPITALISM: BURTON-JONES'S CONCEPTION

Perhaps the most developed model of knowledge capitalism, together with the most worked-out implications for education, comes from a book of that title—*Knowledge Capitalism: Business, Work, and Learning in the New Economy* by Alan Burton-Jones (1999).[6] Burton-Jones states his thesis in the following way:

> The fundamental proposition of the book is that among the various factors currently causing change in the economy, none is more important than the changing role of *knowledge*. . . . As the title of the book suggests, knowledge is fast becoming the most important form of global capital—hence "knowledge capitalism." Paradoxically, knowledge is probably the least understood and most undervalued of all economic resources. The central theme of this book is, therefore, the nature and value of knowledge and how it is fundamentally altering the basis of economic activity, thus business, employment, and all of our futures. The central message is that we need to reappraise many of our industrial era notions of business organization, business ownership, work arrangements, business strategy, and the links between education, learning and work.

He argues that the distinctions between managers and workers, between learning and working, are becoming blurred so that we all become owners of our own intellectual capital, or knowledge capitalists—at least in the Western advanced economies. And he goes on to chart the shift to the knowledge economy, new models of knowledge-centered organization, the imperatives of knowledge supply (as opposed to labor supply), the decline in traditional forms of employment, and the knowledge characteristics of work. He argues that "economic demand for an increasingly skilled workforce will necessitate a move to lifelong learning" (vii) based upon the learning imperative, including the use of learning technologies, which will lead to the development of a global learning industry and to profound "changes to the relationships involving learners, educators and firms" (vii). Burton-Jones addresses himself to the question of how governments might assist in the transition to the knowledge economy by focusing on knowledge acquisition (education, learning, and skills formation) and knowledge development (research and innovation) policies, suggesting that while most of the changes have occurred as a spontaneous response to the demands of the market rather than through state intervention, the state has an important role to play. He is less enthusiastic than Stiglitz or Thurow about the proposition that the increasing importance of knowledge in the economy might lead to a reversal of current trends and produce an increasing role for the state.

KNOWLEDGE CAPITALISM OR KNOWLEDGE SOCIALISM?

Of the three accounts of knowledge capitalism we have briefly presented, Stiglitz's arguments are perhaps the most important for understanding what we call "knowledge cultures." As we argued in chapter 1, the distinction between the knowledge economy and the knowledge society is too dualistic. The object of economics of knowledge is knowledge as an economic good and the properties governing its production and reproduction. Insofar as the knowledge economy discourse is seen as a basis for the structural transformation of the economy focusing on the production, distribution, and transfer of knowledge, it cannot base its understanding on the industrial economy or, indeed, employ traditional neo-classical assumptions. Knowledge does not behave in the same way as other commodities as the exchange, use, and sharing of knowledge may not deplete its value but actually enhance it. *Knowledge capitalism* reifies the economic at that historical point when a shift to the "sign" economy, or the importance of symbolic goods in general, blurs the distinction between economy and culture. The discourse of the knowledge society focuses on the social origin of ideas and their effects on society and the social relations of knowledge including its institutions. It is concerned with new forms of social stratification evident with the production of knowledge and the emerging international knowledge system. It is also concerned with questions of access and distribution, and with associated rights. Our preferred term *knowledge cultures* encourages a greater interdisciplinary approach based in part on the understanding that we must understand the new logic of cultural consumption where consumers are no longer passive but act as co-producers of knowledge, information, and cultural goods. We use the term *knowledge cultures* in the plural because there is not one prescription or formula that fits all institutions, societies, or knowledge traditions. In this situation, perhaps, we should talk of the ways in which knowledge capitalism rests upon conditions of knowledge socialism, at least upon the sharing and exchange of ideas among knowledge workers.

Our speculative hypothesis, not investigated at any length in this chapter, is that knowledge capitalism will exhibit different patterns of production, ownership, and innovation according to five basic regional models of capitalism. These five regional models, based in part on different cultural understandings of knowledge and learning, not only represent cultural differences in the meaning and value of knowledge but also provide a major index for regional differences in education policy.

We can talk of Anglo-American capitalism, European social market capitalism, French state capitalism, and the Japanese model. Clearly, one might also talk of an emergent fifth model based on China's market socialism. A recent World Bank study, for instance, has suggested that the Chinese government must take on the new role of architect of appropriate institutions and provider of incentives to promote and regulate a new socialist market economy based on knowledge (see Dahlman and Aubert 2001).[7]

Yet the notion of the knowledge economy also represents something of an anomaly. Even in the face of widespread policies of privatization, education in most OECD countries remains overwhelmingly public, that is, state owned and regulated. As we argue more fully in chapter 5, the dominant mode of the organization of knowledge is still largely state owned, even if there has been a steady erosion of traditional state providers at all levels and in all areas of education. Clearly, as firms and other nonstate organizations edge themselves further into the traditional preserve of state education, public ownership and regulation of knowledge will diminish. In addition to an increase in the privatized distribution, delivery, and sources of knowledge, there has already emerged a welter of public-private partnerships, particularly in science and engineering fields. There is the continued likelihood that governments will permit greater experimentation in forms of provision, regulation, and funding with the emergence of public-private partnerships, community-owned and/or religiously oriented institutions, and a raft of private enterprises that not only directly substitute for traditional state educational activities—especially with the growth of private business and management schools—but that also interface with the state sector in the area of technical support. There are myriad forms of privatization that parallel each other, from vouchers to outsourcing. This emergence of profit, not-for-profit, community, and state organizations indicates that there will be many struggles—legal and ethical—over knowledge ownership, creation, distribution, access, and archiving. In the age of knowledge capitalism, the problem of knowledge cannot be separated from the problem of the accumulation of capital; these two are increasingly interdependent and inextricably bound up together in ways that imperil "pure" state forms of knowledge production and exchange. The picture is further complicated through the progress of an emerging intellectual property rights regime developed and promulgated, in particular, through the World Trade Organization and negotiations of trade policy, including the General Agreement on Trade in Services (GATS), which came into force in 1995. These new trade rules, designed to encourage international competition, include all manner of service activity and describe those services universally considered to be essential to human health and development, such as education and health care. The implications for knowledge institutions, especially higher education and libraries, are enormous and point toward "knowledge wars" between "information-rich" multinationals and small dependent states, and toward future global struggles over the commercialization and commodification of information, knowledge, and associated services.

NOTES

1. A version of this paper was given as a keynote address to the World Comparative Education Forum Economic Globalization and Education Reforms, Beijing Normal University, October 14–16, 2002.

2. This observation seems questionable in view of the restructuring of national curricula to focus on basic skills of numeracy and literacy, the standards-based movement, the proliferation of work-based education programs, the introduction of technology studies, the emphasis on science, the reform of teacher training, the registration and new accountability of teachers, and the like, which have accompanied globalization.

3. There is a huge literature criticizing globalization and suggesting alternatives. See, for example, Appadurai (2001), Bello (2001), and Mandle (2003).

4. The emphasis on tacit knowledge is developed out of the work of Polanyi (1958, 1967), which is also strongly developed in terms of the concept of practice in both Heidegger and Wittgenstein. The emphasis on practice, perhaps, is a major distinguishing characteristic of much twentieth-century philosophy, sociology, and cultural analysis (see, e.g., Turner, 1994), with a focus on the practical over the theoretical and the "background practices" against which theoretical knowledge is articulated and/or codified. The concept of practice, mostly unexamined, figures largely in education and pedagogy and in the relatively new concept of "communities of practice" that has been developed in the context of business and organizational learning.

5. This section on Stiglitz draws on the section "Analytics of the Knowledge Economy" from Michael Peters's recent paper "Universities, Globalisation and the Knowledge Economy" (Peters, 2002f).

6. For a recent article by Burton-Jones, see the inaugural issue of the web-based new start-up journal *Policy Futures in Education*, edited by Michael Peters and available at Triangle Publications from 2003 (www.triangle.co.uk). The inaugural issue is devoted to "Education and the Knowledge Economy," with contributions from Paul A David and Dominique Forey, Gerarde Delanty, Steve Fuller, and many others.

7. Dahlman and Aubert (2001) argue that improving education is perhaps the most critical reform for the medium and long runs.

4

National Education Policy Constructions of the Knowledge Economy

INTRODUCTION

We live in a social universe in which the formation, circulation, and utilization of knowledge presents a fundamental problem. If the accumulation of capital has been an essential feature of our society, the accumulation of knowledge has not been any less so. Now, the exercise,
production, and accumulation of this knowledge cannot be dissociated
from the mechanisms of power; complex relations exist which must be
analysed.

—Michel Foucault, *Remarks on Marx*

Today, education stands at the heart of the knowledge economy and is
seen as the means for a major structural transformation from the industrial to the knowledge economy. In part this is a consequence of a theory of structural transformation that suggests that labor and capital are
not the only two important forces of production and that they are being
replaced by information and knowledge as the primary wealth-creating
assets. This theory indicates that technology and knowledge have transformed patterns of work and the organization of labor such that, like capital, knowledge and information can be easily circulated around the
globe, and they provide the basis for competitive advantage, especially
when linked to processes of innovation.[1] Both the World Bank and the
OECD have long emphasized how important improvements in education
are to labor productivity and national economic growth. The World Bank,
for instance, asserts,

Education is central to development. It empowers people, strengthens nations, and is key to the attainment of the Millennium Development Goals. Already the world's largest external financier of education, the World Bank is today more committed than ever to helping countries develop holistic education systems aimed both at achieving Education for All (EFA) and building dynamic knowledge societies that are key to competing in global markets through Education for the Knowledge Economy (EKE).

The World Bank clearly subscribes to this theory, and it parses EKE in the following terms:

> Education for the Knowledge Economy (EKE) refers to World Bank assistance aimed at helping developing countries equip themselves with the highly skilled and flexible human capital needed to compete effectively in today's dynamic global markets. Such assistance recognizes first and foremost that the ability to produce and use knowledge has become a major factor in development and critical to a nation's comparative advantage. It also recognizes that surging demand for secondary education in many parts of the world creates an invaluable opportunity to build up in large scale a workforce that is well trained and capable of generating knowledge-driven economic growth (http://web.worldbank.org/WBSITE/EXTERNAL/TOPICS/ EXTEDUCATION/0,,contentMDK:20161496~menuPK:540092~pagePK:148956 ~piPK:216618~theSitePK:282386,00.html).

Education is the principal means of developing "highly skilled and flexible human capital" for effective competition in global markets.

A whole string of theorists from the discourses of economics, management, and business studies now see education as the panacea to development for both first and third world, or developing, countries. Knowledge, skills, and competencies of knowledge workers are all important. These theoretical insights, with little refinement, examination, or reality checking, have become the basis for the reform of education and the restructuring of national education systems.

These observations and predictions are hardly novel. In the mid-1980s, Charles Handy charted the future of work in a book of the same title. Among other things, he suggested that

- the full-employment society was becoming the part-employment society;
- "labour" and "manual skills" were yielding to "knowledge" as the basis for new business and new work;
- "industry" was declining and "services" were growing in importance;
- "hierarchies" and "bureaucracies" were losing appeal;
- "networks" and "partnerships" were gaining appeal; and

- the one-organisation career was becoming rarer and job mobility and career changes more fashionable. (Handy 1984, x)

Handy assumed that we were facing more than a cyclical adjustment; the employment society was ending. Further, he sought new meanings and patterns of work, inevitably turning toward education as the panacea, as not only the means for generating new wealth, credentials, and technology, but also as a creator of labor-intensive employment and a good in itself—a mark of any civilized society (Handy 1984, 133). In promoting a new education agenda based upon greater choice, flexibility, and variety, he argued for the "home as classroom" and the "workplace as school" (146–47).

Quoting the new master futurists Drucker, Cairncross, Canter, and Leadbeater, Hargreaves (2000) has focused on the transition to a knowledge economy, particularly with regard to its consequences for educational systems and schools. He predicts that while the development of literacy (including information technology [IT] literacy) and numeracy will remain part of the core curriculum, the school as an institution will come under increasing pressure to promote new forms of knowledge, namely,

- meta-cognitive abilities and skills—thinking about how to think and learning how to learn;
- the ability to integrate formal and informal learning;
- declarative knowledge (*knowing that*) and procedural knowledge (*know-how*);
- the ability to access, select and evaluate knowledge in an information-soaked world;
- the ability to develop and apply several forms of intelligence (as suggested by Howard Gardner and others);
- the ability to work and learn effectively and in teams;
- the ability to create, transpose and transfer knowledge;
- the ability to cope with ambiguous situations, unpredictable problems and unforeseeable circumstances; and
- the ability to cope with multiple careers—learning how to "redesign" oneself, locate oneself in a job market, and choose and fashion the relevant education and training.

Overall, Hargreaves emphasizes "knowledge management" as playing a vital role in the move to become the "learning society." To him, part of the answer for an effective education system is to train (his word) all education leaders in knowledge management. In essence, it seems that knowledge management will help us to transfer knowledge within and between institutions. It may also assist teachers in making their professional knowledge more explicit and available for others, a knowledge that is typically tacit (and a discourse of which we are highly suspicious).

Observations such as these on the future of work and education have been around for many years, although the explicit theoretical attempt to link knowledge and economy through redesigning national systems is a recent twist to an old policy narrative.[2]

Taking inspiration from Foucault, in this chapter we intend to investigate this new policy twist by identifying and examining the different discursive strands and policy constructions of three different nations and their implications for education policy. We will be taking the United Kingdom, Scotland, and New Zealand as representative examples of advanced liberal states. In OECD countries, there is a strong family resemblance with regard to such policies. The situations in the United Kingdom, Scotland, and New Zealand are simply examples of those in a much larger range of countries that have developed similar policies, including Australia, Canada, and Euroland.[3]

By *knowledge economy*, we mean to stress the received (mainstream) view with certain characteristics that we have renamed as

- the economics of abundance,
- the annihilation of distance,
- the deterritorialization of the state,
- the importance of local knowledge, and
- investment in human capital.

We will discuss these characteristics in more detail below. This received view is largely untested and is adopted without subjection to critique. In this policy-oriented chapter, we are primarily concerned with *how* this knowledge economy, in part, prescribes education policies. We will thus not be exploring the theoretical cadences of Foucault's studies of the human sciences or Lyotard's "logic of performativity" in the postmodern condition (as dealt with by Peters 1995, 1996, 2001c). In the final section, we do however indicate several lines of critique that might be followed in future work in this area.

DISCOURSES OF THE KNOWLEDGE ECONOMY

A number of separate discourses from economics, management theory, futurology, and sociology can be identified as having contributed to shaping the present policy narrative of the knowledge economy.

The Economics of Information and Knowledge

The discipline of economics has contributed at least five important strands of discourse to this narrative. These are mostly associated with the rise to prominence of the neoclassical second (1960s–1970s) and third (1970s until today) Chicago schools.[4] We have already mentioned these:

- the economics of information, pioneered by Jacob Marschak (and coworkers Miyasawa and Radner) and George Stigler (1961), who won the Nobel Memorial Prize for his seminal work in the "economic theory of information";
- Fritz Machlup's (1962) groundwork and development of "the economics of the production and distribution of knowledge" (see Mattessich 1993);
- the "economics of human capital," developed first by Theodore Schultz (1963) and later taken up by Gary Becker (1964) in the New Social Economics;
- public choice theory, developed under James Buchanan and Gordon Tullock (1962); and
- new growth theory, which highlighted the role of education in the creation of human capital and the production of new knowledge, and explored the possibilities of education-related externalities not specified by neoclassical theory. See, for example, Romer (1991) and Solow (2000).

We might also mention the application of free-market ideas to education by Milton and Rose Friedman (1962), although their form of monetarism has lost relative importance.

Management Theory

Management theory plays a strong role in relation to the knowledge economy, from the advent of Taylorism and the development of a system of mass production, to new theories on the organization of work that include the following:

- new forms of teamwork,
- just-in-time production systems,
- lean production,
- *kaizen* (or "continuous improvement"),
- total quality management,
- eco-management, and
- benchmarking.

Also relevant is a new concept of continuous change described under the label of "the flexible firm," involving more innovative, horizontal, and flexible structures based on so-called high skill, high trust, and increased involvement of employees.

Knowledge management is one critical field that has emerged recently and is displaying rapid growth. The author of one site has described this field as embodying "organizational processes that seek synergistic combination of data and information processing capacity of information technologies, and the creative and innovative capacity of human beings" (see www.brint.com/km/whatis.htm). Knowledge management is part and parcel of the new theoretical discourse that has matured in relation to the central concept of the knowledge economy.

Sociology of Knowledge and Education

Another major strand stands as a critique of the positive economics strand and focuses on the sociology of knowledge and education—two fields that have provided grand theories concerning the place of knowledge and education in the modern world. For instance, Nico Stehr (1994) has traced the concept of the "knowledge society" to Robert E. Lane's (1966) "knowledgeable society," Peter Drucker's (1969) *The Age of Discontinuity*, and Daniel Bell's (1973) *The Coming of Post-Industrial Society*. Stehr (6) chooses to label the now emerging form of society as a "knowledge society" because "the constitutive mechanism or the identity of modern society is increasingly driven by 'knowledge,'" and "'knowledge' . . . challenges as well as transforms property and labor as the constitutive mechanisms of society" (7). In agreement with Giddens (1991), Stehr (viii) has commented on the sociological importance of knowledge as the new factor of production:

> There should be a new agenda for social science today because the age of labor and property is at an end. Nonetheless, modern society is still widely conceived in terms of property and labor. Labor and property have an extended and close association in social, political and economic theory and reality. In practice, individuals are forced to define their identities on the basis of their relation to these factors. However, as labor and property (capital) gradually gave way to a new constitutive factor, namely knowledge, older struggles and contests, centered for instance on the ownership of the means of production, also make room for rising sentiments of disaffection with beliefs and values once associated with labor and property and ultimately result in very different moral, political and economic debates and conflicts.

To Stehr's list of influential works, we would add the early classics *The Post-Industrial Society* (Touraine 1974) and *Information Society as Post-industrial Society* (Masuda 1981).[5]

Sociology of the Labor Process

Sociological studies of the nature of work, particularly the literature on the labor process, date from Harry Braverman's (1974) *Labor and Monop-*

oly Capital, in which he theorized the deskilling and intensification of management control. Thompson (1989) provides the best overview of this debate and the various phases it has passed through up until the more recent flexible specialization theory (but see also Wardell et al. 1999).

Futurology, Futures Research, Forecasting, and Foresight

This is a relatively new constellation of fields and disciplines that address the impact of world trends and develop visions of the future with the aim of bridging business, science, technology, and government. These fields have impacted strongly on policy; for instance, in 1994, the United Kingdom launched the Foresight program (see www.foresight.gov.uk, which features a list of futures sites).[6]

Communications and IT

This body of literature on communications and IT resists simple classification or characterization, as contributions come from a wide range of disciplines, including electrical engineering, computing science, telematics, informatics, and cybernetics. "Soft" promotional work by large multinational companies such as IBM and Microsoft—carried out in the name of business—have penetrated education like no previous media form. In addition to these "mainstream" communications and IT discourses, which directly contribute to the received notion of the knowledge economy, more critical literatures exist. These include the recent monumental work of Manuel Castells on the "information age" (Castells 1997, 1998, 2000b) and contributions by Peters and Roberts (1998) and Blake and Standish (2000).

These are clearly disparate disciplines—fields and discourses that operate with different assumptions, employ different methodologies, and reach different and sometimes opposing conclusions. The art of policy scholarship is intended, in part, to gain awareness of these different strands as they influence policy narratives, to disentangle them, and to comment upon inconsistencies. On the other hand, policy development or formulation makes the best of what is available. This can entail weaving often incomplete, partial explanations and new and largely untested approaches to construct policy approaches and narratives with a coherent definition of vision (within the political parameters of government policy manifestos). It seems that the knowledge economy is an idea whose time has come; nudged and patrolled by world policy institutions like the World Bank, OECD, IMF, and the like, national governments the world over have earnestly taken on the task of transforming their economies and societies in accordance with its implicit prescriptions.

DEFINITION AND CHARACTERISTICS
OF THE KNOWLEDGE ECONOMY

Before examining national policy constructions built around the notion of the knowledge economy, we shall briefly consider its accepted definition. Although we have paraphrased the main characteristics, we should emphasize that we are simply representing the claims made for or about the knowledge economy by others.

Policy Definitions

In the United Kingdom's white paper titled *Our Competitive Future: Building the Knowledge Driven Economy*, a knowledge-based economy is defined as

> one in which the generation and the exploitation of knowledge has come to play the predominant part in the creation of wealth. It is not simply about pushing back the frontiers of knowledge; it is also about the more effective use and exploitation *of all types of knowledge* in *all manner of activity*. (Department of Trade and Industry 1998b)[7]

It is suggested that knowledge is more than just information, and it cites a distinction between codified and tacit knowledge. Codifiable knowledge can be written down and easily transferred to others, whereas tacit knowledge is "often slow to acquire and much more difficult to transfer."

In another example, New Zealand's Ministry of Research, Science and Technology recently completed a comprehensive review of the public priorities for good science and technology under the umbrella of the Foresight project. The ministry defines *knowledge economies* as

> those which are directly based on the production, distribution and use of knowledge and information. This is reflected in the trend towards growth in high-technology investments, high-technology industries, more highly-skilled labour and associated productivity gains. Knowledge, as embodied in people (as "human capital") and in technology, has always been central to economic development. But it is only over the last few years that its relative importance has been recognised, just as that importance is growing. (Ministry of Research, Science and Technology, 1998)

This definition is accompanied by a description of the "knowledge revolution," with reference to Alvin Toffler, Peter Drucker, Don Tapscott (*The Digital Economy*), Nicholas Negroponte (*Being Digital*), Charles Handy, Kevin Kelly, Hazel Henderson, and Paul Hawken (for a critical discussion of the Foresight project, see Peters and Roberts 1999, 66–73).

According to the Ministry of Research, the knowledge economy differs from the traditional economy with respect to an emphasis on what we earlier referred to as the "economics of abundance," the "annihilation of distance," the "deterritorialization of the state," the "importance of local knowledge," and "investment in human capital."

UNITED KINGDOM: BUILDING THE KNOWLEDGE-DRIVEN ECONOMY

Understanding based upon these characteristics has recently helped shape national policy constructions of the knowledge economy in the West (e.g., in the United States, the United Kingdom, Ireland, Australia, Canada, and New Zealand) and in the developing world (most notably in China and Southeast Asia). For example, in the 1998 white paper titled *Our Competitive Future*, the United Kingdom's Department of Trade and Industry acknowledges the fact that knowledge was included by the World Bank as a theme in its 1998 *World Development Report*:

> For countries in the vanguard of the world economy, the balance between knowledge and resources has shifted so far towards the former that knowledge has become perhaps the most important factor determining the standard of living. . . . Today's most technologically advanced economies are truly knowledge-based. (Department of Trade and Industry 1998b)

In this white paper, the Department of Trade and Industry also notes that the OECD has drawn attention to the growing importance of knowledge, indicating that the emergence of knowledge-based economies has significant policy implications for the organization of production and its effect on employment and skill requirements. The Department of Trade and Industry also suggests that other countries, including the United States, Canada, Denmark, and Finland, have already identified the growing importance of knowledge and have reflected this in their approaches to economic policy.

Further, the report emphasizes new growth theory, charting the ways in which education and technology are now viewed as central to economic growth. Neoclassical economics are limited in that they do not specify how knowledge accumulation occurs and thus cannot acknowledge externalities. They also fail to consider human capital, such that education has no direct role. In contrast, new growth theory has highlighted the role of education in the creation of human capital and in the production of new knowledge (for example, see Solow 1956, 1994). On this basis, new growth theory has explored the possibilities of education-related externalities.

In short, while the evidence is far from conclusive at this stage, there is a consensus emerging in economic theory that:

a. education is important for successful research activities (e.g., by producing scientists and engineers), which in turn is important for productivity growth, and
b. education creates human capital, which directly affects knowledge accumulation and thus productivity growth (see Department of Trade and Industry 1998b, sec. 3.4ff).

According to the report, not only do research and development expenditures provide a positive contribution to productivity growth, but education is important in explaining the growth of national income (see also Romer 1986, 1990).

The white paper emphasizes that a knowledge economy is neither a return to interventionist strategies of the past nor a naive reliance on markets. In his foreword to the white paper, Tony Blair expresses the role of government thus:

> The Government must promote competition, stimulating enterprise, flexibility and innovation by opening markets. But we must also invest in British capabilities when companies alone cannot: in education, in science and in the creation of a culture of enterprise. And we must promote creative partnerships which help companies: to collaborate for competitive advantage; to promote a long term vision in a world of short term pressures; to benchmark their performance against the best in the world; and to forge alliances with other businesses and with employees. (Department of Trade and Industry 1998a)

In education, Blair places a strong emphasis on the culture of enterprise and on building the skills of entrepreneurship, which differs little if at all from the policy emphases initiated by Lord Young under the Thatcher government. He places equal emphasis on the promotion of research; on industry-education relationships, especially in higher education; on workplace learning; and on building a culture of learning (including the establishment of individual learning accounts).

The following is a brief illustration of the "fit" of this economic policy orientation for education policy in Scotland and New Zealand.

SCOTLAND: TARGETING EXCELLENCE FOR THE KNOWLEDGE ECONOMY

In 1999, the Scottish Office released a white paper titled *Targeting Excellence: Modernising Scotland's Schools* (Scottish Office 1999). We have adopted the above subheading from a chapter in this white paper, which includes the following excerpt:

> The knowledge economy will pose challenges and opportunities. Knowledge and know-how are taking over from buildings and machinery as the most valuable assets of business. The speed at which information can cross the globe, the sophistication of modern products and services, and the sophistication of the modern consumer all point to increasing globalisation of the economy, and to increasing customisation of goods and services to meet peoples' individual needs. Innovation, fresh thinking, the acquisition and application of knowledge, and high levels of customer awareness are likely to be among the critical factors in achievement in the future. Competitive advantage will come from the application of intellect and knowledge to business problems. The skills Scotland will need to be successful can and should be fostered and grown in schools.

In this document, the Scottish Office lists a number of initiatives already under way, including:

- implementation of the National Grid for Learning by 2002;
- investment in training teachers in the use of ICT;
- development of the Scottish Virtual Teachers' Centre;
- development of a "Think Business" program to bring entrepreneurs into the classroom;
- promoting enterprise skills in schools;
- support for the National Centre, Education for Work and Enterprise; and
- investment in industry and enterprise awareness for teachers and schools.

The Scottish Office also identifies the next steps, namely,

- extension of the National Grid for Learning to enhance lifelong learning, particularly support for community access;
- creation of new guidelines for improving work experience;
- creation of new guidelines for careers education; and
- expansion of the Education for Work and Enterprise agenda.

NEW ZEALAND: EDUCATION FOR THE KNOWLEDGE ECONOMY

The Information Technology Advisory Group (ITAG), appointed by the minister for information technology, recently published a report entitled *The Knowledge Economy* (Information Technology Advisory Group 1999).

The executive summary of this report features the following assertions:

> More than 50 per cent of Gross Domestic Product (GDP) in the major OECD economies is now based on the production and distribution of knowledge. We are leaving the Industrial Age behind and moving into the Information Age.
>
> In the US, Australia, the United Kingdom, Canada, Finland, and Ireland, the growth of the Internet and other related new technologies have become the catalyst for the creation of "knowledge economies." . . .
>
> Countries that have encouraged their people through education and life-long learning and by investing heavily in research and development (R&D) are well positioned to take advantage of these new global markets. Australia, Finland, Ireland, Canada, Singapore, and the United States are countries which have embraced the knowledge economy (some still with a strong commodity sector), and are experiencing strong GDP growth as a result. There is much we can learn from them. (Information Technology Advisory Group 1999)

In this report, ITAG makes some interesting claims about knowledge: "know-how" and "know-who" are considered more important than "know-what"; knowledge gained by experience is as important as formal education and training; and lifelong learning is vital for organizations and individuals. ITAG (1999) goes on to suggest that intellectual capital is the source of competitive advantage for firms and that information and communication technologies "release people's creative potential and knowledge." The group also details what New Zealand's competitors are doing and indicates that Ireland has accomplished a great deal by:

- investing heavily in education, especially technical education;
- correcting major imbalances in government finances and putting fiscal and monetary policies in order;
- controlling excessive costs and keeping wage increases moderate;
- opening up the economy and privatizing many state-owned enterprises;
- positioning Ireland as the "hub" between Europe and the global marketplace (Ireland trades 153 percent of its GNP);
- enacting strong legislation designed to open up previously sheltered activities to competition in the interests of consumers;
- creating incentives and stimulating the economy through lower taxation.

ITAG cites that New Zealand faces six crucial issues, the first five of which arguably concern education. For the purposes of this discussion, however, we will quickly focus upon the first issue as dealt with in the report. Specifically, ITAG (1999) makes four significant conclusions regarding the new economics in relation to education:

1. A lack of investment in human rather than physical capital prevents poor countries from catching up with rich ones. Educational attainment and public spending on education are correlated positively to economic growth (Barro and Sala-i-Martin 1995; Benhabib and Spiegel 1994).
2. School quality—measured, for example, in terms of teacher pay, student-teacher ratio, and teacher education—is positively correlated to future earnings of students (Card and Krueger 1992).
3. Education has an important role in the growth of national income. Lifelong learning is also crucial (Aghion and Howitt 1998).
4. People migrate from places where human capital is scarce to places of abundance (Lucas 1988). "Human capital flight" or "brain drain" can lead to a permanent reduction in income and growth in the country of emigration relative to that of immigration.

On the basis of this analysis, ITAG suggests that New Zealand needs more technical graduates and increased ICT literacy (and a greater number of ICT courses) for students and teachers.[8]

TOWARD A CRITIQUE

A certain tedium has crept into official policy documents and academic papers that derives from the new hyperdiscourse and seemingly endless inflated claims that entertain the prospect of the "new" knowledge economy and its implications for education. This may be because under the combined impact of economic globalization, the rapid spread of the new information technologies, and the promotion of a neoliberal paradigm of free trade, there has in fact been an accelerated set of changes occurring in the economy, in the nature of "work," and in education. It is as though world policy institutions, extranational political organizations, and national governments have been trying to devise policies that can embrace the nature of these changes, but apparently reality has made even the best predictions obsolete.

In this general context, the language of policy takes on a different kind of tone, especially when the same entrenched clichés about "the future" seem to occur in document after document. Policy, in other words, has become the "language of futurology," steeped in hyperbole and laced with prediction. The rules of this policy language game seem based upon the invention of new metanarratives—overarching concepts or visions of the future—as a method of picturing these changes and presenting a coherent policy narrative. Thus, the terms *postindustrial society, information society* (which have been around since the late 1960s), and *global information economy* abound in policy documents. More recently, the terms *knowledge* and *learning*—conceptualized in relation to both *society* and *economy*—have come to occupy center stage in national policy documents concerned with mapping the impact of global trends and with encouraging greater competitiveness and more synergistic relationships between education and the economy.

Before we briefly indicate the lines of our critique, we should add that we are not against the notion of the "knowledge economy" or its cognates "knowledge society" and "learning society" in toto, nor their employment as a direction for education policy. However, before such notions can be supported or opposed, the relevant concepts need to be clarified. There are benign and less benign versions of these concepts. For instance, one view of the knowledge economy—understood within the social democratic tradition—posits the economy as subordinate to the state and the question of sovereignty. Based on this model, the accompanying notion of the "knowledge society" provides grounds for both the reinvention of education as a *welfare right* and the recognition of *knowledge rights* as a basis for social inclusion and informed citizenship. This view can be contrasted with that of the "knowledge economy" as simply an ideological extension of the neoliberal paradigm of globalization, where the term stands for a stripped-down functionalist view of education in service of the multinationals.

Our first criticisms are conceptual. These new policy language games, on the whole, do not make standard philosophical distinctions (e.g., between "knowledge" and "information"), nor do they operate with the robust concepts of "learning" and "knowledge." More importantly, no analytical distinction is drawn between "knowledge economy" and "knowledge society," which is as fundamental as the distinction between "economy" and "society." The latter notion, for instance, might enable us to talk of education and knowledge rights in the new "knowledge economy" and therefore address questions of social inclusion more directly.

These national policy constructions revolve around a narrow, instrumental approach to the economics of knowledge and to intellectual culture in general, which does not acknowledge or sufficiently differentiate among various definitions of "knowledge": economic, sociological, and philosophical. These policy documents often obfuscate the issues by using the terms *knowledge* and *information* interchangeably. Traditional analytic philosophers argue that the concept of knowledge has three conditions: a belief condition, a truth condition, and a justification condition. In other words, for a statement to count as knowledge, it must satisfy the conditions of belief, truth, and justification. While it has its difficulties, this philosophical account of knowledge—of great importance in defining *education* in analytic philosophy—does not distinguish between "knowledge" and "information." However, "information" considered as data transmitted from a sender to a receiver does not necessarily have to satisfy the belief, truth, or justification conditions. Thus, "education for the information economy" and "education for the knowledge society" take on quite different meanings.

Second, the meaning of the concept of the "knowledge economy" is not yet clearly defined. If it means more than a certain percentage of the working population employed in "knowledge" occupations, then it is necessary to conceptually explore the links between "knowledge," "economy," and "learning." This is especially necessary if the term signals an emerging phenomenon, as many of the change merchants believe.

Also, it is clear that the empirical evidence for the knowledge economy as a new stage of capitalism or for a new "weightless" economy is still weak at best, as are the empirical connections between the processes involved. Can capital be infinitely substituted for manual and skilled labor? Can knowledge become a new factor of production, as some scholars claim, or have new forms of intellectual and human capital become important? What is the relationship between investment in human capital and economic growth or productivity? What are the differences between state and private forms of investment in human capital, especially in relation to higher education? Should education be seen solely as a form of investment in human capital?

In this respect, the landmark research on the concept of the "learning society" undertaken by the United Kingdom's Economic and Social Research Council under the directorship of Frank Coffield (i.e., *The Learning Society Programme* 1994–2000) resulted in some important evidence on higher, vocational, and workplace education, and the intersection or transition between education and work (see Coffield 1995). Coffield (1999) has spoken of "breaking the consensus" that prevails in the United Kingdom, a consensus built on the tenets of a narrowly construed education policy that is based upon a simplified version of human capital theory and that incorporates the notions of both "lifelong learning" and the "learning society."

In his 1999 address, Coffield examined the problem of human capital theory and its legitimation as policy, and he began to discuss alternative visions of the "learning society." As implied in the title of his recent work (Coffield 2000), he has now taken both this critical contestability of current policy and its visionary element a considerable step further. He explains,

> One of the achievements of the programme is to have explored critically the concept of a learning society and, by examining the definitions used by the 14 projects, it is possible to discern at least 10 contrasting ways in which the term is used. (Coffield 2000, 1:7)

Table 4.1 describes the ten ways listed by Coffield:

Table 4.1.   Coffield's List of Meanings of *Learning Society*

1. skills growth
2. personal development
3. social learning
4. a learning market
5. local learning societies
6. social control
7. self-evaluation
8. centrality of learning
9. a reformed system of education
10. structural change

This demonstrates how cognate concepts like the "learning society" (which is a soft policy focus of the knowledge economy) can take on plural meanings and practices.

Third, the discourse of futurology often embraced by such policy discourses is at once populist and ahistorical. It should be remembered that the discourses of futurology and of futurisms (in the plural) have always been defining features of modernism and modernity and that these discourses gain prominence at the end of each century. They are essentially millennium products. Often such policy discourses are grounded in the corporatist management theory of scenario building, and thus it is not always clear in these future-oriented narratives who is telling the story or whose interests are at stake.

A new form of knowledge managerialism has quickly developed, and its proponents have taken upon themselves the policy expertise for deciding the new meanings of the concepts of "knowledge" and "learning" in their novel constellations within the economy. Most often, these discourses do not consider the history of the notion of the "knowledge society" or its theoretical antecedents in the "postindustrial society" and the "information society," which are not uncontested terms. Rather, they are value- and theory-laden concepts that have been part of social and cultural theory for more than thirty years. The document writers also run terms together, failing to distinguish the discursive strand of the economics of information, knowledge, and education.

Moreover, with the coalescing of literatures in policy documents of this kind, often what occurs is the predominance of an economic definition of knowledge that then serves to construct education policies without careful thought given to other approaches or the criticisms they might generate. Even in terms of the limited approach of economics of knowledge, the documents do not tend to recognize knowledge as a global public good (for example, see Stiglitz 1998b, 1999a, 1999b, 1999c).

Fourth, there are important changes concerning the shifting nature of work and its organization. National policy constructions of the "knowledge economy" are based on the assumption that it is the future basis for national competitiveness and success in the global economy and that it will provide the necessary new jobs for successive waves of "knowledge workers." While unemployment levels in the United Kingdom are historically at their lowest level in many years, the questions of the intermediate and long-term shift in the nature of work, work organization, and new forms of employment related to the knowledge economy require much more reflection and empirical research.

For example, Rifkin (1998) argues convincingly on the basis of empirical data for the "end of work" in his analysis of the U.S. economy. He suggests that as automation becomes more sophisticated, the primary, secondary, and tertiary labor forces (i.e., the knowledge sector) will face massive displacement. Rifkin suggests that the current technological revolution and labor-saving mechanisms have driven down wages and threatened livelihoods. Others have suggested that the social consequences of the disappearance of work are most obvious in America's inner cities (Wilson 1980, 1987).

The shift from industrial capitalism to information or knowledge capitalism is transforming the West into "workless worlds," where only an elite technical labor force will find jobs. In this context, we must rethink the purpose of civil society, particularly the role of national education systems. As Rifkin (1998) argues,

> Corporate downsizing, increasing automation of the manufacturing and service sectors, the shift from mass to elite workforces, growing job insecurity, the widening gap between rich and poor, an aging population, and globalization of the economy are creating a host of new uncertainties and challenges for millions of Americans as well as American businesses. At the same time, government at every level is being fundamentally transformed. The "welfare state" is being pared down, and entitlement programs are shrinking. The social net is being streamlined and overhauled, and government subsidies of various kinds are being reduced or eliminated.

He also posits that "the so-called third sector is likely to play a far more expansive role as an arena for job creation and social-service provision in the coming century." What Rifkin calls the "end of work" is the end of "work" under industrial capitalism, and as André Gorz (1999) (the utopian Marxist sociologist) claims, we must learn to think of work in the philosophical and anthropological senses:

> We must dare to prepare ourselves for the Exodus from "work-based society": it no longer exists and will not return. We must want this society, which

is in its death-throes, to die, so that another may arise from its ruins. We must learn to make out the contours of that other society beneath the resistances, dysfunctions and impasses which make up the present. "Work" must lose its centrality in the minds, thoughts and imaginations of everyone. We must learn to see it differently: no longer as something we have—or do not have—but as *what we do*. We must be bold enough to regain control of the work we do. (1)

For Gorz, work in a genuine sense is the means to self-realization. In the Hegelian and Marxist senses, the nature of work is tied up not only with "practico-sensory activity" but with *poiesis* and self-creation.[9]

Finally, perhaps most importantly, we must not become so locked into national policy constructions and their ideological narratives that, as servants of the state, we spend all our time satisfying its policy requirements and have no time for informed critique or for perceiving the social consequences of the policies. In this regard, we think that the observations of Lynne Chisholm (1999) should be considered carefully:

> New information and communication technologies offer ultimately non-controllable access to diverse and plural worlds—yet they do not assure the acquisition of the ethical and critical faculties needed for personal orientation and balance in negotiation of those worlds. . . . Knowledge societies thus theoretically offer "unprecedented means to empower social actions and to add to the self-transforming capacity of society" [Stehr]. Yet in practice they appear to be highly susceptible to recreating and reinforcing systematic social inequalities and to exacerbating economic and social polarisation. (3)

In the opening quotation of this chapter, Foucault discusses the formation, circulation, and utilization of knowledge as a fundamental problem and compares the accumulation of knowledge to that of capital. These remarks, made in the late 1970s, help us to chart the genealogy of his own project in relation to the emergence and shift of *epistemes* or distinctive formations of systems of knowledge. It was in this period that he coined the term "power/knowledge." Both the quoted remark and his studies on the history of systems of thought are wonderfully prescient. Certain knowledge formations did exist before capitalism. However, perhaps, at this juncture (with full-blown notions of the "knowledge economy" looming large in policy terms), it is now impossible to pursue the question of knowledge separately from the question of capital.

ACKNOWLEDGMENTS

We would like to thank Malcolm MacKenzie and Cathy Fagan at the University of Glasgow; a number of people, including Paul Standish, who attended a seminar at the University of Dundee; and two anonymous reviewers for the *Journal of Educational Enquiry* for their helpful comments on an earlier draft. Michael Peters presented this paper through the Educational Studies Seminar Program at the University of Dundee in the autumn term, December 12, 2000.

NOTES

1. See, for example, this "theory" as it appears in the web pages of "Knowledge Economy" at www.enterweb.org/know.htm (accessed December 5, 2005). This is a confused story since not too much attention is given to principles of knowledge capitalism; to the concept of intellectual property and the global emergence of intellectual property rights regimes; or to notions of human, intellectual, and social capital.

2. For instance, see the European Commission's white paper *Teaching and Learning: Towards the Learning Society* (1995) and "The European House of Education—Education and Economy, a New Partnership" (Working Document SEC 796, May 21, 1999).

3. In August 2000, Michael Peters spent a month in China, during which time he examined the restructuring and current reform of Chinese universities in relation to the "knowledge economy."

4. See cepa.newschool.edu/het/schools/chicago.htm.

5. There is a strong sociological literature that focuses on contemporary analyses of individualization processes, including the work of Beck (1992); Beck, Giddens, and Lash (1994); and Giddens (1991). The sociology of postindustrialism overlaps with more philosophical debates on modernity and postmodernity (see Habermas 1987; Lyotard 1984) and studies of globalization (e.g., Amin 1996; Burbules and Torres 2000 [for education]; Held 1995).

6. One of the earliest and most well-known futures studies was Alvin Toffler's (1972) collection and his subsequent work. See also the 1999 book Michael Peters coauthored with Peter Roberts called *University Futures*, and a recent excellent collection entitled *Global Futures* (Pieterse 2000). Pieterse distinguishes among the mainstream managerial approach to futures based on forecasting and risk analysis; critical approaches to futures that are critical of dominant futures reflecting institutional vested interests; and the alternative futures approach, which seeks to be inclusive without being alarmist.

7. The web links mentioned are as follows:
   - The Foresight Project—www.morst.govt.nz/uploadedfiles/Documents/Publications/policy%20discussions/success.pdf;
   - For tertiary education in New Zealand, see New Zealand Ministry of Education Tertiary Education Strategy 2002–2007 (Wellington: Office of the Associate Minister of Education), www.minedu.govt.nz;
   - This program initiated by the New Zealand Ministry of Research, Science and Technology no longer has a web archive but exists now only as a scholarship program;
   - Knowledge management—www.brint.com/km;
   - New Zealand Trade Development Board—www.tradenz.govt.nz; and
   - Business Information Zone—www.bizinfo.co.nz.

8. In hindsight, ITAG's report became part of a wider national government innovation and enterprise strategy that led into the elections held November 27, 1999.

9. Philosophers of education have had little to say about work, its centrality for society and education, or the new forms it will take in the knowledge economy. For some recent discussions of the philosophy of work and its importance for education, see White (1997) and Winch (2000). Before we can begin to understand new forms or develop education policies based on the future of work, we need to become more aware of the theology of work, the history of the concept "work," and the ideology of work.

5

Universities, Globalization, and the New Political Economy of Knowledge[1]

INTRODUCTION

Higher education has become the new starship in the policy fleet for governments around the world. The public policy focus on higher education in part reflects a growing consensus in macroeconomics toward new growth, or endogenous growth, theory based on the work of Solow (1956, 1994); Lucas (1988); and Romer (1986, 1990, 1994), which argues that the driving force behind economic growth is technological change (i.e., improvements in knowledge about how we transform inputs into outputs in the production process). Knowledge about technology and levels of information flow are now considered critical for economic development and can account for differential growth patterns. In short, universities are seen to be a key driver toward the knowledge economy. Accordingly, higher-education institutions have been encouraged to develop links with industry and business in a series of new venture partnerships. This emphasis in higher-education policy also accords with initiatives to promote greater entrepreneurial skills and activity within so-called national systems of innovation. This chapter focuses on the economic importance of higher education as a key component of the knowledge economy. It discusses the genealogy and contributing strands to the newly emerging discourse and considers universities in the knowledge-driven economy by reference to the UK white paper *Our Competitive Future*. It also considers the arguments advanced by Joseph Stiglitz (ex–chief economist of the World Bank) for the "analytics of the knowledge economy" and discusses universities in terms of "knowledge cultures." Finally, the chapter provides a critique of the policy discourse on the knowledge economy as a basis of the new challenges facing universities under knowledge capitalism.

Proposition 1: Globalization constitutes a new kind of struggle over the meaning and value of knowledge.

In a recent essay, which is developed in his book *Marx's Revenge* (2002), the Indian economist and UK Labour peer, Lord Meghnad Desai discusses the resurgence of capitalism and the death of statist socialism (the subtitle of his book). In his account, which revives an approach from classical political economy, Desai describes globalization as a phase of capitalism. According to his organicist approach, which both Adam Smith and Karl Marx share, a view which is more fiercely propounded by Hayek in the twentieth century, "The economy is an organism which is the result of human action but not of human design" (Desai 2002). Such a view sees "the entire short Twentieth century as a deviation from the true nature of capitalism" and the new phase of globalization as "not 'the end of history' but a resumption of the Nineteenth century global capitalism" (Desai 2002). Thus, for Desai, globalization is neither ideology nor utopia.

The organicist view stands in marked contrast to the mechanistic view, which holds that the economy (or society) is

> a result of a deliberate if faulty design and holds that certain agents—capitalists/corporations, government/politicians, bankers/jews [sic]—as responsible for the design and operation of the machine that is the economy. Thus in this view, globalisation could be a creation of Western powers or global/transnational/multinational corporations. *Their* ideology would be the hegemonic ideology. It would then be programmatic to regulate/overcome/abolish such malevolent agents and establish a world government or New New Deal etc. (Desai 2002)

Desai sets out the differences between the organicist and mechanist views in a table (see appendix 1) that contrasts the nature of capitalism, society, the state, and the market.[2]

Desai provides a comprehensive analysis of capitalism during the twentieth century in terms of three phases: (1) 1914–1945—deglobalization characterized by the rise of Fascism/Bolshevism and the growth of the territorial social state; (2) 1945–1971—the golden age of Keynesianism, Stalinism, and decolonization; and (3) 1971–1989—the crisis of Keynesianism. After 1989, we have passed into an era characterized by the resurgence of capitalism in its global phase. Desai suggests that the days of the old mechanistic paradigm, which sees "globalisation as malfunctioning, ideological, hegemonic and unequalising," have passed, and now we should see globalization in terms of the organicist paradigm, as

> a self organising process not designed by any one or even many corporations or governments but as an incessant seeking for profits in a gale of creative destruction. It is refashioning what was an Interstate [International] Order into a Global Process whose end is not predictable. Yet if the organicist view blames no single agency for the functioning of capitalism, it neither offers hope of a better world in the near future. In Marx's vision, there is incessant class struggle as capitalism reproduces itself. There is a distant end to capitalism and a serious self conscious, self organising society emerges at the end. (2002)

We are less interested in the historical details of Desai's analysis than in his revival of classical political economy and his inspired and daring conjunction of Marx and Hayek. In particular, we want to use his brief summary to highlight the content of the first proposition with which we began the chapter, although the "three moments" of knowledge capitalism as we present them here do not depend on Desai's characterization of globalization. Like Desai, we wish to revive classical political economy, and his organicist conjunction of Marx and Hayek is full of presentiment for an analysis of the knowledge economy, which he does not explore in a sustained way. We differ from Desai in the emphasis we give to the knowledge economy as a significant element of globalization. We call this approach the "new political economy of knowledge." Jean Jacques Rousseau wrote *A Discourse on Political Economy* in 1755 beginning with these words:

> The word Economy, or OEconomy, is derived from *oikos, a house*, and *vomos, law*, and meant originally only the wise and legitimate government of the house for the common good of the whole family. The meaning of the term was then expanded to the government of that great family, the State. To distinguish these two senses of the word, the latter is called *general* or *political* economy, and the former domestic or particular economy (see www.constitution.org/jjr/polecon.htm).

New political economy we consider new because it applies to the knowledge economy as opposed to the traditional or industrial economy. If the knowledge economy operates differently from the industrial economy— if knowledge as a commodity behaves differently from other commodities, as is the strong claim by a number of economists—then we also need a new political economy of knowledge to map its dimensions and analyze its effects.

KNOWLEDGE CAPITALISM AS AN ASPECT OF GLOBALIZATION

> Proposition 2: Knowledge capitalism is the latest phase of globalization.

For the sake of time and space, and their compression, we shall advance or simply assert a series of interrelations that makes the case for knowledge capitalism as the latest phase of globalization (see table 5.1). These assertions should also clarify why globalization might be considered a new kind of struggle over the meaning and value of knowledge, although we shall elaborate on this point below.

The three moments we shall call the "capitalization of knowledge," the "deterritorialization of information," and the "technologization of education." All three lead to new struggles over the meaning and value of knowledge in ways that clearly implicate universities. Before tackling the latter half of this proposal—the bit that mentions the university—let us briefly return to Hayek as a starting point for understanding the revolution in the economics of knowledge and information that characterized the twentieth century.

HAYEK AND THE ECONOMICS OF KNOWLEDGE[3]

> Proposition 3: The international knowledge system is a spontaneous result of human action but not of human design.

Friedrich von Hayek (1899–1992) is probably the single most influential individual economist or political philosopher to shape what is now understood as neoliberalism, although he is best regarded as, and considered himself, a classical liberal.[4] Hayek's own theoretical direction sprang out of the so-called Austrian school established by Carl Menger, Eugen Boehm-Bawerk, and Ludwig von Mises during the first decade of the twentieth century. What distinguished the Austrian school from the classical school of political economy pioneered by Adam Smith and David Ricardo was their subjective, as opposed to an objective, theory of value. Leon Walras (1834–1910) of the French Lausanne school presented economics as "the calculus of pleasure and pain of the rational individual," and Carl Menger, developing the theory of subjective value, launched what some have called a "neoclassical revolution" in economics. Menger

Table 5.1   Knowledge Capitalism as an Aspect of Globalization

1. The rise of the sign or symbolic economy (knowledge capitalism) based on the combined logics of abundance and dispersal:
   a. Unlike most resources that are depleted when used, information and knowledge can actually grow through sharing, exchange, and application.
   b. Capital in the symbolic form of information can be speedily transferred in deregulated twenty-four-hour virtual finance markets, allowing international currency speculation and increased geographical spread and mobility of FDI.
   c. Displacement of the manufacturing industry from its old locations in the North to selected locations—Asia, Latin America—in the South and a dematerialization of industrial products (the weightless economy).
2. Communications and information technologies diminish the effect of distance, making possible "action at a distance in real time":
   a. The radical concordance of image, text, and sound, and the development of a new information/knowledge infrastructure.
   b. The emergence of a global media network linked with a global communications network.
   c. The emergence of a global Euro-American consumer culture and the rise of global edutainment giants in music/film/TV.
3. Investment in human capital and key competencies as a source of value in knowledge-based institutions, with an emphasis on knowledge being locked into systems or processes:
   a. The technological transformations of "leading" sciences—which where the major developments in informatics and modern theories of algebra, computer languages, communication theories and cybernetics, phonology and theories of linguistics, problems of information storage, retrieval and data banks, telematics, and problems of translation—are significantly *all language based.*
   b. New legal, ethical, and economic problems concerning knowledge creation, transmission, and distribution highlighted in the emergence of international intellectual property rights regimes and the recent GATS agreements within the international knowledge system.
   c. The promotion of new knowledge cultures and knowledge/technology transfer policies through the corporatization of the university, the encouragement of new public-private partnerships, and the concept of lifelong education.

Source: The table, of our construction, is based upon a variety of sources, including Desai (2002), especially items 1b and 1c; David Skyrme Associates (www.skyrme.com/insights/21gke.htm); and Lyotard (1984), especially items 3a and 3b. For an application to Scotland, see, for instance, *Scotland: Towards the Knowledge Economy* (summary at www.scotland.gov.uk/library/documents-w9/knec-02.htm); "Targeting Excellence for the Knowledge Economy" (chapter 3 of *Targeting Excellence—Modernising Scotland's Schools*); and *Enterprise and Lifelong Learning Committee, 9th Report 2002, Final Report on Lifelong Learning,* and on knowledge/technology transfer policies, see SHEFC's circular letter at www.sfc.ac.uk/library/11854fc203db2fbd000000ed4d901da8.

questioned the notion of perfect information that was seen to underlie *homo economicus* by both classical and neoclassical economists.

Hayek's work also emphasized the limited nature of knowledge: the price mechanism of the "free" market conveys information about supply and demand that is dispersed among many consumers and producers and cannot be coordinated by any central planning mechanism. His early work emphasized that the key to economic growth is "knowledge," and this insight provided him with the grounds for casting doubt on socialism and state planning, and for advocating that the market was the best way to organized modern society. In an early paper entitled "Economics and Knowledge" delivered to the London Economic Club in 1936, Hayek contended,

> The empirical element in economic theory—the only part which is concerned not merely with implications but with causes and effects and which leads therefore to conclusions which, at any rate in principle, are capable of verification—consists of propositions about the acquisition of knowledge.

This insight, in part, he attributes in a footnote to Karl Popper's notion of falsification outlined in the 1935 German edition of *The Logic of Scientific Discovery*, thus indicating a close relationship to his distant cousin that helped determine the intellectual history of the twentieth century. Hayek provided an analysis of the tautologies that comprise formal equilibrium theory, arguing that the extent to which these formal propositions can be filled out with empirical propositions about how we acquire and communicate knowledge determines our understanding of causation in the real world. With that statement, he distinguished the formal element of economics as the pure logic of choice—a set of tools for investigating causal processes. The problem he addressed receives its classical formulation in the following question: "How can the combination of fragments of knowledge existing in different minds bring about results which, if they were to be brought about deliberately, would require a knowledge on the part of the directing mind which no single person can possess?" And he proceeds to offer a solution in terms of the now celebrated notion of spontaneous order: "The spontaneous actions of individuals will, under certain conditions which we can define, bring about a distribution of resources which can be understood as if it were made according to a single plan, although nobody has planned it." This is also an answer, he surmises, to the problem of the "social mind."

In 1945, Hayek returned to the problem of knowledge in a paper entitled "The Use of Knowledge in Society," in which he poses the problem of constructing a rational economic order and criticizes the approach derived from an economic calculus that assumes we all possess the relevant information, that we start out from a given system of preferences, and that we command complete knowledge of available means. By contrast, he maintains that the problem is not merely one of how to allocate given resources, but rather "it is a problem of the utilization of knowledge which is not given to anyone in its totality." Hayek emphasizes the importance of knowledge of particular circumstances of time and place, which constitutes the unique information that every individual possesses, and he champions practical and contextual, or "local," knowledge ("unorganized knowledge") against scientific or theoretical knowledge—taken as an understanding of general rules—in economic activity. This "local knowledge" is the sort of knowledge, he hastens to add, that cannot be made into statistics or be conveyed to any central authority.

Hayek's 1945 paper, then, is considered the classic argument against central planning and the state. It is an argument that he develops through the notion of evolutionary economics, for he considers the pricing system as an institution that has developed as a means of communicating information, where "prices act to coordinate the separate actions of different people in the same way as subjective values help the individual to coordinate the parts of his plan." This he takes to be the central theoretical problem of all social science—as Whitehead puts it—not the habit of thinking about what we are doing, but the number of important operations we can perform without thinking about them, a kind of spontaneous system that has developed as practices and institutions over time. Some have argued that Hayek's genius was to recognize that liberal democracy, science, and the market are such spontaneous self-organizing systems, based on the principle of voluntary consent and serving no end beyond themselves.

We started with Hayek for a number of reasons. First, his work on the economics of knowledge is generally regarded as the starting point for contemporary economics of knowledge and information.[5] Second, Hayek's liberal constitutionalism provided the blueprint for the form of liberalism understood as a critique of state reason that presaged the rationale for restructuring the state during the high point of the Thatcher-Reagan era. Third, Hayek was important not only intellectually but also historically and organizationally. In 1947, Hayek set up the very influential Mont Pelerin Society, an international organization dedicated to restoring classical liberalism and the so-called free society, including its main institution, the free market. Hayek was concerned that even though the Allied powers had defeated the Nazis, liberal government was too welfare oriented, a situation, he argued, that fettered the free market, consumed wealth, and infringed on the rights of individuals. With the Mont Pelerin Society, Hayek gathered around him a number of thinkers committed to the "free market," including his old colleague Ludwig von Mises, as well as some younger American scholars who were to become prominent economists in their own right—Rose and Milton Friedman, James Buchanan, Gordon Tullock, and Gary Becker—and who went on to establish the main strands of American conservative, monetarist, and neoliberal economics. Fourth, in education research and policy, very little attention has been given by educationalists to economics per se, or to the economics of education and knowledge. Indeed, broadly speaking, only those who embrace a political economy approach or some variant of it come close to economic questions, but not in any formal sense do they approach an understanding of neoclassical economics and its contemporary variants or demonstrate either an awareness of the history of economics or its powerful contemporary policy effects in education.[6]

EDUCATION IN THE KNOWLEDGE ECONOMY

> Proposition 4: If knowledge is a global public good, then governments (and universities) have a key role to play in the knowledge economy.

We previously noted how OECD understands the dynamics of the knowledge-based economy and the importance of knowledge networks in relation to national innovation systems. The OECD accepts that government has a strong role to play in promoting public investment in the infrastructure of education, science, and technology.

Similar arguments profiling the centrality of knowledge to the economy and the important role of education have been made by a variety of scholars. In his recent book *Globalization and It Discontents*, Joseph Stiglitz (2002) indicates that in his advisory role at the World Bank and the White House, there was a close link between the policies he advocated and his earlier theoretical work in economics, much of it related to the economics of information—in particular, "asymmetries of information"—and market imperfections. He writes,

> The standard models that economists had used for generations argued either that markets worked perfectly—some even denied the existence of genuine unemployment—or that the only reason that unemployment existed was that wages were too high, suggesting the obvious remedy: lower wages. Information economics, with its better analyses of labor, capital and product markets, enabled the construction of macroeconomic models that provided deeper insights into unemployment, models that explained the fluctuations, the recessions and depressions, that had marked capitalism since its beginnings. (xii)

Stiglitz goes on to talk of the failures of both markets *and* government, and to criticize the International Monetary Fund, whose decisions he claims "were made on the basis of what seemed a curious blend of ideology and bad economics" (xiii). He suggests that structural adjustment policies, as part of the neoliberal version of globalization promoted by the IMF, were both outmoded and inappropriate and were prescribed "without considering the effects they would have on the people in the countries told to follow these policies" (xiv).

The way ahead for Stiglitz is not to abandon globalization—which is "neither feasible nor desirable" (214)—but to reshape its potential for good and to reshape international economic organizations to ensure that this is accomplished. While the market model has prevailed, he argues that we must recognize that there is not just *one* market model; there are marked differences between the Japanese, American, German, and Swedish market systems. There is room to recognize the role of governments not only in mitigating market failures but also in ensuring social justice. He argues for international public institutions based on a form of global governance that will entail a change of voting rights and greater transparency. His reforms of the apparatus of international institutions and the global financial system grow out of his own theoretical interests in the economics of knowledge and information.

We have previously noted how in his role as chief economist of the World Bank, Stiglitz drew an interesting connection between knowledge and development, with the strong implication that universities as traditional knowledge institutions have become the leading future service industries and need to be more fully integrated into the prevailing mode of production—a fact not missed by countries like China who are busy restructuring their university systems for the knowledge economy. Stiglitz asserts that the World Bank has shifted from being a bank for infrastructure finance to being what he calls a "Knowledge Bank." He writes, "We now see economic development as less like the construction business and more like education in the broad and comprehensive sense that covers knowledge, institutions, and culture" (Stiglitz 1999a, 2). He goes on to argue that the "movement to the knowledge economy necessitates a rethinking of economic fundamentals" because, he maintains, knowledge is different from other goods, in that it shares many of the properties of a *global* public good. This means, among other things, a key role for governments in protecting intellectual property rights, although appropriate definitions of such rights are not clear or straightforward. It also signals the dangers of monopolization, which, Stiglitz suggests, may be even greater for knowledge economies than for industrial economies.

UNIVERSITIES, GLOBALIZATION, AND THE KNOWLEDGE ECONOMY

Proposition 5: Paradoxically, at a point historically when the interventionist state has been rolled back and governments have successfully eased themselves out of the market, they find themselves as the major owners and controllers of the means of knowledge production in the new knowledge economy.

On the strength of this analysis, what conclusions can we draw for the role of the university in the knowledge economy? We have offered a set of conceptual criticisms and have questioned policy constructions of the knowledge economy that revolve around a narrow, instrumental approach taken to the economics of knowledge and to intellectual culture in general, which does not acknowledge or sufficiently differentiate among various definitions of knowledge. In particular, we emphasized differences between the concepts of "knowledge" (as justified, true belief) and "information" (as data that does not satisfy any of the three conditions of truth, belief, or justification). We also questioned the empirical basis for the knowledge economy and criticized a discourse of futurology that uncritically embraces a knowledge managerialism that both operates on the basis of an easy distinction between knowledge managers and knowledge workers and primarily focuses on the commercial principle of embedding knowledge in processes. We emphasized that knowledge has strong cultural and local dimensions as well as global dimensions. The role of the university in the knowledge economy in respect to the former relate to nation building, regional development (taken in a broad sense), the protection of social rights, and the preservation of community; whereas in respect to the latter, beyond its commercial functions, the university might also seek to expand its Enlightenment role through the development of a genuinely global civic community based on extensions of the concept of citizen rights above the level of the state. In earlier chapters, we coined the term *knowledge cultures,* and we suggested that we must come to understand the organization of knowledge in both its industrial and postindustrial forms and under a variety of regional capitalist models. New knowledge technologies offer new pedagogical possibilities and "ultimately non-controllable access to diverse and plural worlds—yet they do not assure the acquisition of the ethical and critical faculties needed for personal orientation and balance in negotiation of those worlds," and they often reinforce rather than ameliorate existing social inequalities (Chisholm 1999, 3).

With the massive sweep of neoliberal reforms that have restructured and privatized the state sector, national education systems remain overwhelmingly part of the public sector, both state owned and state controlled. This is despite the recent wave of reforms in education proclaiming the "end of the comprehensive era" and emphasizing choice and diversity through forms of privatization or joint public-private funding partnerships such as the Private Finance Initiative (PFI) in the United Kingdom. Moreover, state provision of an increasingly "massified" system of formal education is still the dominant form of the organization of knowledge. Advocates of knowledge capitalism argue that state systems are struggling to release themselves from older, predominantly industrial organizational forms to take advantage of more flexible and customized forms of delivery underwritten by developments in ICT (e.g., Burton-Jones 1999). Paradoxically, at a point historically when the interventionist state has been rolled back and when world governments have successfully eased themselves out of the market, governments find themselves as the major owners and controllers of the means of knowledge production in the new knowledge economy. While some economists and policy analysts have argued that there are new grounds for reappraising the role of the state in the knowledge economy (Stiglitz 1999a, 1999c; Thurow 1996), most governments have pursued policies that have followed a process of incremental and parallel privatization designed to blur the boundaries between the public and the private, between learning and work.

In the age of knowledge capitalism, we can expect governments in the West to further ease themselves out of the public provision of education as they begin in earnest to privatize the means of knowledge production and experiment with new ways of designing and promoting a permeable interface between knowledge businesses and public education at all levels. In the last decade, educationalists have witnessed the effects of the Hayekian revolution in the economics of knowledge and information—we have seen the attack on "big government" and have experienced reductions of state provision, funding, and regulation. In the age of knowledge capitalism, the next great struggle after the "culture wars" of the 1990s will be the "education wars," a struggle not only over the meaning and value of knowledge both internationally and locally, but also over the means of knowledge production.

NOTES

1. A version of this essay was presented at the Society for Research in Higher Education annual conference "Students and Learning: What Is Changing?" December 10–12, 2002, University of Glasgow. It draws upon aspects of published work (see Peters 2001b, 2002b, 2002e, 2002f, 2002g, 2003a).

2. See the excellent website on globalization set up at LSE under Desai's Center for the Study of Global Governance (old.lse.ac.uk/collections/globalDimensions) for a series of recent articles by leading experts and politicians.

3. This section draws on Peters (2002b).

4. For Hayek's two papers on knowledge, along with other full texts, commentary, and scholarly articles, see www.hayekcenter.org/friedrichhayek/hayek.html.

5. This is not to say that there is general agreement on Hayek's economics of knowledge. See Zappia (1999), who uses Bowles and Gintis's recent survey of "contested exchange economics" to argue for socialist alternatives to the competitive market mechanism in using information.

6. There are exceptions to the rule: Mark Blaug is an influential economist who consistently has worked in the field of education, as are Bowles and Gintis, who have been very influential. See the web page for the recently established Centre for the Economics of Education, funded by the Department of Education and Skills and set up as a partnership by the London School of Economics and the London Institute (cee.lse.ac.uk/index.html).

6

The Theater of Fast Knowledge: Performative Epistemologies

INTRODUCTION: THE NEW ECONOMY AND FAST CAPITALISM

This chapter first theorizes fast knowledge in relation to fast capitalism through the work of the American sociologist George Ritzer (2000), whose analysis of the fast-food industry in *The McDonaldization of Society* has a ready application to education. In the second section, we specifically draw out the aspect of the *theater* of fast knowledge by focusing on the management of performance and the relation of performance management to fast knowledge.

Speed is of the essence; it defines contemporary capitalism as "fast" capitalism (see Gee, Hull, and Lankshear 1996). As a single principle, speed annihilates distance, thus increasing access to global markets and promoting the mobility of factors of production to such an extent that now some would argue that it imperils "free trade." Speed defines the essence of finance and information capitalism.[1] The mobility of capital has greatly increased private capital flows in the symbolic form of information that can be speedily transferred in deregulated twenty-four-hour virtual finance markets, allowing international currency speculation and increased geographical spread of foreign direct investment (FDI).

In the information economy, the effect of location is diminished as virtual marketplaces and virtual organizations offer the benefits of speed and agility, round-the-clock operation, and global reach. Knowledge and information "leak" to where demand is highest and barriers are lowest, and thus laws and taxes are difficult to apply on a solely national basis. New information and communications technologies have accentuated and augmented aspects of the traditional industrial economy, making international transactions even more efficient and promoting flows of capital, goods, labor, and services at the speeds of sound and light.[2] This has led to the unparalleled growth of e-commerce and e-business—that is, to electronically mediated business transactions that create and transform relationships for value creation among organizations and between organizations and individuals. International Data Corporation (IDC) estimated the value of global e-commerce in 2000 at US$350.38 billion and projected it to climb to US$3.14 trillion by 2004.[3] At the same time, there has been a growing convergence of specific technologies into new integrated systems. The radical and globalized concordance of image, text, and sound has created new IT, media, telecommunications, and information/ knowledge infrastructures and a global media network reflecting the emergence of a Euro-American dominated global consumer culture with the rise of multinational edutainment conglomerates in music, film, and television.

The term *new economy* refers to the "transforming impact of digital technologies and the internet on business" at the micro level, which, especially in the U.S. context, has seemingly changed the rules of business; and, after a decade-long upswing, the new economy meant "inflation-free growth, higher productivity and the end of the business cycle" (Williams 2001, 398). Clearly, during the 1990s, capital markets and financialization played a central role in the development of the new economy. The impact of new digital technologies permitted liberalization of world capital markets and simultaneously enabled high-tech Internet and telecommunications companies to develop rapidly and make massive gains. The dynamic relationship between capital markets and digital technologies temporarily sustained a financial ecosystem that seemed to call into question the rules of the old game, creating a U.S. innovation system based on large-scale venture capital investment. In this environment, economists talked of the "economics of abundance"—the economics of knowledge and information is not one of scarcity, we were told, but rather one of abundance, for, unlike most resources that are depleted when used, information and knowledge can be shared and can actually grow through application. Thus, for instance, Joseph Stiglitz (1999a) suggests that "movement to the knowledge economy necessitates a rethinking of economic fundamentals," because knowledge behaves differently from other commodities. Knowledge, once discovered and made public, operates expansively to defy the normal "law" of scarcity that governs most commodity markets. As we have seen, this leads Stiglitz to emphasize that knowledge shares many of the properties of a *global* public good because it is nonrivalrous.[4] In its immaterial form as ideas or concepts, there are no costs to sharing knowledge or adding new users. Only once it has become materially embodied or encoded does knowledge represent a cost, and yet at the same time, new technologies have dramatically reduced the costs of dissemination and distribution.

These developments have led some economists to emphasize the growing importance of an international knowledge system as a source of labor value and productivity, research, and technological innovation. They stress the growth of intellectual, human, and social capital, all forms of capitalization of the self. Human capital, or "competencies," is the key component of value in the knowledge-based economy, and one of the principal aims of knowledge management is to "extract" it from people's heads and to lock it into systems or processes as soon as possible, where it has a higher inherent value and cannot "walk out the door." In knowledge capitalism, knowledge creation, diffusion, and innovation are all important. This acknowledges the centrality of knowledge and information to the processes of the sign economy and the symbolic society, and, in particular, "the application of such knowledge and information to knowledge generation and information processing/communication devices, in a cumulative feedback loop between innovation and the uses of innovation" (Castells 2000b, 32).

Fast knowledge, then, is a central element in knowledge capitalism, both as content and as technology that refines the very system responsible for its ever-increasing fast circulation. Fast knowledge is an inextricable part of finance capitalism and through the model of the copy (copyright, patent, and trademark) is controlled through the emerging structures of international property rights regimes such as GATS (General Agreement on Trade in Services) and TRIPS (Trade-Related Aspects of Intellectual Property Rights), which include educational services. Fast knowledge also increasingly defines aspects of the international knowledge system determining the speed and efficiency of knowledge creation, transmission, and distribution. We have witnessed this kind of development in education through the growth of the Internet since the late 1990s and the new educational uses it permits—the increasing use of e-mail for academic communication; the growth of scholarly e-publishing of journals and books; the rise of e-learning, videoconferencing, texting, and blogging; and the development of knowledge networks and mobile learning works (see Peters 2003b). Fast knowledge has changed our educational institutions and academic practices. It has become part of an outputs-driven performance culture based on a "logic of performativity" (Lyotard 1984). In Britain and elsewhere, research assessment counts publications in a publish-or-perish climate, which not only determines faculty and institutional reputation, but also levels of research funding. Universities have become theaters of fast knowledge, driven by the ethos of performance in teaching and research and with conferences that now restrict presentations to bite-size bits no longer than fifteen minutes, sometimes including discussion, for example, AERA (American Educational

Research Association). One of the beauties of the PESGB (Philosophy of Education Society of Great Britain) conference is that it has, to date, resisted such moves, allowing approximately forty-five minutes for presentation and discussion per paper, despite the increasing number of conference participants.

FAST CAPITALISM, FAST KNOWLEDGE, AND THE MCDONALDIZATION OF EDUCATION

According to Eric Schlosser in *Fast-Food Nation* (2002), the farm activist Jim Hightower first warned of "the McDonaldization of America" in the early 1970s. At that stage, McDonald's operated about a thousand burger-based fast-food outlets/restaurants. By comparison, today it operates thirty thousand and opens almost two thousand new ones each year. It hires about a million people and is the largest owner of retail property in the world, operating more playgrounds than any other *private* organization in the United States. Schlosser writes that McDonald's "is responsible for the nation's bestselling line of children's clothing (McKids) and is one of the largest distributors of toys" (4). Ronald McDonald has almost universal recognition by American kids, with only Santa having a higher recognition factor. Schlosser, like Ritzer, analyzes the industrialization of the restaurant, commenting negatively on the frozen, canned, dehydrated, or freeze-dried state of the food delivered to the restaurant and the low and declining hourly rate received by McDonald's workers. Most of all, Schlosser is concerned about the way fast food is aggressively marketed to children— "an industry that both feeds and feeds off children" (9).

Schlosser picked up on some of the criticisms of McDonald's and the effect of fast food on the culture and construction of postwar America that George Ritzer had made when he first published *The McDonaldization of Society* in 1993. This chapter uses an updated 2000 edition. After a couple of decades of musing about a process by which principles first developed in the fast-food industry came to dominate American society and subsequently became more deeply ingrained in other cultures around the world, Ritzer (2000) produced a work of social criticism following in the footsteps of Max Weber (1930) and his analysis of the rationalization process.[5]

McDonaldization as a process therefore is more about the development of a set of principles of fast capitalism than about McDonald's or the fast-food industry per se. The application of these principles to other foods and other types of business, such as toys, fitness, taxes, books, weight loss, car transmissions, and so on, offers a paradigm based on efficiency, calculability, predictability, and control through nonhuman technology. Ritzer's critique is based on what he calls "the irrationality of rationality," by which he means, more generally, "that rational systems inevitably spawn irrational consequences." In effect, McDonaldization also leads to inefficiency, unpredictability, incalculability, and loss of control:

> Contrary to McDonald's propaganda and the widespread belief in it, fast-food restaurants and their clones in other areas of society are not reasonable, or even truly rational, systems. They spawn many problems for customers, including inefficiency rather than efficiency, relatively high costs, illusory fun and reality, false friendliness, disenchantment, threats to health and the environment, homogenization, and dehumanization. McDonaldization does have advantages, but these irrationalities clearly counterbalance and even overwhelm them. (Ritzer 2000, 145)

While McDonaldization offers many advantages, it also has a downside. In the case of McDonald's, Ritzer mentions the adverse effects on the environment and other ecological problems, dehumanizing assembly-line conditions for working and eating, and the "fatness" or obesity crisis. Part of the strength of Ritzer's analysis is that it examines the forces driving McDonaldization, tracking it as a local phenomenon and relating it to wider changes in American society. He also relates McDonaldization to globalization, which he considers a form of Americanization and an agent of cultural imperialism that may threaten local customs. If Ritzer's thesis holds water, then it offers a set of insights, more generally, into the principles of fast capitalism and their application to the so-called knowledge economy, or what we have called "fast knowledge." It also offers a ready critique of fast knowledge.

Ritzer also briefly considers a number of other theoretical perspectives for viewing McDonaldization, including postindustrialism, post-Fordism, and postmodernism, all of which share the assumption that somehow we have passed beyond the modern. He concludes that McDonaldization fits Fredric Jameson's (1981) five characteristics of postmodern societies—association with late capitalism, superficiality, waning of emotion or affect, loss of historicity, and reproductive technologies—but he does not think that we face a mode of production that is fundamentally different. He does acknowledge, however, that McDonald's, along with malls and Disney World, is an example of "new means of consumption." Developments in the postwar era have revolutionized the ways we consume by rationalizing the structures of consumption. Clearly this has effects on the self (see Gee et al. 1996).

Ritzer explores the precursors of McDonaldization by reference first to Weber's theory of rationality and the increasing bureaucratization of everyday life; then to the Holocaust (mass-produced death), scientific management or Taylorism, and the development of the assembly line; and finally to the housing industry in the United States and the development of shopping centers or malls. For Ritzer, then, McDonaldization represents a culmination of trends and processes of rationalization rather than something entirely new. He devotes a chapter to each of the major principles in the development of the fast-food industry.

During the process, he makes several references to education that amount to a preliminary examination of fast knowledge. For example, he explains that the contemporary university, dubbed the "McUniversity" by critics (Parker and Jary 1995), has succumbed to the pressure for greater efficiency (evidenced in machine-graded multichoice examinations) and streamlining of the educational process—publishers provide free manuals and sets of questions with textbooks, increasingly as computer programs (Ritzer 2000, 49). While many academics may jocularly talk about working in an academic "factory," the development of customized textbooks and the e-publishing of courses and course materials have led scholars like David Noble (2001) to talk of universities as "digitalized diploma mills." The efficiency emphasis, Ritzer's first principle, is aimed at streamlining the process, simplifying the product, and putting customers (students) to work.

The emphasis on the quantity rather than the quality of products (an aspect of his second principle of calculability) is detectable not only in the fast-food industry but also in higher education, where

> most courses run for a standard number of weeks and hours per week. In the main, little attention is devoted to determining whether a given subject is best taught in a given number of weeks or hours per week. The focus seems to be on how many students (the "products") can be herded through the system and what grades they earn rather than the quality of what they have learned and of the educational experience. (Ritzer 2000, 66)

Ritzer explores calculability in the standardization of grades, scores, ratings, and rankings in higher education, a feature, one might argue, that has become strengthened over recent years with the introduction of league tables for schools and universities in Britain and elsewhere as a result of the Research Assessment Exercise (RAE) and other national assessment and monitoring mechanisms. Ritzer points to "credentialization," to student evaluations of courses and the intrusion of quantitative measures not only in teaching but also in research, where publications are counted, journals are ranked, and citation analysis has become a new methodology for plotting academic reputation. McDonaldization suffers from the illusion of quantity and from a process that reduces production and service to numbers.

The third principle is predictability, which necessitates creating predictable settings, scripting interactions with customers, making employee behavior predictable, and creating predictable products and processes, which Ritzer exemplifies by reference to an educational example of what he calls "cookie-cutter textbooks," and an example from entertainment that he calls "McMovieworld." Control, the fourth principle, refers to the control of employees and customers, as well as of the process and the product.

Ritzer provides us with a comprehensive model of fast knowledge in relation to education. His analysis enables us to identify elements of fast education—its operating principles based on efficiency, predictability, calculability, and control—and its critique, the irrationality of rationality. The empirical question for educationalists is, first, to identify the ways in which education has become a consumption good—that is, how students, parents, and (even) teachers and employees have become consumers—and, second, to analyze the ways in which the institutions and structures of education have revolutionized the institutions and structures of education consumption. These are major research questions. A critical theoretical issue is whether fast knowledge is just a further rationalization of industrial education processes or whether it represents something fundamentally new, perhaps even a generically new form of capitalism.

In looking to the future, Ritzer also provides us with a practical guide for dealing with McDonaldization that has application in the world of education: the promotion of different forms of capitalism—"caring capitalism" and the elimination of the worst excesses; the collective "fight-back" of class actions; national heart savers; high-quality regional movements emphasizing traditional values ("slow food"); "save-the-children" individual strategies; and so on.

A further development of fast knowledge, and, considering its recency, understandably one that is not explored by Ritzer, is fast publishing. The *Economist* (2003) report on "fast publishing" focused on an invitation in central London to write a book in a day under the proposed titled of "Strategic Thinking in Tactical Times." The invitation came from Joe DiVanna who runs the consulting firm Maris Strategies out of Cambridge. At the London conference, DiVanna divided the thirty people (a selection of bankers, management consultants, and company strategists) into three teams and first subjected them to nine fifteen-minute lectures by experts before engaging them with a preexisting structure based on three chapters, each of three sections, entitled "The Strategic Individual," "Developing the Strategic Corporate Competency," and "Moving the Strategic Agenda into Actionable Initiatives." After sessions dominated by flipcharts and "a buffet lunch with fine wines," DiVanna

> revealed how the real work would begin: each author would take three topics, one per chapter, and undertake to write 400 words on each by the next morning. After all the talk of passion in the workplace and emotional commitment, it was hard to refuse. With 30 people writing over 1,200 words, that would be at least 36,000 words by dawn. Never mind the quality, feel the width. (117)

The raw material was posted on a website for a month. DiVanna edited and added to the material and delivered the final manuscript of 60,000 words to Palgrave Macmillan, which will reportedly sell the book for £50 (US$87), with an initial print run of five hundred. Such may well be expected of academics in the near future.

KNOWLEDGE MANAGEMENT IN THE NEW ECONOMY: THE SOURCES OF PERFORMATIVITY RESEARCH[6]

It is one of the uninvestigated central ironies of the new critical science driven by French theory that one of its major sources of theoretical inspiration is British analytic philosophy and especially the "linguistic" philosophy of J. L. Austin and Ludwig Wittgenstein.[7] Both Lyotard (1984) and Foucault (1978), for example, use and adapt Wittgenstein's conception of "language games" to describe the fragmentary nature of the social bond, the crisis of legitimation of scientific knowledge in the "postmodern condition," and the strategic and political nature of "games of truth." Derrida and Lyotard, though for different purposes, draw explicitly on Austin's (1975) notion of the "performative," first formulated in *How to Do Things with Words*. Derrida (1977, 1998) embraces Austin's category and theory of the performative as the basis for the new humanities, and Butler (1990, 1993) extends this use in gender studies to indicate that gender is constituted by performative acts that come to form a "coherent" gender identity. Lyotard (1984) appropriates Wittgenstein's philosophy of language games as a basis for his analysis of the problem of the legitimation of knowledge and education in the postmodern condition and draws on Austin to formulate and predict a new culture of performativity for higher education.

Lyotard's prophetic prognosis on the nature of knowledge and its management in higher education has become a theoretical springboard for educational theorists to analyze performativity as a more general condition affecting not only the whole of the education sector but also, more widely, newly consumer-driven public services across the board. At the same time, management theorists and business schools picking up on similar socioeconomic structural changes in capitalism have developed notions of performance—"performance management" and "performance culture"—in a parallel though generally theoretically unreflexive discourse.[8] The genealogies of *performance* reveal multiple and disparate sources in performance studies (Carlson 1996) and, almost simultaneously, in both Austin (1962) and Marcuse, who coined the term *performance principle* in 1955 to name the reality principle of postindustrial societies (see McKenzie 2001b). Yet it is Lyotard's use of *performativity* and *the logic of performativity* that gets referred to in the field of educational studies.

The remainder of this chapter elucidates the theoretical sources of the performative in Austin and performativity in Lyotard before making some more general remarks on performance culture and its place in management theory. It is part of our argument that educationalists need to theorize the term *performance*, to recognize its conceptual homes and its intersectoral linkages across disciplines and across public service, if they are to properly locate the term and understand its historical significance for framing the present.

J. L. Austin (1911–1960) was an Oxford ordinary language philosopher who developed much of the theory of speech acts. A speech act is an action performed by means of language, involving such diverse speech acts as describing, asking a question, making a request or order, or making a promise. Austin (1962) outlines a theory of performatives in *How to Do Things with Words*, in which the action that the sentence describes (nominating, sentencing, promising) is performed by the sentence itself. As J. O. Urmson makes clear in his editor's preface, *How to Do Things with Words* comprised the William James Lectures originally delivered by Austin at Harvard University in 1955, although the views on which they were based were developed in 1939. It has to be remembered that between 1952 and 1954, Austin gave lectures at Oxford under the title "Words and Deeds." In *How to Do Things with Words*, Austin distinguishes between *constative* and *performative* utterances in terms of *saying* and *doing*, a distinction that challenges the age-old assumption in philosophy that to say something is to state something with the intention of effectively decoupling performatives from the truth-falsehood dichotomy. He argues that there are many utterances that do not easily fit into the category of statements, that is, the class of sentences that purport to describe a state of affairs, which Austin calls "constatives." There is a class of expressions that Austin calls performatives that are not statements and yet against verificationist sympathies have sense. Austin provides a number of examples of these performative sentences in which words are deeds, so to speak. Austin finally abandons the distinction between constative and performative utterances for a more carefully worked out theory of illocutionary forces.

Jean-François Lyotard is considered by most commentators, justly or not, as the non-Marxist philosopher of "the postmodern condition" (sometimes referred to as "postmodernity"). His *The Postmodern Condition: A Report on Knowledge* (1984), originally published in Paris in 1979, became an instant cause célèbre. The book crystallized in an original interpretation a study of the status and development of knowledge, science, and technology in advanced capitalist societies. *The Postmodern Condition* was important for a number of reasons. It developed a philosophical interpretation of the changing state of knowledge, science, and education in the most highly developed societies, reviewing and synthesizing research on contemporary science within the broader context of the sociology of postindustrial society and studies of postmodern culture. Lyotard brought together for the first time diverse threads and previously separate literatures in an analysis that many commentators and critics believed to signal an epochal break not only with the so-called modern era but also with various traditionally "modern" ways of viewing the world.

The Postmodern Condition, as a single work considered on its own merits, is reason enough for educational philosophers and theorists to devote time and effort to understanding and analyzing Lyotard's major working hypothesis: "that the status of knowledge is altered as societies enter what is known as the postindustrial age and cultures enter what is known as the postmodern age" (1984, 3). He uses the term *postmodern condition* to describe the state of knowledge and the problem of its legitimation in the most highly developed societies. In this, he follows sociologists and critics who have used the term to designate the state of Western culture "following the transformations which, since the end of the nineteenth century, have altered the game rules for science, literature and the arts" (3). Lyotard places these transformations within the context of the crisis of narratives, especially those Enlightenment metanarratives concerning meaning, truth, and emancipation that have been used to legitimate both the rules of knowledge of the sciences and the foundations of modern institutions.

By "transformations," Lyotard is referring to the effects of the new technologies since the 1950s and their combined impact on the two principal functions of knowledge—research and the transmission of learning. Significantly, he maintains that the leading sciences and technologies have all been based on language-related developments—theories of linguistics, cybernetics, informatics, computer languages, telematics, theories of algebra, and the like—and their miniaturization and commercialization. In this context, Lyotard argues that the status of knowledge is permanently altered: its availability as an international commodity becomes the basis for national and commercial advantage within the global economy, and its computerized uses in the military is the basis for enhanced state security and international monitoring. Knowledge, as he admits, has already become the principal force of production, changing the composition of the workforce in developed countries. The commercialization of knowledge and its new forms of media circulation, he suggests, will raise new ethico-legal problems between the nation-state and the information-rich multinationals, and will widen the gap between the so-called developed and third worlds.

Here is a critical account theorizing the status of knowledge and education in the postmodern condition that focuses upon the most highly developed societies. It constitutes a seminal contribution and an important point of departure to what has become known—in part due to Lyotard's work—as the modernity-postmodernity debate, a debate that has involved many of the most prominent contemporary philosophers and social theorists (see Peters 1996). It is a book that directly addresses the concerns of education, perhaps more so than any other single poststructuralist text. It does so in a way that bears on the future status and role of education and knowledge in what has proved to be a prophetic analysis. Many of the features of Lyotard's analysis of the postmodern condition—an analysis well over twenty years old—now appear to be accepted aspects of our experiences in Western societies.

One way his analysis has been prophetic is that the postmodern condition marks the decline of modernity's grand narratives, in particular the way the "progress" of Western capitalist technoscience has been culturally embedded in deeper metaphysical fables about reason and freedom rather than globalization, flexibility, social regulation, and performativity. The story of Western capitalist technoscience was supposed to lead to the gradual but inevitable unfolding of the progress of knowledge in emancipation. Lyotard, however, hypothesizes that this story became simply too incredible to believe when in the 1960s it was clear that the transition to the postindustrial society (or knowledge economy) was no longer a smooth, necessary, inevitable, and desirable movement. He maintained that the postmodern condition was based on failing hope for

> the existence of a modern era that dates from the time of the Enlightenment and that now has run its course: and this modern era was predicated on the notion of progress in knowledge, in the arts, in technology, and in human freedom as well, all of which was thought of as leading to a truly emancipated society: a society emancipated from poverty, despotism and ignorance. But all of us can see that the development continues to take place without leading to the realization of any of these dreams of emancipation (Lyotard 1984, 37).

In this transitional period, Lyotard argues, science and technology are falling under the sway of "another language game, in which the goal is no longer truth, but performativity—that is, the best possible input/output equation" (37).

It is clear that Lyotard is referring to performance and a logic of performativity that are cornerstones of the new technoscientific capitalist knowledge economy:

> There is no denying the dominant existence today of techno-science, that is the massive subordination of cognitive statements to the finality of the best possible performance, which is the technological criterion. But the mechanical and the industrial, especially when they enter fields traditionally reserved for artists, are carrying with them much more than power effects. The objects and the thoughts that originate in scientific knowledge and the capitalist economy convey with them one of the rules which supports their possibility: the rule that there is no reality unless testified by a consensus between

partners over a certain knowledge and certain commitments. This rule is of no little consequence. It is the imprint left on the politics of the scientist and the trustee of capital by a kind of flight of reality out of the metaphysical, religious and political certainties that the mind believed it held. This withdrawal is absolutely necessary to the emergence of science and capitalism. (Lyotard 1984, 76–77)

THE POLITICAL ECONOMY OF PERFORMATIVITY[9]

In the new BBC4 series *The Commanding Heights: The Battle for the World Economy* based on the book by Daniel Yergin and Joseph Stanislaw, the chancellor, Gordon Brown, who heads up the key policy-making IMF committee, tells Yergin,

> The problem for the Left in the past was that they equated the public interest with public ownership and public regulation, and therefore they assumed that markets were not in the public interest. . . . [Markets] provide opportunities for prosperity, but equally they're not automatically equated with the public interest.

He goes on to say,

> The idea that markets must work in the public interest, the idea that governments have a responsibility for the level of employment and prosperity in the economy, the idea that governments must intervene on occasions—these are increasingly the ideas of our time.

The chancellor accepts globalization as a fact of life but tells Yergin, "The question is, can we manage it in the interests of a few or in the interests, as I want it to be, of all the people of the world." His desire is not only to eliminate poverty at home but also to double aid to the Third World. In his capacity as chairman of the IMF committee, he aims to improve mechanisms of international financial institutions for crisis prevention and early warning systems.

The crucial element in the chancellor's recorded statement is his hedging acceptance that markets can be made to work in the public interest and that government intervention may be required in areas of employment and prosperity. There is the strong tacit acceptance that for the most part government will not need to intervene and that for the most part, once the consumer mode of delivery for public services has been set up, government quasi-markets or marketlike arrangements will function smoothly and in the public interest. This means, in effect, business as usual for education and health. It means also, to quote the title of a major new joint AHRB/ESRC (Arts and Humanities Research Council/Economic and Social Research Council) program, the promotion of "Cultures of Consumption" (see www.consume .bbk.ac.uk). The executive summary for the program begins,

Consumption has returned to the centre of public affairs, government policy making, and intellectual life in recent years, in Britain as well as more globally. Consumption and related issues of consumers' rights and interests, consumer culture and consumer policy inform today [*sic*] major debates about the future of democracy and the nation-state, wealth and welfare, economic governance, the role of new technologies and the environment, and the changing relationship of commerce and culture in contemporary societies. (see revised specification at www.consume.bbk.ac.uk/about.html).

The AHRB/ESRC research program contextualizes itself by reference to the British government's white paper *Modern Markets: Confident Consumers*, released in 1999, which sets a new agenda both to promote open and competitive markets and yet to provide people with the skills, knowledge, and information they need to become demanding consumers, especially those who are socially excluded and those on low incomes who can least afford to make a bad purchase.

Clearly, the white paper presages issues relating to Third Way policy concerning the consumer as a new social actor in the PFI public-private partnerships that are now redesigning consumer-driven public services and attempting to encourage a better alignment between consumption and citizenship. These consumer-driven public services signify the end of large, monolithic, "one-size-fits-all" institutions and a move toward smaller, more flexible, "customized" public services, with also greater public accountability harnessed to a set of more workable democratic relationships between the market, consumer advocacy, and public policy.

Increasingly, under neoliberalism and the Third way in the United Kingdom, risk and security management is associated with the new consumer welfare regime where an entrepreneurial self invests in herself—a form of prudentialism—and calculates the risks and returns on this investment in her education, health, employment, and retirement. This process we describe as both self-constituting and self-consuming (Peters 2003b). It is self-constituting in the Foucauldian sense that choice making shapes us as moral, economic, and political agents. It is self-consuming in the sense that the entrepreneurial self creates and constructs herself through acts of consumption. Take, for instance, the example of a self-investment in an advanced degree undertaken over a period of four to five years, where the entrepreneurial self is paying for the degree his/herself (let's assume $3,400 per year for five years). This is an investment in one's future, and it is made after a process of deliberation, of weighing up a range of factors including future security and employment prospects (a clear form of risk calculation and management). The investment is made in the self—in an activity that traditionally is held to be personally trans formative—although it is made over a period of time, and its success as an investment requires active participation (work on the self) by the subject. Certainly it differs from the normal acquisitive model of consumerism, and one could argue that the purchase of (and investment in) services differs markedly from the purchase of commodities.

The neoliberal regime is in part supported by the rise of enterprise culture and what we have called "enterprise education" (Peters 2001a), which began under Thatcher's government. Blair's Third Way is an attempt to go beyond neoliberalism and its conflation of autonomy with possessive, individualized consumerism and to subordinate the security of the producer to the freedom of the consumer. As Daniel Leighton (2003) notes, "The goal is to save the welfare state but to do so by privileging the efficiency of the private sector and the sovereignty of the consumer."

Tony Blair's speech on public-service reform to workers in the public sector on October 16, 2001, defined the elements of a Third Way program to remodel the government-citizen relationship along consumer lines: "The key to reform is re-designing the system around the user—the patient, the pupil, the passenger, the victim of crime." And later in the speech, he defines its principles thus:

> First, high national standards and full accountability. Second, devolution to the front-line to encourage diversity and local creativity. Third, flexibility of employment so that staff are better able to deliver modern public services. Fourth, the promotion of alternative providers and greater choice.
>
> All four principles have one goal—to put the consumer first. We are making the public services user-led, not producer or bureaucracy led, allowing far greater freedom and incentives for services to develop as users want. (*Guardian* 2001)

Blair makes the following comments about education in relation to the four principles. Concerning standards and accountability,

> In education, there are national tests in the basics for all 7, 11 and 14 year-olds; regular inspection of schools; and national strategies including literacy and numeracy hours to ensure basic minimum standards of teaching and learning school by school.

Concerning devolution and diversity,

> Specialist schools—schools which build a real center of excellence in one area while continuing to teach the whole curriculum—also represent significant change. Schools achieving highly in one respect tend to perform better across the board—GCSE results in specialist schools are nearly 10 percentage points higher than in non-specialist comprehensives with a single intake. Our programme of diversity in secondary education is therefore vital to the future, which is why we have set a target of at least 1,500 specialist schools by 2005 as a staging post to specialist status for all secondary schools ready for it.

Concerning flexibility of employment,

There are new training salaries for new post-graduate teacher trainees, a performance bonus of £2,000.00 to nearly 200,000 classroom teachers. . . . In education, we have established the new National College for School Leadership.

And concerning greater choice,

The fourth of our reform principles is the provision of far greater choice to the consumer—not just formal choice, but the ability to make that choice effective.

In education that means not only a wider variety of schools, but also expansion of successful schools and encouragement of the very successful to take over schools or set up new schools, so that more parents are able to secure their first preference school for their child.

The four reform principles—standards and accountability, devolution and diversity, flexibility of employment, and greater choice—define what Catherine Needham (2003) calls "the consumerisation of citizenship," supported by an increasingly promotional and top-down form of communication, consultation focused on the "self-regarding individual" without collective discussion, and a form of service delivery based on the combined objectives of maximizing "customer satisfaction and expanding individual choice and competition."

In large measure, the four reform principles, considered in conjunction with the emulation of private-sector efficiency and consumer sovereignty, also determine what we have called the "culture of performativity," which provides the insider professional with a picture of the consumer-driven public sector. The driving question from the *outside*, though, is whether Third Way New Labor can go beyond neoliberalism and loaded definitions of freedom in purely consumer terms to revitalize and perhaps redefine elements of traditional social democracy: participation and active engagement, access and equality, collective identity and mobilization, and social justice. The pressing question from the *inside* is whether the culture of performativity provides the best conditions for service and knowledge workers in the new economy—for teachers, lecturers, nurses, doctors, and all manner of education and health professionals.

MANAGING PERFORMANCE

Jon McKenzie (2001b) has offered an explanation of performance considered as a new social attitude in his recently published text *Perform or Else: From Discipline to Performance*. He argues that the concept of "performance" is now widely recognized in business and the commercial world as a conceptual tool for assessing human and technological standards and that it is fast becoming the dominant social model of evaluation. According to McKenzie, traditional philosophical distinctions are becoming less influential, and performance "effectiveness" and "efficiency" are growing in power as the new conventions for defining the basis of measuring what is right, true, and good (178–79). He writes,

> For better or for worse, I have come to think that we are entering an age of global performance. We can understand performance as a stratum of power/knowledge by extrapolating from Foucault's well-known genealogy of discipline. While disciplinary mechanisms produce unified subjects through a series of institutions (school, factory, prison, hospital), each with its own discrete archive of statements and practices, performative power blurs the borders of social institutions by connecting and sharing digital archives. Financial information, criminal records, medical files, and school transcripts once stored in separate metal file cabinets are now being uploaded to silicon databases and electronically networked. (6)

Following Richard Schechter (2000), McKenzie theorizes performance as a formation of power and knowledge, and in doing so, he warns us of the growing objectification and alienation of human labor. He asks whether we have entered an age of global performance and remarks that *performance* has emerged as a crucial term in at least three different areas of social life: economics, technology, and art. He goes on to explain, "Far from existing in disconnected spheres, these paradigms increasingly overlap and intersect: just as theatre takes place in institutional contexts constrained and enriched by technological and economic imperatives, the theatrical model has come to inform organizational theory and web design." He writes,

> I theorize performance not only as transgressive cultural praxis but also as a global formation of power and knowledge, one that challenges us to perform—or else. Performance in this sense extends and displaces the disciplinary power analysed by Michel Foucault. Its politics are post-colonial rather than colonial, its infrastructures electronic as well as industrial, its economies dominated by services more than manufacturing. Factory labour and tradeoff commodities have obviously not disappeared: instead they have been overcoded by "soft wares," forms of immaterial production found in communications, finance, healthcare, and social work. (McKenzie 2003)

For McKenzie, performance management draws upon the paradigm of cultural performance and substitutes for scientific management or Taylorism, which was the dominant organizational paradigm developed in the early part of the last century for a manufacturing-based, nationally oriented, and highly industrialized economy. Performance management, in contrast to scientific management, no longer produces highly centralized bureaucracies; rigid, top-down management styles; or perceived controlling, hierarchical, and conformist organizational cultures. Rather it

> attunes itself to economic processes that are increasingly service-based, globally oriented and electronically wired. Since the end of the Second World War, theorists from Herbert Simon to Edwards Deming to Peter Drucker have argued for decentralized structures and flexible management styles, styles that, rather than controlling workers, empower them with information and training so they may contribute to decision-making processes. The principles regularly cited in management are not uniformity, conformity, and rationality, but diversity, innovation, and intuition. (McKenzie 2001b, 6)

As he remarks later, performance management doesn't sell itself as scientific, but rather, adopting the paradigm of cultural performance, it redescribes itself as an *ars poetica* of organizational practice, which is evident in texts like *Corporate Renaissance: The Art of Reengineering* (Cross et al. 1994), *Jamming: The Art and Discipline of Business Creativity* (Kao 1998), and *Cultural Diversity in Organizations* (Cox 1993). This new soft power of management theory and practice recognizes performance as having acquired a normative force. McKenzie's analysis of it as a formation of power and knowledge enables us to appreciate a theorizing of performative power that extends beyond the realm of cultural production into discourses and practices that have the normative force to structure our organizations and the institutions of work, learning, and leisure. And while there are different semantic ranges involved, together with different sites of pragmatic installation, as McKenzie argues, the soft power of performance also enables us to recognize the integration of cultural, management, and technological systems.

Higher education is a crucial subsector where these types of performative power intersect, especially when framed by the policy template of the knowledge economy, for in the knowledge economy, the cultural and the symbolic are paramount. This is the very idea behind the so-called sign economy, which is no longer based on raw materials but rather on the transformation of ideas and symbolic resources by means of intellectual, human, and social capital.

In this environment, the three spheres of the economic, technical, and cultural are increasingly brought into close alignment as performative power combines the rational calculation of ("high-performance") technical systems and databases with the domain of affective management based around personal experience and social interaction. Performance management in this context first came to light under the development of performance measurement systems developed by the performance indicator movement, and later under New Public Management, which drew on principal agency theory and transactional cost analysis.

Performance management is an ideal system for knowledge management, especially where one of the main aims for the knowledge manager is to extract knowledge from people's heads (often tacit knowledge that is difficult to codify) and embed it in intellectual systems or processes as soon as possible, both protecting it as intellectual property under copyright, patent, or international trade law and putting it into commercial service to make a profit. It is, classically speaking, concerned with appropriating the knowledge surplus, and performance management often utilizes the soft psychotherapeutic technologies in the affective domain, alongside traditional peer-review mechanisms and collegial exchange, and in combination with simple counts and computer or accounting methodologies (including the weighting and mathematization of soft variables like "reputation") to produce departmental, faculty, and institutional performance "profiles" and institutional, national, and international league tables.

NOTES

1. This conceptualization is developed from figure 1, "The Knowledge Economy as an Emerging International System," in Peters (2003b).

2. Some theorists have emphasized "speed" as a dimension of contemporary post-Fordist capitalism, for instance, David Harvey (1989), who talks of "space-time compression." See also the work of the French theorist Paul Virilio (1985), who writes of "space-time technologies."

3. Definition and data taken from Andam's "e-Commerce and e-Business," accessed September 23, 2003, at www.eprimers.org/e-comm.

4. Knowledge, while nonrivalrous, can be *excluded* from certain users, which is the other property of a pure public good, through the protection of intellectual property. The term *intellectual property* emerged only in the nineteenth century, when its modern use was determined in court judgments defining copyright. In this sense, "intellectual property" was not meant to be a property right in the general sense of the term but rather referred to a U.S. federal policy that "granted a limited trade monopoly in exchange for universal use and access" (Vaidhyanathan 2001, 21).

5. The original article of the same title was published in 1983 in the *Journal of American Culture* 6:100–107. For his response to critics, see Ritzer (1994, 1999).

6. Parts of this section on Lyotard are drawn from Michael Peters's "Lyotard and Philosophy of Education," www.vusst.hr/ENCYCLOPAEDIA/lyotard.htm.

7. This is not to suggest that Wittgenstein might also be seen as a philosopher of the Austrian counter-Enlightenment and in terms of fin de siecle Vienna (see Janik and Toulmin 1973; Peters and Marshall 1999).

8. Such unreflexive discourse is not always the case. Management theorists are using Foucault and Lyotard increasingly. See, for instance, Stephen Probert's (2003) use of Lyotard and Foucault in his article "Knowledge Management: A Critical Investigation" in the *Electronic Journal of Business Research Methods*.

9. Parts of this introduction draw on Peters (2003b).

7

The New Pedagogy and Social Learning[1]

INTRODUCTION: IDENTIFYING THE NEW PEDAGOGY

It is a curious fact that those pedagogical practices in which we engage every day as teachers and that are so familiar to us somehow remain resistant to scrutiny, research, and theory. This is why we have chosen to focus on current pedagogic research on and practice of the so-called new pedagogy. The term has been used by the Tavistock Institute, which recently made its final report to the British Economic and Social Research Council, entitled *Review of Current Pedagogic Research and Practice in the Fields of Post-Compulsory Education and Lifelong Learning* (Cullen et al. 2002), as part of its synthesizing analysis commissioned as necessary background to the council's Teaching and Learning Research Programme, Phase III—Emerging Themes (see www.tlrp.org). The program is perhaps the most comprehensive and influential on teaching and learning in post-compulsory education ever attempted in Britain.

Current research on pedagogy and learning is greatly variable across different learning sectors. There is nothing that resembles a theoretical orthodoxy, and related discourses are normative and value laden with debates arguing for the primacy of one approach over another rather than about the appropriateness of different practices for different settings and purposes. Yet within this eclecticism, a new pedagogy is emerging that draws on constructivist and postmodern theory. Within the constellation of the new constructivist pedagogy, four main types of pedagogic method can be identified: expository, interactive, conversational, and experiential. Perhaps the most important feature of this new paradigm is how, under the influence of postmodernism, the whole educational enterprise is perceived differently; the very nature of knowledge and educational research is altered. The curriculum, both its content and its process, reflects this influence in a move away from propositional knowledge toward knowledge seen as contextualized, contingent, and more immediately applicable. While the core issues concerning learners, learning, and teaching may not have changed, the societal context within which the questions are posed has become transformed. This is the basis of a review that a recent report from the Tavistock Institute gives about current pedagogic research and practice in the postcompulsory education sector. Yet we might expect that the review findings apply much more widely across education. It is an influential report from a prestigious institute—an institute of human relations that R. D. Laing, the Glaswegian existential psychiatrist, was associated with during the 1960s while conducting research on the families of schizophrenics.

The institute was interested in providing an overview, in identifying the key research questions, and in locating the gaps as a basis for its conclusions and policy recommendations. The report, one would think, should be of interest to teachers, policy makers, and educational researchers. Yet its conclusions are not surprising, although they are shocking in that after years of effort so little should be known about pedagogy in postcompulsory education, or any other sector for that matter. In the preamble, the review itemizes a set of realities that underlie pedagogic research and practice:

> Firstly, there is little established "evidence base[d] culture" in teaching and learning. Secondly, pedagogic understandings are shaped by different—and sometimes conflicting—patrimonies across each sector. Thirdly, however, there has been a significant—and complex—degree of "inter-breeding" between the sectors of post-compulsory education, and it is often difficult to attribute a particular set of pedagogic "outcomes" to particular sources of evidence. Fourthly, practices are either grounded in day to day minutae of "chalkface" learning delivery (and hence ungrounded in theory) or, conversely, are tied to a particular "grand learning theory" and are unsubstantiated in practice. (Cullen et al. 2002, 4)

Patrimony is a term listed in the glossary as *learning patrimony*, with the following meaning: "The cultural and historical forces that shape philosophy, policy and theory and practices around learning in a particular space and time. At the macro level, an example is the school curriculum in a particular country" (Cullen et al. 2002, 8). The glossary lists some thirty-two terms from educational psychology (e.g., *cognitive theory*); adult education (e.g., *andragogy*); constructivism (itself a term, attributed to John Dewey); critical theory; sociology of education (e.g., *social capital*); and postmodern theory (e.g., *performativity*), as though these terms constitute a new vocabulary of pedagogic research. To be sure, some of the terms might constitute part of the conceptual vocabulary for the new pedagogy,[2] although it is necessary to separate out a critical theory/pedagogy strand (focused around Freire and, more recently, Habermas) from a post-structuralist (rather than "postmodern") strand (focused around Lyotard and Foucault), and to acknowledge more widely a postmodern theory/ pedagogy strand that mistakenly gets conflated with poststructuralism. Curiously, perhaps, neither critical pedagogy nor poststructuralism gets mentioned explicitly.

Yet we should also understand the self-imposed limitations of the Institute's Review: first, it is restricted to current research and practice in post-compulsory education and lifelong learning, and second, it is a review of the literature (books, journals, web-based material, abstracts, conferences, and interviews with experts and practitioners). Given these limitations, a major problem arises for the reviewers in that the elements of the new pedagogy, insofar as they are exemplified in constructivism and postmodern theory, originate outside the field of postcompulsory education and lifelong learning, in the fields of Continental philosophy (critical theory and poststructuralism), constructionist psychology and sociology, pragmatism (especially Dewey), and nonfoundational epistemology. And yet there are many general texts in educational theory and philosophy that focus on these strands that the reviewers might easily have acknowledged.[3]

Our purpose in this chapter is to identify the main elements of the new pedagogy identified in the Tavistock Institute's review and to briefly discuss them; second, this chapter also provides an analysis of the review's weaknesses and entertains a different (philosophical) account of social learning. In what follows, we want to focus specifically on constructivism (as opposed to postmodern theory) as one of the two elements said to constitute the new pedagogy. In the Tavistock report, there is no attempt made to analyze the conjunction of constructivism and postmodernism as the two main elements of the new pedagogy, and had there been time we might have examined this relationship more carefully: sometimes it is said that postmodernism is a form of constructivism, or that it works with constructivist nonfoundational epistemologies, or that individual theorists like Michel Foucault are constructivists, but then all these formulations are crude and only indicate the nature of the complexity of the relationship that needs to be clarified if anyone is to understand the Tavistock Institute's synthetic claims concerning the new pedagogy.

ELEMENTS OF THE NEW PEDAGOGY

The main elements of the new pedagogy are itemized in the executive summary of the Tavistock Institute's review (Cullen et al. 2002, 11–17) as follows:

- A new pedagogy, drawing on constructivism and postmodernism, has emerged.

- This pedagogy views not only knowledge but also the whole educational enterprise differently.
- Yet the "core issues and propositions about learners, learning and teaching have not altered" (12)—only the societal context within which we now pose the questions has changed.
- "Performativity" is "creating tensions between the social and the highly individualistic consumer ethic identified as the key to postmodernity, and between the rediscovery of learning as a social activity and the rise of self-directed and virtual (web-based) pedagogies" (12).
- Little is known about knowledge management—"knowledge production is lagging behind the evolving 'new pedagogy'" (13).
- "The key driver in the 'new pedagogy' is recent government policy, within which learning has been explicitly identified as the main catalyst for economic competitiveness and growth." Learning has become "situated within a broader arena, justified by concerns for 'citizenship,' social integration and equity" (13).
- "There has been a marked degree of 'mixing' of methods and practices across different settings and sectors" (13).
- "The reconfiguration of the 'learning setting'" has meant that pedagogies are "much more concerned with: the de-centering of knowledge; the valorisation of other forms of knowledge and ways of knowing; supporting the learner as consumer; working with knowledge as 'social,' distributed rather than individualised; learning rather than education" (13).

The review also identifies gaps in our current understanding of effective teaching and learning practices, including "the nature, and implications of, the re-configuration of the education and training infrastructure in the new post-modern climate" and "how the knowledge-production process operates," with a focus on understanding "what works" and its measurement (16). In addition, the review identifies two gaps:

> The nature and effects of post-modern "distal-proximal interactions" on pedagogic theory and practice (for example the drive towards the "decentering" of knowledge; the focus on assessment and performativity; the demand for "just-in-time" skills; the re-invention of lifelong learning).
> The effects of the introduction of Virtual Learning Environments and information and communication technologies (for example whether they are really new forms of learning, or old, re-packaged pedagogies; whether they imply new learning and teaching roles for all stakeholders; how to assess their effectiveness). (16)

On the basis of this brief description of the main elements of the so-called new pedagogy, we can pursue a number of questions concerning the Tavistock Institute's characterization. First, we want to question whether it is helpful to lay out the new problematic from within the fields of postcompulsory education and lifelong learning as constructed by the review, for the reason that these are fields that have been constructed largely in terms of administrative divisions that largely reflect the impact of government policies. One may inquire whether there is something theoretically distinctive about postcompulsory education. The terms *work-based learning*, *informal learning*, and *lifelong learning* are policy constructions that reflect government priorities rather than any theoretical distinctiveness of the new pedagogy, such as constructivism or postmodernism. The policy constructions may intersect with and draw upon concepts or elements of the new paradigm, but they do not define its working epistemology or its theoretical approach. With these policy constructions, there is a need to unpick the relations between education policy, broadly conceived, where education has become a subset of wider economic policy; other broad policy areas; and especially economic and social policy, political theory, and educational theory and practice.

Second, it is not clear just how *new* the new pedagogy is, given that its origins, as suggested by the report, lie in Dewey's philosophy of education, the work of G. H. Mead, Freire's critical pedagogy, and the work of Piaget and Vygotsky, as fathers of the first "revolution" in cognitive psychology. Third, the report acknowledges nothing of the complexity or the intellectual difficulties that accompany education discourses on the theme of constructivism. If constructivism is one of the major influences on the new pedagogy, then we are obliged to ask what it is—what are the dominant theories, what are its origins, and what are the main issues of contention? Only if and when we can identify these, it might be argued, will we be able to talk meaningfully about an empirical research agenda.[4]

THE EDUCATIONAL AND CULTURAL STAKES OF CONSTRUCTIVISM

In this chapter, we have chosen to focus on constructivism as one of the two main elements of the new pedagogy identified by the Tavistock report, because while so much has already been written on this topic, it is not well understood. The report itself is woefully inadequate in this respect, and even as a synthetic review it provides little help to teachers, researchers, or policy makers. Constructivism is an epistemology, a pedagogy, a social methodology, a movement in art history, and a loose set of ideas deeply embedded in twentieth-century European sciences, humanities, and culture. Academic disputes about social constructivism erupted into heated public debates in the 1990s about the nature of science and mathematics—the "science wars"[5]—which various commentators claim represent fundamental challenges to knowledge and education in the Western tradition. These science war disputes, for instance, have surfaced in highly publicized polemics over Paul Gross and Norman Levitt's (1998) *Higher Superstition* and Alan Sokal's postmodern spoof that was accepted by the journal *Social Text*[6] and that later became the basis for the academic best seller *Intellectual Impostures* (Sokal and Bricmont 1998).[7]

This is how the philosopher Richard Rorty (1999) characterizes the debate:

> Occasionally we read about a war that is supposed to be going on among philosophers. The war, we are told, is between those who believe in truth and rationality and those who do not. The latter—the bad guys—are sometimes called postmodernists, sometimes irrationalists and relativists, and sometimes social constructionists. The good guys believe that science tells us the way things really are; they take the paradigm of rationality to be scientific inquiry, just as the paradigm of truth is the result of that inquiry.

He goes on to say that the good guys, like E. O. Wilson and Paul Gross, "ask us to see natural science as a model for other human activities" and "are deeply suspicious of philosophers of science" such as Bruno Latour and Thomas Kuhn "who describe conflicts between scientific theories in the same terms they use to describe conflicts between moral or political opinions."

> Bad guys, like the people Sokal fooled, think that "postmodern philosophy"—roughly, the anti-metaphysical doctrines common to Nietzsche, Foucault, Heidegger and Derrida—has "unmasked" science. Starting with the claim that homosexuality, the Negro race, and womanliness are social constructions, they go on to suggest that quarks and genes probably are too. "Ideology" and "power," they say, have infiltrated sterile laboratories and lurk between the lines of arcane journals of mathematical physics. The very idea of scientific objectivity, they say, is self-deceptive and fraudulent.

If there has been a raging storm of protest and debate concerning constructivism (and postmodernism), why is it promoted in our teacher education programs, embraced so strongly by teachers, and endorsed by education authorities? The stakes and consequences of this debate for education are enormous: why did the Tavistock report not advertise these stakes more widely, or at least signal these debates?

D. C. Phillips (1995, 192) notes, "Arguably it [constructivism] is the dominant theoretical position in science and mathematics education," and Peter Slezak (2000, 1) emphasizes the educational stakes of this debate when he writes,

> Undeniably, if radical social constructivist doctrines are correct, the implications for science education are revolutionary for, on these views, knowledge

is merely consensus upon arbitrary convention; and education involves not learning as a cognitive process of reason and understanding, but merely conformity to power and political interests.

Slezak's characterization of constructivism here is of course highly biased, especially when he suggests that the doctrine holds that "knowledge is merely consensus upon arbitrary convention," for he is a good enough philosopher to know that both "consensus" and "convention" are troublesome philosophical terms that have generated a huge analytic literature from Wittgenstein to Lewis and Dummett. Constructivism is probably the most popular and the most misunderstood theory in education. It is the new orthodoxy. As Michael Matthews (2003, 349) writes,

> Although constructivism began as a theory of learning to the effect that knowledge cannot be transmitted from teacher to learner but must be constructed anew by each learner, it has expanded its dominion, becoming a theory of teaching, a theory of education, a theory of educational administration, a theory of the origin of ideas, a theory of both personal knowledge and scientific knowledge, and even a metaphysical and ideological position. Constructivism has become education's version of a grand unified theory.

Matthews's observation can be evidenced in the work of the great Harvard cultural psychologist Jerome Bruner. In his *Culture of Education*, Bruner (1996) mentions constructivism as one of the central tenets that distinguishes the culturalist theory of mind from the computational theory, which is based on a model of information processing. He writes in this regard,

> Culture, then, though itself man-made, both forms and makes possible the workings of a distinctively human mind. On this view, learning and thinking are always situated in a cultural setting and always dependent upon the utilization of cultural resources. (4)

He goes on to draw up the contrast between the culturalist and the computational theories of mind in terms of a conception that embraces the tenets of *perspectivism* (the meaning of a statement is relative to its perspective); *constraints* (forms of meaning are constrained by our "native endowment" and the nature of language); *constructivism* ("The 'reality' we impute to 'worlds' we inhabit is a constructed one" [19]); *interaction* (intersubjectivity, or the problem of knowing other minds); *externalization* (the production of oeuvres, or works); *instrumentalism* (the political context, e.g., education for skills); *institutionalism* (that education in the developed world takes place in institutions); *identity and self-esteem* (as he says, "perhaps the most universal thing about human experience is the phenomenon of 'Self,' and we know that education is crucial for its formation" [35]); and *narrative* (narrative as a mode of thought).

For Bruner, then, constructivism is one of the central tenets of cultural-
ism, the theory of mind that defines an approach to education that op-
poses the computational theory. As he writes,

> Education is not simply a technical business of well-managed information
> processing, nor even simply a matter of applying "learning theories" to the
> classroom or using the results of a subject-centered "achievement testing." It
> is a complex pursuit of fitting a culture to the needs of its members and of fit-
> ting its members and their ways of knowing to the needs of the culture.
> (Bruner 1996, 43)

In a very strong sense, the culturalist theory of mind and educational
paradigm defines the endpoint of Bruner's career trajectory, beginning
with individual intrapsychic processes of knowing; through various
stages of the cognitive revolutions during the Cold War period under the
influence of Luria, Vygotsky, and Piaget; to cultural theories of development reflecting the combined influences of Mead, Dewey, Jakobson, Mey-
erson, the Annales school, and Nelson Goodman. It is only through this
approach, based firmly on constructivism, that psychology and pedagogy
can approach their next challenge—intersubjectivity, or the problem of
knowing other minds.

Bruner, in other words, in the course of his career moved from the position of a constructivist psychologist focused on the individual's learning
to a cultural constructivist preoccupied with the question of intersubjectivity. It is this link between constructivism and the social—between constructivism, the new pedagogy, and social learning—that interests us particularly. For we find ourselves largely in agreement with Bruner,
endorsing and wanting to explore further the connections between constructivism and social learning, and for similar reasons but under quite
different influences. Our sources of inspiration are, first, the philosopher
Ludwig Wittgenstein, particularly his later philosophy (see Peters and
Marshall 1999), and, second, the philosophers Nietzsche and Heidegger
(see Peters 2002h; Peters, Marshall, and Smeyers 2001). Third, we take our
reference point from the work of the poststructuralist philosophers Jean-
François Lyotard, Michel Foucault, and Jacques Derrida (see Peters 1995,
1996, 2000b, 2001e, 2001f; Trifonas and Peters 2003). We found Wittgenstein's private-language argument and his social philosophy of language
convincing at an early stage in our careers.[8] Many social constructivists in
the philosophy of mathematics, the philosophy of language, and the sociology of knowledge take their lead from Wittgenstein and regard him as
a protoconstructivist. It would take too long to lay out all the reasons why
we regard Nietzsche and Heidegger as sympathizers for social constructivism, and yet their status as forefathers of French poststructuralism,
along with Saussure and Jakobson, speaks to a form of constructivism

that decenters the individual author, thinker, or learner to emphasize the text, the discourse, the archive, or the episteme.

Constructionism and postmodernism are elements of a historical watershed that underlies the development of philosophy and the "cultural turn" in the social sciences that occurred in the latter half of the twentieth century. We might sloganize this movement in twin methodological imperatives: the linguistic turn, the significance of representation, and the so-called social construction of reality, on the one hand, and the attempt to overcome the dualisms, the search for certainty and essences, and the subjectivism that are the legacy of Cartesian thought, on the other. Constructionism contains elements of both. We have used the word *constructionism* rather than *constructivism* in this context for reasons that will become plain later. In discussing these varieties of constructionism, we will not seek to resolve the problems or contradictions but rather, simply, to complexify and problematize them with the aim of producing a "survey"—a perspicuous conceptual mapping so that we can recognize the intellectual genealogy of the terms and get a better critical purchase on them. We must realize that *construction, constructionism*, and *constructivism* are family-resemblance terms that are dynamic and culturally embedded in the history of twentieth-century Western culture, especially the broad movement of European formalism, which enters into dialogue with structuralism and encompasses developments in mathematics, logic, epistemology, linguistics, poetics, biology, and aesthetics.

Nowhere in the discourse on constructionism do we find an account of construction in aesthetics, architecture, or the arts, which we find curious, given that it has assumed various forms and even explicit ideologies and manifestos during the twentieth-century history of the avant-garde in movements as different as cubism, Italian and Russian futurism, and Russian constructivism.[9] Clearly, constructivism cannot be easily separated from the history of the European avant-garde, from the broad movement of formalism, or from the history of modernism. In these art discourses, the metaphors of construction as building, assembling, and making stand ultimately for the act of creation itself.[10]

CONSTRUCTIVISM IN EDUCATION—A FIRST LOOK

In educational theory and practice, constructivism is often loosely associated with the cognitive constructionists and is also read back against the work of John Dewey, Carl Rogers, and even Jean-Jacques Rousseau.[11] Here is a typical account of constructivism in education:

> Focusing on a more educational description of constructivism, meaning is intimately connected with experience. Students come into a classroom with

their own experiences and a cognitive structure based on those experiences. These preconceived structures are either valid, invalid or incomplete. The learner will reformulate his/her existing structures only if new information or experiences are connected to knowledge already in memory. Inferences, elaborations and relationships between old perceptions and new ideas must be personally drawn by the student in order for the new idea to become an integrated, useful part of his/her memory. Memorized facts or information that has not been connected with the learner's prior experiences will be quickly forgotten. In short, the learner must actively construct new information onto his/her existing mental framework for meaningful learning to occur. (Hanley 1994)

Often constructivism appears in the form of a set of pedagogical principles. For instance, there are many lists that are intended to pick up the main characteristics of constructivist learning environments, such as, provide multiple representations of reality to avoid oversimplification and to represent the complexity of the real world; emphasize knowledge construction instead of knowledge reproduction, and authentic tasks in a meaningful context rather than abstract instruction out of context; base learning on real-world settings or cases instead of predetermined sequences of instruction, which encourages reflection on experience; and support collaborative construction of knowledge through social negotiation, not competition, among learners for recognition.

Often principles of learning are distilled in the form of handy hints for teachers, such as, "learning is an active process in which the learner uses sensory input and constructs meaning out of it"; "learning consists of both constructing meaning and constructing systems of meaning"; "the crucial action of constructing meaning is mental: it happens in the mind"; "learning involves language: the language we use influences learning"; "learning is a social activity"; "learning is contextual: we learn in relationship to what else we know, what we believe, our prejudices, and our fears"; "it is not possible to assimilate new knowledge without having some structure developed from previous knowledge to build on"; "learning is not instantaneous"; and "motivation is a key component in learning."[12] Yet these are mere assertions that neither always reference their source nor seek to resolve theoretical differences among the views from which they are derived.

Constructivism in most of its epistemological forms confronts a number of theoretical difficulties that have not yet been adequately resolved: the sheer eclecticism of many constructivist positions, including pedagogical constructivism; the ongoing debate with realism; and the problem of humanism or the humanist philosophy of the subject that assumes both a transparency—an agency—and that the subject is the author of his own semantic intentions. In education, D. C. Phillips (2003, 239) usefully distinguishes two different foci of interest in contemporary constructivism. As he writes,

> Many constructivists have as their interest individual learners (such things as the psychological mechanisms that play a role in their learning, and to what degree social factors contribute); other constructivists focus on the way in which the public bodies of knowledge (disciplines such as the sciences, mathematics, economics, history) are "socially constructed."

He remarks that the former acknowledge past historical influences going back to Vico, Kant, and Rousseau and include the twentieth-century thinkers Piaget, Vygotsky, Montessori, Dewey, and von Glasersfeld (see Phillips 2000).

The notion of constructionism as an epistemological doctrine is given a particular expression in the term *radical constructivism*, which is associated with the names of Heinz von Foerster (second-order cybernetics), Humberto Maturana (the founder of the theory of *autopoiesis*), Francisco Varela ("enacted" cognition), W. Ross Ashby (cybernetics), and Gordon Pask (conversation theory). It is given the following description on the Radical Constructivism website:

> The notion "radical constructivism" (RC) was coined by Ernst von Glasersfeld in 1974 in order to emphasize that from an *epistemological* perspective any constructivism has to be complete (or "radical") in order not to relapse into some kind of fancy *realism*. The basic tenet of RC is that *any* kind of knowledge is constructed rather than perceived through senses. As such, RC does not present a *metaphysics* in the strict sense as it does not make statements about an outside reality ("No statement" means neither confirming nor denying reality. The subject of much criticism, RC equals *solipsism*, doesn't therefore apply). Now, the idea itself does not originate in EvG. Forerunners of the RC movement in the 18th century were Giambatista Vico, whose dictum "verum ipsum factum" already points in the direction of knowledge construction, and George Berkeley whose claim "esse est percipi" challenges metaphysics. (www.univie.ac.at/constructivism/about.html)

Following Phillips in educational theory, we can identify a number of strands of constructivism: first, *cognitive constructivism*, built upon the work of Piaget, Vygotsky, and the early Jerome Bruner; second, "second wave" social psychology, inspired by the work of Wittgenstein and exemplified in the *discursive psychology* of Rom Harré and others; third, a form of *social constructionism*, which developed out of phenomenology to characterize a variety of approaches in modern psychology and sociology typified by the work of Berger and Luckmann; fourth, a *sociology of knowledge* strand also inspired by Wittgenstein, evidenced in the Edinburgh school; fifth, *radical constructivism* associated with the work of von Glasersfeld and others; sixth, a *postmodern social constructionism* characterized by the work of Kenneth Gergen and John Shotter, who attempt to make the link with postmodernism explicit; and, seventh, *pedagogical constructivism*, which often comprises a set of practices and guidelines loosely and pragmatically based upon elements of these various strands. Pedagogical constructivism also often consists of appeals to the pragmatism of John Dewey without much care for distinguishing the various strands or their conflicting epistemological assumptions.

THE HOUSE OF KANT: ORIGINS OF CONSTRUCTION

Ian Hacking (1999), the Canadian philosopher, suggests that we should distinguish among different kinds of constructivism. He indicates that the great pioneer of construction was Immanuel Kant. Kant's house is a very, very big house, containing many rooms. Kant, as Hacking remarks, was truly radical in his day, and he worked within the realm of reason, even if some of the many metaphors of construction derived from his work, which have served to express many kinds of philosophy, work against reason. Hacking provides us with a conceptual mapping of constructionism in epistemology, the philosophy of science, mathematics, the sociology of knowledge, psychology, and moral theory. Hacking's account appears to be, at least in part, a historical one, for he provides an intellectual history of the idea of constructionism that is an internalist history more Kuhnian than Foucauldian. He argues,

> We have logical constructions [Russell's logical atomism], constructivism in mathematics [dating from Kant's puzzle over the status of synthetic a priori statements], and following Kant, numerous strains of constructivism in ethical theory, including those of John Rawls and Michel Foucault. (41)

After Kant, he begins with Russell's logical constructions and indicates the connection to logical positivism, especially Carnap's *Aufbau*, noting, "The roots of social constructionism are in the very logical positivism that so many present-day constructionists profess to detest" (42–43).

As heir to Russell, the notion of "construct," standing for theoretical entities, found its way via logical positivism first into the philosophy of the social sciences and then into the philosophy of experimental psychology, where, standardly, notions like "intelligence" were called constructs. In the psychology of Lee Cronbach in the mid-1950s, the term found its way into psychological testing in the form of the term *construct validity*—a history suppressed in psychology's own self-history, as Hacking remarks. Its links to education and pedagogy in this logical positivist form are clear, given the influence of Cronbach's work and the significance of the psychological testing industry in education.

Hacking proceeds to talk of the constructionist orientation of Nelson Goodman (1978), whose work also evolved from Russell and Carnap and is based on a notion of "worldmaking," clearly evidenced in the following remark:

> Without the organization, the selection of relevant kinds, effected by evolving tradition, there is no rightness or wrongness of categorization, no validity or invalidity of inductive inference, no fair or unfair sampling, and no uniformity or disparity among sample." (Goodman 1978, 138–39; cited in Hacking 1999, 129)

Goodman's point is that the selection and organization of kinds determines what we call the world, and that this selection and organization comes into being through the "fit with practice" effected by an evolving tradition.

Hacking completes his genealogy of constructionism by briefly examining constructivism in mathematics (from Kant, through Russell and Whitehead, to Gödel's incompleteness theorem and Brouwer's intuitionism) and moral theory, focusing on Kantian derivatives of Rawls's theory of justice and Foucault's doctrine of self-improvement. He devotes an entire chapter to natural science and to the philosophy and sociology of science through the work of the epidemiologist Ludwik Fleck and the social constructionist schools of Edinburgh—under the so-called strong program of Barry Barnes (1977, 1995) and David Bloor (1976)—and Bath, based on the work of Harry Collins (1990) and Trevor Pinch (1986). He mentions also the sociology of knowledge tradition dating from Durkheim and manifesting itself most clearly in Karl Mannheim's (1952) work.[13]

Hacking distinguishes social constructionism, where for the most part *social* is redundant, from these versions, explaining that "*various* sociological, historical, and philosophical projects [aim at] displaying or analysing actual, historically situated, social interactions or causal routes that led to, or were involved in, the coming into being or establishing of some present entity or fact" (1999, 48, emphasis added). He argues that there is no universal social constructionism and that "constructivists, constructionists, and constructionalists live in different intellectual milieus" (49). As can be seen from Hacking's discussion, it is difficult to state the thesis of constructionism with any precision. He provides a useful discussion of *social constructionism* as a code word embroiled in the "culture wars" and "science wars" that have come to dominate intellectual life, suggesting the following formulation:

> Social construction work is critical of the status quo. Social constructivists about X tend to hold that:
>
> (1) X need not have existed, or need not be at all as it is. X, or X as it is at present, is not determined by the nature of things; it is not inevitable.

Very often they go further, and urge that:

(2) X is quite bad as it is.
(3) We would be much better off if X were done away with, or at least rad-
    ically transformed. (Hacking 1999, 6)

Thus, social constructivism, insofar as one can assume a coherent concept, attacks essentialism (about the self, race, or whatever) to imply a
radical contingency, and it is often associated with a revolutionary zeal to
transform the world.[14] As Hacking writes,

> The metaphysics of constructionism denies that creation had an essence, or
> that there is a God's eye view. It is a threat to such a world view. Likewise,
> feminist critics of the natural sciences formed alliances with constructionists,
> in order to undermine the idea that the sciences must proceed along an in-
> evitable, preordained track. (1999, 61)

SOCIAL CONSTRUCTIONISM: THE HOUSE OF HUSSERL?

The term *social constructionism* came to prominence in sociology with
Berger and Luckmann's (1966) *The Social Construction of Reality*, which
was an account of the social phenomenology of knowledge. It was a
groundbreaking text that took as its subtitle "A Treatise in the Sociology
of Knowledge," although the influences were Marx, Weber, Durkheim,
and phenomenological sociology, especially the work of Alfred Schütz,
who had his roots in Husserl and Weber. Berger and Luckmann maintain
that the everyday world is an intersubjective world and claim that while
man produces himself, "man's self-production is always, and of necessity, a social enterprise" (51). Their book is one of the most significant
ever written in the social sciences, ranking with Kuhn's *The Structure of
Scientific Revolutions* and spawning across the social sciences a multidis-
ciplinary program that prefigured many of the debates in the 1980s and
1990s about social constructionism and postmodernism. As Hacking
(1999) observes, the number of imitations of Berger and Luckmann's
book grew rapidly. During the 1970s and down through the 1980s and
1990s, all kinds of things were claimed to be socially constructed: gender,
knowledge, literacy, emotions, illness, authorship, women refuges, youth
homelessness, urban schooling, homosexual culture, brotherhood, the
child viewer of television, nature, and quarks.[15] But when Berger and
Luckmann claimed that our experience of everyday reality is neither a
Kantian a priori nor a psychological product of cognitive processes, they
were not making a claim for a grand unified or universal theory. As
Hacking notes, "They did not claim that nothing exists unless it is socially constructed" (25).

Rather, they maintained that everyday knowledge is constructed at different levels of society from language, including family histories; children's folktales; workplace and professional ideologies; formal theories and paradigms; and, finally, "symbolic universes" or overarching worldviews. To Berger and Luckmann, reality is unknowable except through the prism of experience as interpreted through what they call "plausibility structures." Berger and Luckmann base their work on a set of fundamental propositions: (1) man's consciousness is determined by his social being; (2) knowledge must always be from a certain position or social location; (3) "What is truth on one side of the Pyrenees (mountains) is error on the other" (Blaise Pascal); (4) social facts or institutions should be considered as things (Emile Durkheim); and (5) the sociology of knowledge must concern itself with everything that passes for knowledge in society. The full history of contemporary social science cannot be written without the centrality of this single text and its guiding idea of the social construction of reality. Its effects in the sociology of education were immense, and they spilled over to most content areas.

Berger and Luckmann's social constructionism was ultimately indebted to Husserl and Weber via Schütz. We do not think Hacking makes enough of the house of Husserl, if we can put it this way, for Husserl asks us to focus on the quality of immediate experience and to bracket out our assumptions. He envisages himself as the first explorer of the new field of experience that he names "transcendental subjectivity." Husserl's *Logical Investigations* was an attack on psychologism, and his later work inspired constitutive phenomenology, which develops the method of transcendental phenomenological *epochê* and reduction, and is responsible for suspending acceptance of the pregiven status of conscious life as something that exists in the world, in order both to secure an ultimate intersubjective grounding for the world and to develop positive sciences of it.

In Husserl's house, perhaps in the back room, we can also mention the existential phenomenology of Martin Heidegger, which went beyond Husserl to develop an analysis of human beings as a means to a fundamental ontology, and hermeneutical phenomenology, also due to Heidegger, according to which human existence is interpretative. We mention these developments out of, or even against, Husserl because Heidegger and Nietzsche are probably the principal sources from which Foucault derives his constructionism (and not merely the Kantian ethical self-constitution that Hacking ascribes to him). More importantly, Berger and Luckmann, who worked closely with Schütz and drew strongly on Weber, were associated both with the New School for Social Research and with the Frankfurt school. A particular political tradition is thus intertwined with *The Social Construction of Reality*, one that through various forms of phenomenology is evidenced in the work not only of Hannah Arendt and Karl Jaspers, but also the French, including Gabriel Marcel, Simone de

Beauvoir, Maurice Merleau-Ponty, and Jean-Paul Sartre, and a hermeneu-
tical thread including Paul Ricoeur, Patrick Heelan, Don Ihde, Graeme
Nicholson, Joseph J. Kockelmans, Calvin O. Schrag, Gianni Vattimo, and
Carlo Sini.

SOCIAL CONSTRUCTIONISM: THE WITTGENSTEINIAN MANSION?

After Berger and Luckmann, the term *social constructionism* thereafter was
quickly picked up by social psychologists in the 1970s focusing on the cultural acquisition of language, appealing to the work of Piaget and Vygotsky (e.g., Bruner 1990). Piaget and Vygotsky still remain the central figures
in social constructionist pedagogy. Others, like the New Zealand–born Oxford philosopher Rom Harré (1983, 1986), explicitly followed the pragmatism of G. H. Mead and the language philosophy of Wittgenstein as a
means of criticizing the biological determinism of Piagetian "stages" and
offering, by contrast, a sociocultural analysis of cognitive development.
Notice here that social constructivism is not directly applied to knowledge
but rather to the psychology of human development.

We are very attracted to the style of Wittgenstein's architecture, although we would want to acknowledge some commonalities both with
the house of American pragmatism (James, Dewey, Pierce, and Mead), a
house we do not have the space to inhabit, and with phenomenology in
its various forms. Wittgenstein's influence has been pervasive and often
not well understood. We limit ourselves here to briefly mentioning four
strands: the discursive psychology of Rom Harré, the postmodern constructionism of Kenneth Gergen and John Shotter, the constructivist philosophy of mathematics education of Paul Ernest, and Michael Peters's
postmodern appropriation of Wittgenstein. We are surprised that Hacking does not identify this strand, not Wittgenstein's thought so much as
other scholars' appropriations of his work. In this section, and mainly for
reasons of space, we do not explicitly comment on the strong program of
Barnes and Bloor at Edinburgh. Any full account of the Wittgensteinian
mansion would, of course, have to provide an account of the Edinburgh
school, its Wittgensteinian roots, and its significance in the sociology of
knowledge.

First, then, let us consider Rom Harré, who has been strongly associated
with the move to discursive psychology. Harré and Gillet (1994) provide
a brief account of the shift from what they call "the Old Paradigm" of be-
haviorism and experimentalism, based on an outdated philosophical theory of science and metaphysics, toward psychology as a cognitive science
in its first and second waves. The impetus for change from the old paradigm, they suggest, came from two sources: the "new" social psychology,

which took its start from G. H. Mead, and, more importantly, the "new" cognitive psychology, which developed out of the work of Bruner (1973, 1990) and Miller and Johnson-Laird at Harvard. Harré and Gillet maintain that the second cognitive revolution began under the influence of the later writings of Wittgenstein (1953), which gave a central place to language and discourse and attempted to overcome the Cartesian picture of mental activity as a set of inner processes. The main principles of the second revolution pointed to how psychological phenomena should be treated as features of discourse and thus as public and social activities. Thus, "Individual and private uses of symbolic systems, which in this view constitute thinking, are derived from interpersonal discursive processes" (Harré and Gillet 1994, 27). The production of psychological phenomena, including emotions and attitudes, are seen to depend upon the actors' skills, their "positionality," and the story lines they develop (on positioning theory, see Howie and Peters 1996, and Peters and Appel 1996).

Second, views similar to the discursive strand, utilizing Wittgenstein (among other theorists), were advanced by social psychologists such as John Shotter (e.g., 1993) and Kenneth Gergen (1985, 1991). These views also emphasized a social construction rather than an individualist cognitivist construction. Gergen (2001) acknowledges the sociology of knowledge tradition and maintains that once knowledge became denaturalized and reenculturated, the terms passed more broadly into the discourses of the human sciences. He documents the development of the Sage book series *Inquiries into Social Construction*, which began with *The Social Construction of Lesbianism* in 1987 and, twenty volumes later, ended with *The Social Construction of Anorexia Nervosa* in 1999, and his own book as a conclusion to the series. The series included books on rhetoric, collective remembering, texts of identity, discursive psychology, gender, postmodernism, the self, therapy, and so on. There is a useful chapter written with Lisa Warhus (Gergen and Warhus 2001) entitled "Social Construction and Pedagogical Practice," which talks of "the demise of knowledge as an individual possession" and "the social construction of knowledge," with an emphasis on "indeterminacy," "polyvocality," "contextualization," and "pragmatics." The chapter argues for a move toward "meaning in practice," "reflective deliberation," and "generative relationships."

Of these two social psychologists, Shotter is the one most clearly influenced by Wittgenstein. He describes his own research program as an attempt to overcome the pernicious moral effects of the Cartesian mechanistic paradigm in the human and behavior sciences and its undermining of our intrinsic human relatedness. Since 1980, he says, he has explored the philosophical, empirical, and methodological consequences of our embodied selves and our spontaneous responsiveness both to others and to the world. He calls his stance toward these problems "social constructionist," and he writes,

What strikes me as wrong with current social constructionist approaches, is their still Cartesian, (post) structuralist, dualistic approach to language and to our surroundings—as if we are only in an *external* relationship to them both, rather than having our very being *within them*. Other social constructionist approaches still take the referential-representational function of language as central and merely reverse its direction, so to speak—i.e., instead of our representations being *of* reality, they take it that they our *constitutive* of our realities. Whereas, I have taken the central function of language to be of a relationally-responsive kind. It is in being directly responsive to the bodily expressions of others, we enter into one or another kind of living relationship with them. (pubpages.unh.edu/~jds/BioAndResprog.htm)

As he says, the main influences upon his thought, then, were drawn from Wittgenstein, Vico, Vygotsky, Mead, Bakhtin, Billig, and MacIntyre, and from increasing Wittgenstein's "poetic" methods of inquiry to develop "a whole new *descriptive, participatory* approach to an understanding of social life" (for a selection of recent papers, see pubpages.unh.edu/~jds/page1.htm).

In addition, both Shotter and Gergen were also instrumental in linking social constructionist psychology with the postmodern turn. Yet the "postmodernism" of Shotter and Gergen, at least in its early stages, while critical of the universalist explanations of modernist psychology, tended to embrace a form of (liberal) humanism, whereas the poststructuralist orientation of the critical psychologists (e.g., Walkerdine 1984) was critical of the alleged humanism, individualism, and liberalism underlying social constructionism (see Morss 1996).

Third, take the constructionist philosophy of mathematics advanced by Paul Ernest. Constructionist epistemologies, which may be subject specific, do overlap and coalesce when it comes to questions of pedagogy. Paul Ernest (1999), working in the field of the philosophy of mathematics education, states the social constructivist thesis as follows: "Mathematics is a social construction, a cultural product, fallible like any other branch of knowledge." This view entails two further claims: the allegedly uncontroversial idea that "the origins of mathematics are social or cultural" and the notion that "the justification of mathematical knowledge rests on its quasi-empirical basis."

Equipped with two realist assumptions—the existence of both an independent physical world and a social reality—Ernest suggests that a social constructionist epistemology can be developed from the principles of radical constructionism, which he elaborates as follows:

a. "knowledge is not passively received but actively built up by the cognizing subject";
b. "the function of cognition is adaptive and serves the organization of the experiential world, not the discovery of ontological reality" (Glasersfeld 1989, 182);

c. the personal theories that result from the organization of the experiential world must "fit" the constraints imposed by physical and social reality;

d. they achieve this by a cycle of theory-prediction-test-failure-accommodation-new theory;

e. this gives rise to socially agreed theories of the world, social patterns, and rules of language use; and

f. mathematics is a theory of form and structure that arises within language.

Michael Peters (2002h) has recently published a paper commenting on Ernest's philosophy of mathematics education in the context of the "new Wittgenstein," where he argues that Ernest's attempt to base a social constructionism on Wittgenstein is certainly not a move to which Wittgenstein himself would consent. It is not enough, indeed it is misleading, to say that Wittgenstein bases his account of mathematical certainty on linguistic rules of use and "forms of life," as it is to claim that Wittgenstein argued that "the justification of mathematical knowledge rests on its quasi-empirical basis." Yet, as Peters explains in a footnote to his 2002 paper, this is not to say that he is unsympathetic to the argument Ernest puts forward, only that he entertain doubts concerning its attribution to Wittgenstein and that Ernest's argument, insofar as it is buttressed by appeals to Wittgenstein, fails. Yet see Ernest's more recent work, which spells out the case for a social constructionist philosophy of mathematics (1998, 1999) and provides a provocative and interesting critical account of mathematics education in relation to the justification problem "Why teach mathematics?" (2000). To the traditional aims of reproducing mathematical skill and knowledge-based capability and developing creative capabilities in mathematics, he suggests adding two more: the development of empowering mathematical capabilities and a critical appreciation of the social applications and uses of mathematics, and the development of an inner appreciation of mathematics—its big ideas and nature.

Finally, let us say a word about our own program of research in relation to Wittgenstein,[16] which can be best understood in relation to the emergence of the "new Wittgenstein." The new Wittgenstein coalesces around a series of common interpretive protocols: Wittgenstein is not advancing theories in metaphysics but is employing a therapeutic method; he is helping us to work free of the confusions that become evident when we begin to philosophize; and, at the same time, Wittgenstein is disabusing us of the notion that we can stand outside language and command an external view and that such an external view is both necessary and possible for grasping the essence of thought and language. By contrast, Wittgenstein, on the new reading, encourages us to see that our intuitions about meaning and thought are best accommodated "by attention to our everyday forms of expression and to the world those forms of expression serve to reveal" (Crary and Read 2000, 1). In this new schema for reading Wittgenstein also puts less emphasis on the decisive break in his thought, represented by the *Tractatus* and the posthumous *Investigations*, to emphasize, by comparison, significant continuities of his thought centering around his therapeutic conception of philosophy.

What is more, the new reading emphasizes that his modes of philosophical criticism and the methods he employs serve to highlight and elucidate his therapeutic aim: "the dialectical structure of Wittgenstein's writing makes an internal contribution to the philosophical instruction it contains" (p. 7). This is what we have called the "pedagogical" aspects of Wittgenstein's later philosophy (see Peters and Marshall 1999). It is this aspect, as Crary and Read (2000, 7) point out, that Stanley Cavell's (1976, 1979) early work was first to reveal, and it is a theme that he has returned to again and again.[17]

The new reading that emphasizes the therapeutic character of Wittgenstein's philosophical aims and method, we would argue, is sympathetic to and consistent with the "postmodern" view of Wittgenstein that we present in our recent book *Wittgenstein: Philosophy, Postmodernism, Pedagogy* (Peters and Marshall 1999). Our reading explicitly provides

> an emphasis on a literary, cultural and (auto)biographical reading of Wittgenstein's works, their intertextuality, the expression of the spirit of European (Viennese) modernism in the *Tractatus*, and the anticipation of certain "postmodern" themes in his later works which, on the one hand, cast him in close philosophical proximity to Schopenhauer, Nietzsche and Heidegger and, on the other, project his writings into an interesting engagement with poststructuralist thought. (Peters and Marshall 1999, 19–20)

This cultural reading, in part, was inspired by Cavell's work, which we took as an exemplar in reading Wittgenstein both in relation to the movement of modernism and against Wittgenstein's Viennese cultural background. Cavell's writings also draw widely upon the philosophical tradition and emphasize the parallels between Wittgenstein and many contemporary thinkers, including both Derrida and Foucault.

In our reading, while we do not maintain that there are two Wittgensteins, as in the standard narrative, we do argue that the *Tractatus* is modernist in its formalism, while the *Investigations* anticipates certain "postmodernist" themes (see also Peters and Marshall 2002). The distinction is principally a matter of the style of *doing* philosophy, and it is reflective of the impact of larger cultural forces upon Wittgenstein, and also, significantly, of the six-year break from philosophy (in an institutional sense), which Wittgenstein spent as a schoolteacher. It does not deny that there are significant continuities in his thought, say for instance in his view of philosophy. In this reading, it is possible to argue that the therapeutic aim became more manifest in Wittgenstein's "pedagogical" style and in a view that we call "philosophy as pedagogy" (Peters and Burbules 2002). Yet nowhere in the presentation of this view did we use the term *social constructionism*, nor do we think that *postmodernism* (whatever that elusive term means) necessarily entails social constructionism in any of its versions.

CONCLUSION

Let us return to our starting point—the Tavistock report and its depiction of the "new pedagogy," which, while directed at the field of postcompulsory and lifelong education, can be taken to apply more widely. We have criticized the report on a number of grounds, not least its theoretical understanding of the two components said to form the new pedagogy—social constructionism and postmodernism. Our chapter is a response to the Tavistock report, and we have focused on social constructionism in order to demonstrate its theoretical complexity. If national research councils and other state agencies are to fund and design programs of research, then we need to make sure that such programs are based upon a clear conceptual understanding of the extant theory—how else are funders and policy makers to be able to fund the right programs? What we have tried to demonstrate is the theoretical complexity of constructionism, the cultural and educational stakes of the debates surrounding constructionism, and how deeply embedded they are in twentieth-century Western culture. There are no easy accommodations to be made, no easy compromises. What we must do intellectually is recognize the different strands and movements if we are to understand culturally what is at stake. We must also recognize that this is a genuine intellectual problem that may never be resolved (and certainly not in one chapter).

When we turned to the recommendations of the Tavistock report, we were not surprised to learn that a key conclusion of the review was that "we know very little about 'what works.'" The report thus recommends that "priority should be given to meta analyses and reviews of reviews in order to lay the foundations for an evolving evidence base" (Cullen et al. 2002, 82). We hope this chapter can be seen in this light, although we do not think we should be entirely seduced by the current ideology of "what works" or evidence-based inquiry and policy. There is a crying need for theoretical and conceptual research in education, not least in order to provide the templates by which we can interpret or make sense of data—isn't this part of the message of constructionism in science?

Another conclusion and recommendation in the report states,

A key theme for Phase III should be the relationships between "meta-theories" of psychology, political economy, grand theories of learning, middle theories of learning and practice and how these affect outcomes. (Cullen et al 2002, 82)

This means, of course, engaging in the sort of practice we have discussed in this chapter, yet in regard to constructivism, clearly we need to understand its appropriations in sociology and philosophy as much as psychology, especially given the way in which some of our best psychologists, like Bruner and Harré, are either philosophers or work out of a philosophical tradition.

The Tavistock report mentions several other overarching priorities, including the need for (1) structural analyses to identify the overlaps and linkages of various education sectors; (2) an understanding of how "assessment cultures" and "performativity" drive interpretations of the new pedagogy; (3) research that develops frameworks, typologies, and analytic tools allowing comparisons to be made across different pedagogical configurations; and (4) the utilization of virtual learning environments in teaching and learning. All of these priorities are important and even insightful, but none actually follows from the new pedagogy, and only the last one really begins to address its promise, especially in the context of informal and work-based learning. In Scotland, there is currently much expertise at the levels of the practitioner, the researcher, and the policy maker across a range of disciplines and sectors; the trick is developing methods of identification, innovation, and coordination that can make use of these resources.

Social constructionism is one of the most vexing questions of the age. Among philosophers, scientists, and mathematicians, the idea that reality has an intrinsic structure that inquiry is destined to reveal is now open to contestation in a way that has led to the culture and science wars and to tactics of grandstanding, polemics, ad hominem argument, bitter attacks, and a form of academic conflict that has not progressed or clarified the issues. It is imperative that we do not also allow these wars to bedevil the cultures of pedagogy.

NOTES

1. This chapter was presented as a paper in the Professorial Lecture Series at the Faculty of Education, University of Glasgow, October 19, 2003. We would like to thank Louise Hayward for the kind invitation to be part of this series.

2. Including, arguably, the following: "action learning," "communicative action" (Habermas), "communities of practice," "conscientization," "constructivism," "critical theory," "dialogic reflexivity," "distal forces," "dividing practices" (Foucault), "ethnomethodology," "experiential learning," "learning patrimony," "pedagogy" "performativity" (Lyotard), "phenomenology," "proximal forces," "situated learning," "social capital," "transformative learning," and "virtual learning environment."

3. See, for instance, the sixty-eight books in the Critical Studies in Education and Culture series edited by Henry Giroux and Paulo Freire and published by Bergin & Garvey (an imprint of Greenwood Press), including Michael Peters's *Education and the Postmodern Condition* (Peters 1995). See also the series Studies in the Postmodern Theory of Education, edited by Joe L. Kinchloe and Shirley R. Steinberg and published by Peter Lang Publishers (New York).

4. There is a great deal more in the summary that we would comment on if there were space enough, especially the contradictions among a number of the statements advanced: the third statement seems at odds with statements two, four, six, and eight.

5. *Science wars* is an American term referring to the disagreement between natural scientists and cultural studies theorists over the nature of scientific knowledge. Where scientists see themselves proceeding by experiment and observation to investigate the nature of reality, cultural studies theorists see scientific theory as a social product embedded in a historical context that is shot through with ideology and power relations.

6. www.physics.nyu.edu/faculty/sokal (accessed December 6, 2005).

7. In 1996, Alan Sokal, a physicist at New York University, published a pastiche of postmodern theory in *Social Text*, a cultural studies journal, entitled "Transgressing the Boundaries: Towards a Transformative Hermeneutics of Quantum Gravity." Later, Sokal published "A Physicist Experiments with Cultural Studies" in *Lingua Franca*, owning up to the hoax. See www.physics.nyu.edu/~as2/.

8. Michael Peters completed his Ph.D. thesis on Wittgenstein, *Wittgenstein and the Problem of Rationality: An Historicist Approach for Philosophy of Education*, University of Auckland, unpublished thesis, 1984. Tina Besley was also influenced by Wittgenstein, even though she focused on Michel Foucault.

9. Russian constructivism (1914–1932) is an artistic and architectural movement strongly influenced by cubism, futurism, and Malevich's suprematism, utilizing new "industrial" media and tools to express a new realism ideology to "construct art." The influence of Soviet constructivism can also be seen in the impact of international constructivism on the Bauhaus; on the English sculptors Henry Moore and Barbara Hepworth before WWII, prior to its taking root in the United States in the 1960s; and on the work of Mondrian, among others.

10. It is in this general intellectual environment that we should properly locate the work of the famous "structuralist" linguist Roman Jakobson and the Russian psychologists Lev Vygotsky and Alexander Luria. Vygotsky wrote a book entitled *The Psychology of Art* in 1925, where in the preface he writes, "The search for a way out of the precarious confines of subjectivism has equally characterized Russian art scholarship and Russian psychology during the years of my studies. This tendency toward objectivism, toward a precise, materialistic, scientific approach to knowledge in both fields, gave rise to the present volume" (www.marxists.org/archive/vygotsky/works/1925/preface.htm).

11. See the website of the University of Colorado at Denver School of Education (carbon.cudenver.edu/~mryder/itc_data/constructivism.html) and also the collection of papers on the Maryland Collaborative for Teacher Preparation (www.towson.edu/csme/mctp/Essays.html).

12. See www.artsined.com/teachingarts/Pedag/Dewey.html.

13. This is another significant link to education, in that, escaping Nazi Germany and on invitation from Harold Laski, Mannheim lectured at the LSE on the

sociology of knowledge before occupying the first chair in sociology of education at the University of London.

14. It is curious how little Hacking writes of Wittgenstein in relation to constructionism given that his early work is associated with Russell's logic (the *Tractatus* can be seen as a correction of Russell's logical constructions) and that his later language philosophy underlies the work of the strong program of the Edinburgh sociology of knowledge and the social discursive psychology of Harré and Shotter. It is perhaps even more curious if one accepts a conservative interpretation of Wittgenstein's thought (see Nyiri 1982), which we do not.

15. The list is selected from Hacking's (1999) opening page.

16. We based this brief description of our own research program on Peters (2002h).

17. We have sought to demonstrate the significance of Cavell's work for the philosophy of education. In particular, we have drawn attention to the way in which he emphasizes the importance of the "voice" of the child in the opening sections of the *Investigations* and how the structure of the figure of the child is intimately related to the theme of learning language games (see Peters 2001d).

8

Theorizing Educational Practices: The Politico-Ethical Choices[1]

INTRODUCTION

The notion of "practice" figures as an unanalyzable given in educational literature and activity. Practices are seen as the bedrock of a set of educational activities that are widely regarded as self-evident. The presuppositions of the term are not analyzed or clarified, and rarely is it acknowledged that theories of practice not only shape what we accept as "true" and "normal" but also implicitly constitute a set of politico-ethical choices. In education, the term *practice* is used frequently. In fact, practice is part of a new orthodoxy in education, prioritizing the practical over the theoretical, including "practitioner knowledge," the "reflective practitioner," "situated learning," "communities of practice," "effective educational practices," and the like. This paper comprises four related parts: first, it maps some of the uses of the term *practice* as it figures in educational discourse and theory; second, it considers the turn to practice in contemporary theory; third, by reference to the work of Hubert Dreyfus, it outlines and develops a typology of five competing views of practice, elucidating their politico-ethical implications; and, finally, it highlights the elusiveness of practice as a concept and the difficulties it presents for accounts of professional practice and learning.

THE ELUSIVENESS OF PRACTICE: TURNER'S CHALLENGE

Stephen Turner's (1994) *The Social Theory of Practices* poses a challenge to contemporary theory. He claims that practices "are the vanishing point of twentieth-century philosophy" (1). While the term is widely employed in literary criticism, feminist scholarship, history, anthropology, and social theory, he suggests that the concept of practice is "deeply elusive" (2), and he questions what is being referred to when, for example, Wittgenstein talks of "the inherited background," or social theorists talk of "tacit knowledge" or "presuppositions." Practices, he maintains, are ascribed mysterious properties of being "social" or "shared." To what extent should we take this language seriously, he asks. He tracks out the history of practices in a range of kinship terms of "traditions," "customs," "mores," and "habits" and goes on to claim,

> In postfoundationist writings in the humanities, the diversity of human practices has become a place-holder or filler in the slot formerly occupied by the traditional "foundationalist" notions of truth, validity and interpretive correctness. Truth, validity, and correctness are held to be *practice-relative* rather than *practice-justifying* notions. (9)

His complaint is that when we move away from first principles in traditional philosophy to practices as a way of grounding our framework, we are in fact substituting something that is neither explicit nor universal. He examines the causal aspects of practices, allegedly showing that causes do not identify practices or explain them. To identify or attempt to explain practices as "shared presuppositions" suffers from circular reasoning, he claims, and the major problem facing any account of practice is that there is no available model that accounts for transmission. As he says, "The concept of shared practices . . . requires that practices be transmitted from person to person," yet every causal account to establish sameness, where the same practice is reproduced in another person, leads to ludicrous results.

There are two problems concerning the notion of practice that are especially relevant for educational theory. First, if indeed, as Turner indicates, practice is a slippery concept that demands an account of its *shared* nature, which implies its transmittance, then for professional practice and development, especially the education of teachers, this becomes an important problem. How do we *educate* beginning or novice teachers in the practice of teaching when there is no viable model of transmission?

Second, and associated with this difficulty, there are two related difficulties. If current phenomenological accounts based on Heidegger, Wittgenstein, and Dreyfus are accepted, then professional practice and learning must be considered noncognitive, nonconceptual, and prelinguistic. Under these conditions, how can practice be learned or transmitted? Van Manen (e.g., 1999) provides us with one possible answer in terms of forms of noncognitive knowing. Similarly, "reflection-in-action" accounts of professional practice and learning face objections nicely put by van Manen concerning the paradoxical nature of reflective practice: if it is "retrospective or anticipatory reflection," it is unoriginal but likely; if it is "reflection in action" or contemporaneous, it is original but unlikely.

MAPPING THE MEANINGS OF EDUCATIONAL PRACTICES: CULTURE, SOCIAL, BODILY, AND APPLIED KNOWLEDGE

The concept of "practices" is perhaps *the* neglected underlying concept that signals a whole host of elements concerning the so-called new pedagogy, a term used by a report for the Tavistock Institute as part of a review of current pedagogic research and practice (Cullen et al. 2002). The notion of educational practices includes an emphasis on social construction and postmodern theory that gels with a constellation of new emphases in educational studies more generally. It reflects the central importance of culture—the importance of "cultures" in the plural (e.g., learning and knowledge cultures, evidence-based cultures, organizational cultures) and of "cultures" in the sociological literature that attempt to identify elements of "subcultures," especially in relation to youth. The term also implies a central focus on "the practitioner" and practitioner knowledge, as it is written into programs of "the reflective practitioner" dating from the work of Donald Schön (1987, 1995) and Chris Argyris (Argyris and Schön 1974, 1978; Argyris 1999). This use is carried over to so-called communities of practice (e.g., Wenger 1998), as they have become known in a burgeoning literature, together with the associated notion of "situated learning" (Lave and Wenger 1991). In relation to both of these developments—the cultural turn and the reflective practitioner—the term *practices* has been used to signal the priority of the practical over the theoretical in educational activities. This means, among other things, that education activities are primarily engagements with others in the world; it implies that learning and teaching are fundamentally social activities, "doings," or performances without "inner" processes. The stress on practices also accords with and partially explains the currency of the now taken-for-granted distinction between Mode 1 and Mode 2 knowledge first proposed by Gibbons and colleagues (1994), with its emphasis on applied knowledge and contexts of use. Less obviously, perhaps, these overlapping tendencies in philosophy and social theory that have infiltrated education tend to focus on the increasing importance of an understanding of the body to education, not just the emotions or embodied knowledges and rationalities, but also the body as formations of self and social order. Finally, the use of *practices* also highlights pragmatics in general, in both linguistic and cognitive theory (i.e., practices as pragmatically grounded). These theoretical tendencies, we will argue, derive from a largely unexamined shift in philosophy and social theory to focus on practices as the underlying concept of cultures and communities, which brings social reality to social order and structures.

While we can map these overlapping uses and family resemblances (Wittgenstein 1953) of the term *practices* in relation to education and social theory, it is not the case that the term is used deliberatively or purposively with these meanings or understandings explicitly in mind. Rather the term has been adopted in use without much reflection, and when it is used, it is often without sufficient attention to what the term implies.

Let us provide some recent prominent and influential examples. Herbert J. Walberg and Susan J. Paik (2000) have written a booklet entitled *Effective Educational Practice*, which appears in the Educational Practices Series developed by the International Academy of Education and distributed by the International Bureau of Education (available at www.ibe.unesco.org). Neither the series nor Walberg and Paik theorize the underlying notion of practice. It is a concept that is taken for granted and regarded as a given.[2]

In another example, this time from the field of organizational science, which has appropriated the term *practice* in so-called *communities of practice*, John Sharp (1997) provides the following definition:

> A *Community of Practice (CoP)* is a special type of informal network that emerges from a desire to work more effectively or to understand work more deeply among members of a particular specialty or work group. At the simplest level, CoPs are small groups of people who've worked together over a period of time and through extensive communication have developed a common sense of purpose and a desire to share work-related knowledge and experience.

He discusses the work of John Seely Brown and Paul Duguid in their study of Xerox. He writes,

> The notion of "practice" is critical in CoP, pointing out that the group concentrates on learning that emerges only though working, or actually practicing one's craft. CoPs supplement the book and classroom learning of many trade and professional workers. To learn how one does work in this organization, or in this area, that goes beyond the official "canonical" training for that activity implies that a key part of learning how to work is learning how to communicate and share information within the community of practice. In this sense, learning is about work, and work is about learning, and both are social.

Again, while the term is used, it is not theorized. *Practice* refers loosely to planned collaboration that is meant to generate a common, shared understanding of events and an action orientation for dealing with such events the next time they arise.[3]

A final introductory example comes from the Tavistock Institute, which, as we discussed in chapter 7, recently made its final report to the British Economic and Social Research Council, entitled *Review of Current Pedagogic Research and Practice in the Fields of Post-Compulsory Education and Lifelong Learning* (Cullen et al. 2002) as part of its synthesizing analysis that was commissioned as necessary background to the council's Teaching and Learning Research Programme, Phase III—Emerging Themes (see www.tlrp.org). The Tavistock Institute was interested in providing an overview, in identifying the key research questions, and in locating the gaps as a basis for its conclusions and recommendations. The concept of practice figures implicitly in the review, yet no attempt is made to distinguish the concept or indicate the theoretical stakes in different accounts.[4]

With all three examples, we can clearly see an instrumental focus on the concept of practice as something that indicates a kind of bedrock beyond which we cannot go. The implicit assumption behind these uses of the concept of "practice" is that both learning and pedagogy are fundamentally *shared social activities* that can be identified, unpicked, observed, and improved. The notion of learning and pedagogical practices as shared social activities sometimes takes on an explicit constructivist construction, as in "communities of practice," where the underlying assumption is that organizationally it is possible to create or construct communities based on shared practices and that it is possible to design group learning strategies in organizational settings.

The emphasis on practice in education takes many different and related forms (see table 8.1). We draw a distinction between those forms that are relatively well theorized and those that are not. In the former case, we can distinguish among various related notions of practice advanced directly by theorists or drawn from the work of others outside education. We can identify, for instance, a pragmatic notion of practice as it figures in the work of Dewey, a praxical notion of practice influenced by Marx and the Frankfurt school that shapes Freire's work, and a notion of practice that informs the work of Bourdieu. We might also acknowledge scholars

Table 8.1. Theories of Educational Practice

Practice as *problem-solving* (e.g., Dewey)
Practice as *praxis* (e.g., Marx, Freire)
Practice as *lived experience* (e.g., life-world phenomenology)
Practice as *reflection in action* (e.g., Schön)
Practice as *phronesis*, or practical judgment (e.g., Aristotle)
Practice as *lebensformen*, or "forms of life" (e.g., Wittgenstein)
Practice as *habitus* (e.g., Bourdieu)
Practice as *noncognitive knowing* (e.g., van Manen)

working in education who have begun to import the notion of practical reason from Aristotle, focusing on his notion of *phronesis*, or from Wittgenstein, in terms of "meaning as use," rule following, and "background practices." We might also mention in this context the work of life-world phenomenologists strongly influenced by Schütz (1972) and Berger and Luckmann (1966) in sociology but ultimately springing from Husserl and Heidegger. Yet even with these theorized accounts in education, rarely is the notion of practice analyzed or clarified. There is no systematic approach to these theorized accounts or to the ethico-political implications of the theory of practice embraced. Any account of practice in education would first need to systematically differentiate among these different accounts.

THE CONTEMPORARY TURN TOWARD PRACTICES

The present emphasis on practices—the contemporary turn to practices— can be traced, perhaps, to the contemporary turn to Aristotle, to the continuing influence of Marx, and to the currency of both Heidegger and Wittgenstein.[5] The theory of practice is embedded in the priority of practical engagement with the world, a materialist social ontology, and a view of language as practice based. This broad view has its origins in an account of practical reason beginning, perhaps, with Aristotle (2000), who in the *Nicomachean Ethics* (Book VI) talks of *"phronesis"* as the ability to use the intellect practically. Practical reason is to be distinguished from theoretical reason in that the former is directed to a practical and especially a moral outcome and results in an action rather than a proposition or a new belief (see Dunne 2001).

It is not possible to talk of practices without the mention of Marx, for his materialist social ontology has influenced thinkers like Heidegger as well as contemporary practice theorists like Bourdieu (1977, 1990, 1998) and Freire (1972). His texts are strewn with references to the priority of the practical. The second thesis on Feuerbach reads, "The question whether objective truth can be attributed to human thinking is not a question of theory, but a *practical* question" (Marx 1969, 283). His point is that we are practically bound up with the world we are contemplating and are therefore already part of a whole set of social relations and material conditions. The touchstone for Marx is, of course, the concept of labor, broadly considered as the means of self-realization and creative self-development. In Marx's anthropology, the concept of labor prefigures the human body as the source of social life. Thus, Marx "does not explain practice from the idea but explains the formation of ideas from material practice" (Marx 1974, 58). The materialist view of history that Marx embraces holds that the "social being" determines consciousness: as he writes, "Life is not de-termined by consciousness, but consciousness by life" (47) and "it is not the consciousness of men that determines their being, but on the contrary, their social being that determines their consciousness" (Marx 1963, 182). Yet, as he says in "The Eighteenth Brumaire," "Men make their history, but they do not make it just as they please; they do not make it under cir-cumstances chosen by themselves, but under circumstances directly en-countered, given and transmitted from the past" (1963, 97). Language is also practical, and historical practices lie at its foundation.

Heidegger was to emphasize the practical over the theoretical and also claimed to find his source for firsthand practical understanding in Aristotle (Sheenan 1993, 81). As Harrison Hall (1993, 128) notes, "The practical world is the one that we inhabit first, before philosophizing or engaging in scientific investigation," and "the world in the traditional sense can be understood as derivative from the practical world." Hei-degger's emphasis on the priority of the relational context of practical activity is also mounted as a critique of traditional Cartesian ontology, which pictures the world as comprising subjects as minds whose men-tal representations (ideas) attempt to capture an independent (material) reality. Philosophy and science on this view are concerned with ways of guaranteeing the accuracy of our representations. We can only avoid the problem of knowledge (skepticism) and the problem of value (how things have value) by avoiding traditional Cartesian metaphysics, which wants to privilege the thinking subject (Hall 1993, 129). In par-ticular, Heidegger questions the claim made by Plato that moral knowl-edge must be explicit and disinterested. As Hubert Dreyfus (1993, 293–94) argues,

> Heidegger questions both the possibility and the desirability of making our everyday understanding totally explicit. He introduces the idea that the shared everyday skills, concerns, and practices into which we are socialized provide the conditions necessary for people to make sense of the world and of their lives. All intelligibility presupposes something that cannot be fully articulated—a kind of knowing-how rather than a knowing-that. At the deepest level such knowing is embodied in our social skills rather than our concepts, beliefs, and values. Heidegger argues that our cultural practices can direct our activities and make our lives meaningful only insofar as they are and stay unarticulated background practices. As Heidegger puts it in a later work, "The Origin of the Work of Art," "Every decision . . . bases itself on something not mastered, something concealed, confusing; else it would never be a decision."

Wittgenstein, too, came to accept in his later work that philosophy, like language, was, as Rorty (1993, 344) expresses the point, "just a set of indefinitely expansible social practices." Rorty goes on to make the comparison between Heidegger and Wittgenstein explicit:

> Early Heidegger and late Wittgenstein set aside the assumption (common to their respective predecessors, Husserl and Frege) that social practice—and in particular the use of language—can receive a noncausal, specifically philosophical explanation in terms of conditions of possibility. More generally, both set aside the assumption that philosophy, might explain the unhidden on the basis of the hidden, and might explain availability and relationality on the basis of something intrinsically unavailable and unrelational. (347–48)

David Bloor (2001) explains that rationalism is the philosophical tradition that accords priority to theory over practice, and conservatism is the tradition sometimes referred to that accords priority to practice over theory. We prefer Bloor's alternative descriptions—Enlightenment and Romantic— for the reason that not all accounts of the priority of practice are conservative; witness, for instance, the accounts by Bourdieu and Foucault. As Bloor indicates, rule following would seem to be a paradigm case of rationalism, yet for Wittgenstein, rule following is a practice, and its normative aspect derives from the consensus between different rule followers, which can be understood only in naturalistic terms as facts about our "natural history."

Both Heidegger and Wittgenstein are important because with their emphasis on background practices—how the present, and our skills and understandings, always take place against a cultural background that in principle is not intelligible or able to be articulated in a principled way— the very project of the "reflective practitioner" becomes problematic. The contemporary turn to practices in education not only reflects the broader turn to practices in philosophy and social theory, but in the mainstream it turns to practices naively and generally without theoretical sophistication. Indeed, we might hypothesize that the "reflective practitioner" has become ideology, and as its ideological force has grown, so the institutional ossification of the doctrine has become more obvious and more dangerous.

In the introduction to a recent edited collection entitled *The Practice Turn in Contemporary Theory*, Theodore Schatski (2001) indicates that underlying the adoption of the term *practice* in contemporary theory is the desire to move away from dualistic ways of thinking. He characterizes the philosophical work of Ludwig Wittgenstein, Hubert Dreyfus, and Charles Taylor (the latter two both heavily influenced by Heidegger) as an attempt to overcome the object-subject dualism and to "highlight non-propositional knowledge and illuminate the conditions of intelligibility" (1). Talk of practices for sociologists such as Pierre Bourdieu, Anthony Giddens, and the ethnomethodologists, he advises us, is a way of avoiding the dualism of action and structure as well as the determinism of objectified social structures and systems. In the hands of "cultural theorists" like Michel Foucault and Jean-François Lyotard, Schatzki maintains, practices provide a means for theorizing language as a discursive activity against structuralist and semiotic notions of language as a structure or system. Social scientific studies of science that picture science also as an activity (in the work of Andrew Pickering and Joseph Rouse) use the notion of practices to counter representational accounts of science and to challenge "humanist dichotomies between human and nonhuman entities" (1). Clearly, there has been a major paradigm shift in contemporary thought linked to the theorization of practice. While there is, Schatzki claims, "no unified practice approach" (2), most theorists identify practices as fields of human activity, defined as the skills, tacit knowledges, or presuppositions that underlie activities. And while most theorists focus on *human* activities, there is a significant posthumanist trend, especially in science and technology studies, that wants to construe practices as involving an interface with machines and scientific instruments. Finally, Schatzki contends,

> Most practice theorists would agree that activity is embodied and that nexuses of practices are mediated by artefacts, hybrids and natural objects, disagreements reign about the nature of embodiment, the pertinence of thematizing it when analyzing practices, the sorts of entities that mediate activity, and whether these entities are relevant to practices. (2)

As he elaborates, forms of human activity are anchored in accounts of the body, and typically theorists will maintain that "bodies and activities are 'constituted' within practices" (Schatzky 2001, 2). In so doing, practice theorists tend to adopt a materialist social ontology emphasizing the way human activity depends on shared skills or understandings, typically viewed as embodied. The fundamental philosophical claim involves the assertion of the priority of practical engagement and understanding of the world over any form of theoretical contemplation, understanding, or speculation. The priority of practical engagement and understanding follows from an emphasis on the body and on embodied knowledge, rationality, and understanding, which takes place through the skilled body, through the acquisition of shared embodied know-how. If actions are embedded in practices and individuals are constituted within practices, then practice theory pits itself against contemporary theoretical approaches that privilege the individual, language as a signifying system, the lifeworld, institutions or roles, or structures or systems in defining the social. These phenomena can only be correctly elucidated and analyzed through the field of practices, which Schatzki defines as "the total nexus of interconnected human practices" (2). He also addresses the problem of social order in terms of practices but raises the question of what orders the field of practices itself. These metaquestions concerning the kinds of ontology that constitute accounts of practices lead to further questions concerning the ethics and politics associated with these accounts, which are crucial to identify in theories of professional practice and development.

DREYFUS AND FIVE COMPETING VIEWS OF PRACTICES

Following the American phenomenological philosopher Hubert Dreyfus, it is possible to identify five competing views of practice and the extent to which they are unified or dispersed, and integrated or disseminatory. The outline of these five approaches sets up a rich set of connections between theories of practice and the ethico-political commitments they embody. Perhaps what is required in pedagogical theory and practice, above all, is an account of practices.

The five points in table 8.2 are taken from an essay by David Stern (2000, 67–68) and are based upon a handout, as Stern indicates in a footnote (358n33), provided by Dreyfus at the National Endowment for the Humanities (NEH) Summer Institute on Practices on July 24, 1997.

Table 8.2.   Background Practices: The Ethico-political Implications

1. Stability (Wittgenstein, Bourdieu). The practices are relatively stable and resistant to change. Change may be initiated by innovators or may be the result of "drift," but there is no inherent tendency in the practices for this to happen. The consequence is either a conservative acceptance of the status quo or a revolutionary prescription for change.
2. Articulation (Hegel, Merleau-Ponty). The practices have a telos of clarity and coherence and become increasingly more refined as our skills develop. This leads to political progressivism and Whiggish history, albeit with the recognition that the path to progress will not always lead in that direction.
3. Appropriative gathering, *Ereignis* (Dreyfus's reading of later Heidegger). When practices run into anomalies, we make an originating leap, drawing on marginal or neighboring practices and so revising our cultural style. This supports those who can best bring about such change within a liberal democratic society, such as entrepreneurs, political associations, charismatic leaders, and culture figures.
4. Dissemination, difference (Derrida). There are many equally appropriate ways of acting, and each new situation calls for a leap in the dark. The consequence is a sensitivity to difference, to loosen the hold of past norms on present and future action, and to become aware of the leaps we make rather than covering them up with Whiggish history.
5. Problematization (Foucault). Practices develop in such a way that contradictory actions are felt to be appropriate. Attempts to fix these problems lead to further resistance. This leads to a hyperactive pessimism: showing the contingency of what appears to be necessary and engaging in resistance to established order.

Source: Dreyfus cited in Stern (2000, 67–68).

Dreyfus develops a typology of five competing accounts of practices. We think it is possible to add to these by recognizing contributions from the Aristotelian, Kantian, pragmatic (Dewey), and analytic traditions.

The central question is to determine whether, and the extent to which, these different accounts necessarily overlap in their definition of practice or share similar assumptions. In educational theory, for example, Van Manen (1999) has addressed the question of practice, noting how the term is used in many different contexts—professional practice, education practices, reflective practice, and the like—and he suggests that this usage, which focuses on preferred ways of acting, tacit knowledge, presuppositions, traditions, and so forth, differs from the traditional meaning of *practice* as "practical" or "applied theory." Van Manen argues that the case of reflectivity in teaching has been made unreflectively. Teaching is rarely if ever based on "reflection in action," van Manen maintains, and he disputes Schön's (1995, 54) claim that not only is it true that "we can think about doing something but that we can think about something while doing it." He suggests that the notion of reflective practice, considered in Schön's sense as a practice of reflecting about doing something while doing it, is open to two objections: "the relational structure of the interaction, and the temporal dimensions of the practical contexts in which the action occurs."

Van Manen argues, "Phenomenologically it is very difficult, if not impossible, for teachers to be immersed in interactive or dialogic activities with their students while simultaneously stepping back from the activity." He argues, by contrast, that the practice of teaching involves a form of noncognitive knowing that inheres in our body, in our actions, in the things around us, and in our relations with others. It is a kind of silent practice that cannot be captured in words or propositions and made theoretically explicit. As he argues,

> This noncognitive knowledge is like a silent practice that is implicit in my world and in my actions rather than cognitively explicit or accessible to critical reflection. What Wittgenstein, Heidegger, Dreyfus have suggested is that this silent practice cannot necessarily be translated back into words, propositional discourse. Heidegger proposed provocatively that while *Rede* ordinarily means "talk" in the sense of reason, not all *Rede* manifests itself through words. Dreyfus uses the term *Articulation* to refer to this nonreflective implicit knowing. He says, "one does not have words for the subtle actions one performs and the subtle significations one *Articulates* in performing them." And Wittgenstein suggested that this practical domain of our actions is ultimately nonconceptual, prelinguistic, noncognitive.

Dreyfus's Heideggerian approach to practices is the most developed contemporary example of the phenomenological position and perhaps the most influential approach in education that provides a clear basis to challenge the orthodoxy of the "reflective practitioner," especially the cognitivist approach best exemplified by Schön. Yet, on the basis of this preliminary analysis, we may begin to distinguish between at least seven broad theoretical approaches to educational practices, all of which must be analyzed in relation to one another to reveal the ethico-political choices implicit in their accounts. We might identify these approaches to educational practice as:

1. phenomenological (Wittgenstein, Heidegger, and Dreyfus)—practice as noncognitive, nonconceptual, and prelinguistic;
2. Marxist (Bourdieu and Passeron)—practice as telic or praxical;
3. positivist—practice as "practical" or "applied theory";
4. cognitive—practice as "reflection in action" (Schön);
5. ethical (Aristotle and Kant)—practice as practical judgment or engagement;
6. Deweyean pragmatism—practice as problem solving;
7. poststructuralist—practice as problematization (Foucault) or difference (Derrida).

There remains the very difficult task of sorting out the differences.

ACKNOWLEDGEMENT

We would like to thank Lynn Fendler for a set of constructive criticisms on this chapter.

NOTES

1. A version of this paper appears in *Beyond Empiricism: On Criteria of Educational Research* by Paul Smeyers and Marc Depaepe.
2. They write, for instance, "The practices described in this booklet can generally be applied to classroom subjects in primary and secondary schools. . . . As with all educational practices, of course they can be effectively or ineffectively planned and conducted." The booklet goes on to talk of "powerful" and "consistent" practices in promoting academic learning, clearly assuming that there are good and bad practices. In terms of effective practices, then, we are told that research demonstrates that "learning is enhanced when schools encourage parents to stimulate their children's intellectual development" or that "students learn more when they complete homework that is graded, commented upon and discussed by their teachers" (Walberg and Paik 2000). We do not need to pursue this example here, as it is clear that the term *practice* is employed with little reflection on the status or meaning of practices.

3. CoP entails collaboration and common understandings. The use of the term shifts the epistemology of learning away from the psychological realm and a transfer theory of learning to a sociological realm but does not entail a future-oriented perspective that might enable practitioners to deal with such events next time. CoP is one example of the "new pedagogy." We are grateful to Lynn Fendler for this observation.

4. See, for instance, the quotation from Cullen et al. (2002) on p. 114 of chapter 7.

5. While the Kantian inversion of Cartesian epistemology makes Heideggerian relationality thinkable, we restrict ourselves to the philosophers mentioned.

9

Knowledge Networks, Innovation, and Development: Education after Modernization

If nature has made any one thing less susceptible than all others of exclusive property, it is the action of the thinking power called an idea, which an individual may exclusively possess as long as he keeps it to himself; but the moment it is divulged, it forces itself into the possession of everyone, and the receiver cannot dispossess himself of it. Its peculiar character, too, is that no one possesses the less, because every other possesses the whole of it. He who receives an idea from me, receives instruction himself without lessening mine; as he who lites his taper at mine receives light without darkening me.

—Thomas Jefferson (1861)

INTRODUCTION

Arguments are synchronous and atemporal. Narratives and human beings, even postmodern ones, are time consuming and temporal. Stories, including life histories, inescapably involve temporality, a chronicle or sequence of events, or "emplotment," as Hayden White would say. This chapter is both an argument and a narrative. It is a story about development—personal, human, and economic—and an argument asserting that "development education" can take new forms with different imperatives in the global knowledge economy. The argument is also one concerning the key concepts of "development" and "time"—development education by definition necessarily involves a philosophy of space-time. It entertains the proposition that in the global knowledge economy—under conditions of "knowledge capitalism"—development is less

151

like a continuous, unbroken, linear story separated by chapters or stages and more like a nonchronological, networked communication system based upon a layered complexity. If we adopt the latter description rather than the former, we will come to see development education as a central aspect of postmodernization, which is a term we use as a shorthand to speak of "education after modernization."[1] The term has been used in the social sciences since the early 1990s very much as a couplet to modernization and in the family modern-postmodern, modernity-postmodernity, modernism-postmodernism (see, e.g., Crook et al. 1992; Braun and Klooss 1995; Inglehart 1997).[2] Hardt and Negri (2001) use the term to refer to the "informatization of production." Educational postmodernization is, thus, a form of development very much tied to digitalization and networks, and we have chosen to talk of one form of development education in terms of "knowledge networks." Networks per se help to define postmodernization as a form of development, and, in turn, postmodernization functions in part as a critique of modernization theory and in part as a program for developing networks.

The first part of this chapter focuses on the knowledge economy and attempts to distinguish what is new and different about it compared to the traditional industrial economy (an idea versus an object economy). This section also spells out how important learning is to the knowledge economy, a fact often observed or assumed but rarely explained. The second part, entitled "Education after Modernization," offers a critique of modernization theory and the role that education has increasingly come to play within it. This section of the chapter briefly examines two recent models of development education based on contemporary modernization theory: education as human capital, the theory developed by Gary Becker in the 1960s from Theodor Schultz's agricultural economics, and education as knowledge for development, a position argued for by Joseph Stiglitz and adopted by the World Bank as its official development philosophy. In the final part of the chapter, we will explain and illustrate our arguments by reference to knowledge networks, and, following the work of Lawrence Lessig (2001), we will draw the connection between knowledge networks and innovation or creativity.

THE KNOWLEDGE ECONOMY AND THE ROLE FOR LEARNING

Without further ado, let us turn directly to specifying characteristics of the knowledge economy and begin with restating an influential policy definition. The United Kingdom's white paper *Our Competitive Future: Building the Knowledge-Driven Economy* (Department of Trade and Industry 1998b) defines a knowledge-based economy in the following terms:

A knowledge-driven economy is one in which the generation and the exploitation of knowledge has come to play the predominant part in the creation of wealth. It is not simply about pushing back the frontiers of knowledge; it is also about the more effective use and exploitation *of all types of knowledge* in *all manner of activity*. (emphasis in original)

The report suggests that "knowledge" is more than just information, and it goes on to distinguish between two types of knowledge: "codified" and "tacit." Codifiable knowledge can be written down and transferred easily to others, whereas tacit knowledge is "often slow to acquire and much more difficult to transfer."[3]

The knowledge economy allegedly differs from the traditional economy. To recapitulate, we have earlier characterized these differences acknowledged in the literature by emphasizing the "economics of abundance," the "annihilation of distance," the "deterritorialization of the state," the "importance of local knowledge," and "investment in human capital."

It is argued that the knowledge economy is different from the traditional industrial economy because knowledge is fundamentally different from other commodities, and that these differences, consequently, have fundamental implications both for public policy and for the mode of organization of a knowledge economy. Joseph Stiglitz (1999c), for instance, suggests that "movement to the knowledge economy necessitates a rethinking of economic fundamentals" because, he maintains, knowledge is different from other goods in that it shares many of the properties of a *global* public good. This means, among other things, a key role for governments in protecting intellectual property rights, although appropriate definitions of such rights are not clear or straightforward. It also signals the dangers of monopolization, which Stiglitz suggests may be even greater for knowledge economies than for industrial economies.

Recall that Stiglitz argues that knowledge is a public good because it is nonrivalrous—that is, knowledge once discovered and made public operates expansively to defy the normal "law" of scarcity that governs most commodity markets. Knowledge in its immaterial or conceptual forms—ideas, information, concepts, functions, and abstract objects of thought—is purely nonrivalrous in that there are essentially no marginal costs to adding more users. Yet once materially embodied or encoded, such as in learning or in applications or processes, knowledge becomes costly in time and resources. The pure nonrivalrousness of knowledge can be differentiated from the low cost of its dissemination resulting from improvements in electronic media and technology, although there may be congestion effects and waiting time (to reserve a book or download from the Internet).

While nonrivalrous, knowledge can be excluded (the other property of a pure public good) from certain users. The private provision of knowledge normally requires some form of legal protection; otherwise firms would have no incentive to produce it. Yet knowledge is not an ordinary property right. Typically, basic ideas, such as mathematical theorems, on which other research depends, are not patentable, and hence a strong intellectual property-right regime might actually inhibit the pace of innovation. Even though knowledge is not a pure public good, there are extensive externalities (spillovers) associated with innovations. As Stiglitz notes, the full benefits of the transistor, microchip, and laser did not accrue to those who contributed to those innovations (see also Stiglitz 1998a, 2002).

Stiglitz is not the only economist to argue that knowledge operates expansively to defy the law of scarcity. Indeed, in order to understand this claim, it is helpful to place it in the tradition of the economics of knowledge and information (and of education) that began with Friedrich von Hayek in the late 1930s and progressed through the work of scholars such as Jacob Marschak, George Stigler, Kenneth Boulding, Fritz Machlup, Gary Becker, and many others. New growth theory, articulated by Romer and championed by the OECD, has highlighted the role of education in the creation of human capital and in the production of new knowledge and has explored the possibilities of education-related externalities not specified by neoclassical theory.

The role of learning, in particular, has become recognized by economists and educationalists as important to the knowledge economy. David Hargreaves (2000), for instance, quoting the new master futurists Drucker, Cairncross, Canter, and Leadbeater, focuses on the transition to a knowledge economy and its consequences for educational systems, schools in particular. He predicts that while literacy (including IT literacy) and numeracy will remain part of the core curriculum, the school will come under increasing pressure to provide new forms of knowledge, which he lists as follows: metacognitive abilities and skills—thinking about how to think and learning how to learn; the ability to integrate formal and informal learning, declarative knowledge (or *knowing that*), and procedural knowledge (or *know-how*); the ability to access, select, and evaluate knowledge in an information-soaked world; the ability to develop and apply several forms of intelligence as suggested by Howard Gardner and others; the ability to work and learn effectively and in teams; the ability to create, transpose, and transfer knowledge; the ability to cope with ambiguous situations, unpredictable problems, and unforeseeable circumstances; and the ability to cope with multiple careers—learning how to "redesign" oneself, locate oneself in a job market, and choose and fashion the relevant education and training. He places emphasis on "knowledge management," which he sees as playing a vital role in moving to the "learning society." For him, part of the task of an effective education system is to "train" (his word) all education leaders in knowledge management. In essence, it seems that knowledge management will help us to transfer knowledge within and between institutions, and also to make explicit and share the professional knowledge of teachers, which is often tacit and locked in teachers' heads. We think this is a good description of some of the skills and abilities required, although Hargreaves's analysis needs to be supplemented with a heavy dose of political economy to relate the curriculum production of "flexible learners" to the regime of knowledge production and the mode of regulation. We are also suspicious of easy appeals, without refinement or qualification, to new cognitive science, especially the work of Gardner, and knowledge management. Yet Hargreaves has at least identified that new forms of knowledge are necessary.[4] Our list of the roles of learning reflects some shared features with Hargreaves (see table 9.1).

Table 9.1.   The Role of Learning in the Knowledge Economy

1. Learning has become increasingly important to people, organizations, networks, and firms.
2. The increase of the codification of knowledge and the digitalization of information implies that we are moving increasingly toward learner-centered networked environments with less emphasis on either supervision or teacher-centered education.
3. A corresponding need for information and Web skills—not only access, search, and browsing, but also transmission, storage, and retrieval (i.e., "Internetworking").
4. In the knowledge economy, there is a shift in learning from consuming to using ("rip, mix, burn"), symbolized by performative and digital epistemologies (cf. Wittgenstein: "Now, I know how to go on").
5. In national innovation systems, the emphasis now is on learning to innovate, creativity, problem solving, teamwork, and openness to change.
6. The knowledge economy involves a greater emphasis on informal learning carried out by individuals in their own time, often just-in-time, with open access to the Internet twenty-four hours per day.
7. A greater emphasis on learning-by-doing, learning-by-using, and learning-by-interacting.
8. "Flexible learners" and learning organizations place emphasis on learning through networks while often on the move ("mobile learning works").
9. New forms of learning are increasingly limited by the legal model of the copy (including simulation, copyright, and patent) and intellectual property.
10. Social learning as the deliberate effort to coordinate action of a multitude of institutions and actors working together ("communities of practice").
11. Distributed learning with tailored programs in virtual learning communities.

This strong emphasis on learning is reflected more theoretically in the term *learning economy*.[5] In the modern learning economy,

> the rate of knowledge turnover is high; learning and forgetting are intense, the diffusion of knowledge is fast and a substantial part of the total knowledge stock is changed every year. Furthermore, learning has become increasingly endogenous. Learning processes have been institutionalized and feedback loops for knowledge accumulation have been built in, so that the economy as a whole is learning by interacting in relation to both production and consumption. When economies learn how to learn the process tends to accelerate. (Gregersen and Johnson 1997)

Gregersen and Johnson (1997) argue that the post-Fordist era of the fifth Kondratieff long wave has brought the new learning process into being based on ICTs, "which have dramatically reduced the costs of storing, handling, moving and combining information, and have made different kinds of networking possible." This has changed the process of innovation, thus shortening product cycles and making continual innovation necessary for firm survival. The knowledge infrastructure of universities and schools has profoundly affected innovation by promoting networking and interactive learning. There is also much stronger institutional support for learning and innovation (dealing with intellectual property rights, technological service systems, tax rules, and the like), leading to the development of "a 'learning culture' in which people regard long formal education, repeated re-education and retraining, and even life-long education, as necessary and normal aspects of economic life." In this environment, the role of government policy has changed, and the state has an important role to play in developing

> the means of learning (schools, training systems, etc.), the incentives to learn (intellectual property rights, taxes and subsidies, supporting learning networks, etc.), access to relevant knowledge (libraries, databases, technological service systems, telecommunication systems, etc.), decreasing the costs of forgetting (retraining, labour market mobility, social security, etc.), and, more generally, keeping options open by protecting technological and institutional diversity and promoting an openness to learning from abroad in different fields of knowledge. (Gregersen and Johnson 1997)

EDUCATION AFTER MODERNIZATION

Let us begin this section with a story. On a recent visit to China in August 2000, Michael Peters stayed several days in the center of Beijing at a hotel that had satellite TV. He was in China to talk to Chinese intellectuals about Chinese postmodernization, to learn something about the restructuring of Chinese universities, and to give some lectures at a number of Chinese universities on two topics: postmodernity and the role of education policy in the knowledge economy.[6] One night, sitting in a hotel room, he tuned into CNN's world news to view a magazine piece on information technology. This program detailed two little interventions, or what we call "information experiments." The first concerned a traditional, preindustrial Colombian village located in the interior. It was still tribal, cut off from the rest of the country, and owed its existence to subsistence agriculture. An American anthropologist developed a power source from the local irrigation system, at least enough of one to charge a battery from which the village could run a laptop computer. Now, in this development scenario—in this dramatic leapfrog from the preindustrial to the knowledge economy—the village rapidly became transformed. The most adept at keyboard and computer skills in the village—as it happens, a teenager—downloaded and later developed and sequenced education programs from the best sources on the Web. He acted as a service facilitator and teacher aide in a learner environment. At night, those in the village he had taught helped to hold evening classes with adult agricultural workers, downloading information on crops to help improve their agricultural base.

The other "story," dressed up in CNN American-news hype, concerned some "street kids" of the urban dispossessed in New Delhi slums. A computer engineer who owns his own successful digital company set up a vandal-proof street computer screen with a manual gear stick only. Before long, the street kids who congregated around this street installation had taught themselves sufficient computer skills not only to navigate the Internet, but also, through innovative moves and links, to actually create their own website! There were many other development stories like these.

What these feel-good stories demonstrate is not simply isolated mini successes and the dramatic effects of postmodern global information and communications technologies on traditional societies, but they are also indicative of much grander development scenarios that call into question traditional assumptions. Let us note just two here.

First, they indicate that nonlinear economic development that skips so-called stages is possible, and maybe even desirable, and that postwar modernization theory, based upon a Western homogenous model, has often been damaging not only to "developing countries" but also to an understanding of the process of development. The deconstruction of development discourse, which started in the late 1980s, has revealed the "arbitrary character of the concepts, their cultural and historical specificity, and the dangers that their use represents in the context of the Third World" (Escobar 1995, 13). One group utilizing a "systems of knowledge" approach, which suggests that cultures are characterized by ways of knowing, in addition to rules and values, indicates that "Development has relied exclusively on one knowledge system, namely the Western one" (Escobar 1995, 13). In other words, non-Western knowledge systems were discarded, traditional knowledge structures were ignored, and yet it is these knowledge systems and structures—the source of normative orientations, myths, and traditions—that provided alternatives to economistic and reductionistic ways of thinking.

Second, when we talk of the knowledge economy, we must realize that knowledge has a strong cultural and local dimension as well as a universalistic dimension. It is part of our argument, foreshadowed here, that postmodernization demands the promotion of knowledge cultures together with *cultural knowledges*, the other half of the equation that often gets forgotten in development talk. We should speak, then, of knowledge cultures (in the plural) and cultural knowledges, just as we should acknowledge alongside the knowledge economy, the economy of knowledges.[7]

E. Doyle McCarthy (1996, 108) provides us with a powerful rereading of the sociology of knowledge tradition, going back to the classic texts. Elucidating the central claim of this tradition, that *society is constitutive of human being*, or what Arthur Child called "the intrinsic sociality of mind," she argues that "*knowledge* is best conceived and studied *as culture*," suggesting that "as powerful cultural forms, knowledges also constitute meanings and create entirely new objects and social practices" (McCarthy 1996, 1). Beginning with an observation of how Marx's distinction between the realms of material substructure and cultural superstructure has been superseded in the last half century, McCarthy observes,

> We live in a world almost overwhelmed by its own inventiveness, its own artificiality. Our realities exist in transmission—on screens and cables—and our sense is that those who possess and control knowledges and images and sounds effectively control our realities. Material life, as we understand it today, has become inescapably semiotic; we consume products that serve as signs of things and, more importantly, of ourselves. Our world of things exists no more to communicate, to "say something," than to serve a practical need or function. As theories of discourse have gained ascendancy in the academy, talk . . . talk . . . talk hounds us in daily life. People, led by the "talk shows" of radio and television, never seem to stop talking. In our time are we witnessing the death of conversation by talk? "Culture" also serves to account for our growing sense of "construction" and "difference" in a world that "whatever it is, is no longer One" (Lemert 1994, p. 146).

To claim that *knowledge is culture* is to insist that the sciences—both natural and social—"operate *within* culture—that they contain and transmit and create cultural dispositions" (108).

In other words, we can understand more clearly the collapse of the distinction between what Marxists called base and superstructure, between the economic realm and the realm of culture. Today, at the beginning of the twenty-first century, we see the beginnings of a shift toward the "symbolic economy," where culture, knowledge, and education, broadly defined, become all important to development. Over twenty years ago, Jean-François Lyotard (1984) drew our attention to the way in which all the new developments in knowledge significantly were language based—the development of cybernetics, telematics and informatics, computer algorithms and languages, new algebras, choreographies, and the like. He was pointing to the confluence of what Richard Rorty called the "linguistic turn" and what others have called the "cultural turn."

The critique of modernization theory has emphasized the unexamined assumptions concerning the notion of "progress" clearly embodied in Rostow's stages of growth, which implied an invariant logic of development from subsistence, to sedentary and agricultural, to industrial, and finally to postindustrial, following the Western model best exemplified in the Anglo-American example. Since the inception of modernization in the postwar period, education has come to occupy center stage.

EDUCATION AS DEVELOPMENT
OF HUMAN CAPITAL: GARY BECKER

Simon Marginson (1993, 48ff) indicates that the OECD was responsible for the revision and rediscovery of human capital theory in the late 1980s. Originating in neoclassical economics in the work of J. R. Walsh and later that of Milton Friedman and Simon Kutznets in the 1940s and 1950s, human capital theory was to undergo development in the hands of Theodore Schultz, Jacob Mincer, and Gary Becker in the 1960s. The fundamental claim was that human capital determines the rate of economic growth. Marginson (1993, 40) identifies three phases in the application of human capital theory to government education policy:

> The first phase, in the 1960s, was one of public investment in human capital, dominated by claims about a link between education and economic growth. The second phase was a period of eclipse, in which the earlier policy assumptions were abandoned and the rates of return equations were confined to a modest place with the body of neo-classical theory. The third phase (not completed) saw renewed policy commitment to investment in human capital. But in the free market climate now prevailing, the emphasis is on private rather than public investment.

In the latest phase, education in human capital terms is seen as a source of labor-market flexibility in relation to technological and social change.

Gary Becker (1964), drawing on the work of his teachers at the University of Chicago—Theodore Schultz, Greg Lewis, and George Stigler—began to theorize education as a form of human capital in the early 1960s.

Both Becker and Machlup, along with Milton Friedman, were members of the Mont Pelerin Society, established by the Austrian economist Frederick von Hayek, who had taken up a chair at the University of Chicago in 1950 and exercised a strong influence over the development of contemporary forms of American neoliberalism. As Becker (1997) said in a recent interview, "Chicago always stands for markets, rationality and that markets do things more efficiently than governments do." Since Becker's pathbreaking work, it has been argued that it is primarily a lack of investment in human capital (rather than investment in physical capital) that prevents poor countries from catching up with rich ones. Educational attainment and public spending on education are correlated positively to economic growth (Barro and Sala-i-Martin 1995; Benhabib and Spiegel 1994). Education is also important in explaining the growth of national income, and lifelong learning is seen as crucial (Aghion and Howitt 1998).

THE WORLD BANK: KNOWLEDGE FOR DEVELOPMENT

In 1996, the World Bank embarked on a new vision to become a "Knowledge Bank" that would bring the knowledge revolution to developing countries and act as a global catalyst for creating, sharing, and applying the cutting-edge knowledge necessary for poverty reduction and economic development. In relation to this vision, the World Bank invested in knowledge networks, communities of practice, and information technology within the organization. The bank argued that four critical elements were necessary in order to reap the benefits of the global knowledge economy:

- An *economic and institutional framework*—to provide incentives for the efficient use of existing knowledge, the creation of new knowledge, and the flourishing of entrepreneurship.
- An *educated and skilled population*—to create, share, and use knowledge well.
- A *dynamic information infrastructure*—to facilitate the effective communication, dissemination, and processing of information.
- A *network of knowledge centers*—of research centers, universities, think tanks, and community groups to tap into the growing stock of global knowledge, assimilate and adapt it to local needs, and create new knowledge.

The World Bank recognized that a knowledge infrastructure comprising community development, learning communities, and education networks was necessary in order to make the most of increased connectivity and wider access to information and communications technologies.

The World Development Report *Knowledge for Development* (World Bank 1998), as its former president James D. Wolfensohn summarizes, "examines the role of knowledge in advancing economic and social well being." He indicates that the report "begins with the realization that economics are built not merely through the accumulation of physical and human skill, but on the foundation of information, learning, and adaptation." The World Development Report is significant in that it proposes that we look at the problems of development in a new way—from the perspective of knowledge. Indeed, Joseph Stiglitz, ex–chief economist of the World Bank, who recently resigned over ideological issues, ascribed a new role for the World Bank. He draws an interesting connection between knowledge and development, with the strong implication that universities as traditional knowledge institutions have become the leading future service industries and need to be more fully integrated into the prevailing mode of production—a fact not missed by countries like China who are busy restructuring their university systems for the knowledge economy. He asserts that the World Bank has shifted from being a bank for infrastructure finance to being what he calls a "Knowledge Bank." He writes, "We now see economic development as less like the construction business and more like education in the broad and comprehensive sense that covers knowledge, institutions, and culture" (Stiglitz 1999c, 2).

The World Development Report, *Knowledge for Development*, focuses on two types of knowledge and two problems that are taken as critical for developing countries—*knowledge about technology*, that is, technical knowledge or simply "know-how," such as nutrition, birth control, or software engineering, and *knowledge about attributes*, such as the quality of a product or the diligence of a worker. Developing countries typically have less know-how than advanced countries, which the World Bank report calls "knowledge gaps." Also, developing countries often suffer from incomplete knowledge of attributes, which the report calls "information problems." Development, thus, is radically altered in this conceptualization, where it becomes a matter of narrowing knowledge gaps through national policies and strategies for acquiring, absorbing, and communicating knowledge, and addressing information problems through national policies designed to process the economy's financial information, increase knowledge of the environment, and address information problems that hurt the poor.[8]

Let us briefly note the importance of education to this development recipe. Acquiring knowledge not only involves using and adapting knowledge available elsewhere in the world—best acquired, so the report argues, through an open trading regime, foreign investment, and licensing agreements—but also local knowledge creation through research and development and building upon indigenous knowledge. Absorbing knowledge is the set of national policies that centrally concerns education, including universal basic education (with special emphasis on extending girls' education and that of other disadvantaged groups); creating opportunities for lifelong learning; and supporting tertiary education, especially science and engineering. Communicating knowledge involves taking advantage of new information and communications technology, as the report would have it, through increased competition, private-sector provision, and appropriate regulation.

KNOWLEDGE NETWORKS AND INNOVATION

The knowledge economy has been described as

> a hierarchy of networks, driven by the acceleration of the rate of change and the rate of learning, where the opportunity and the capability to get access to and join knowledge-intensive and learning-intensive relations determines the socio-economic position of individuals and firms. (Houghton and Sheehan 2000, 11)

On this conception, taken from the OECD (1996b), the firm becomes a learning organization that seeks to promote interfirm interactive learning and that, with the support of government, enters into collaboration with other firms, universities, and other research organizations to eventually develop a national innovation system. Networks and clusters are thus important geographical and locational factors, and government policy has attempted to build clusters around groups of universities to facilitate complementarity and innovation (e.g., Silicon Valley, the Oxford-Cambridge corridor) in order to maximize network externalities.[9]

In this context, it is also important to mention the recent development of network economics, which focuses on the provision, efficiency, and desirability of network services and network-based applications using concepts of interconnection, interoperability, and intermediaries.[10] The economics of networks began in the mid-1970s with Roland Artle, Christian Averous, Lyn Squire, and Jeffrey Rohlfs, who developed the concept of demand externalities, demonstrating the possibility of alternative market allocation. This literature received a renewed impetus after the breakup of AT&T in 1984, and market allocation inefficiencies were linked to consumer expectations and switching costs developed by Michael Katz, Carl Shapiro, Christian van Weizsäcker, and Paul Klemperer. By the 1990s, the economics of networks had helped to explain global changes in information industries following the liberalization of world telecommunications and the development of new forms of dynamic competition, together with their anticompetitive consequences (for example, the unchallenged position of Microsoft in the global software industry). Increasingly, the economics of networks must take onboard Internet 2 and the White House's Next Generation Internet Program.[11]

Crucial to understanding the development potential of networks and their relation to innovation and the generation, transmission, and exchange of knowledge is the concept of the network itself. In terms of the architecture of networks and network design, we can look to national systems of transport, electricity, and telephony as early prototypes that permitted the increasing speed of movement of goods, ideas, and people. Indeed, all these networks in some way became part of the wider infrastructure out of which the present global telecommunications system emerged. In terms of networks, we must differentiate between the resource and its physical infrastructure and use. Ivan Illich was an early theorist to point to this argument when he drew the distinction between manipulative and convivial institutions. He was indirectly addressing the question of network design in convivial institutions that permitted people to access the system when they wanted to rather than being forced to do so, and thus, he was also discussing the critical question of control versus freedom in basic network and institutional design.

Lawrence Lessig (2001) in *The Future of Ideas* has suggested that digital technologies have dramatically changed the conditions of creativity. "Consumers" or users do more than simply consume, as he suggests the advertisement from Apple Computers indicates when it instructs its users to "rip, mix, burn" (referring to "sampling" as in creating your "own" music). The future of ideas and "the fate of the commons in an interconnected world" (the subtitle of his book) is a question of freedom and control in relation to the development of the Internet. As he writes,

> The argument of this book is that always and everywhere, free resources have been crucial to innovation and creativity; that without them, creativity is crippled. Thus, and especially in the digital age, the central question becomes not whether government or the market should control a resource, but whether a resource should be controlled at all. (14)

Lessig defines "free" through the concept of the intellectual commons and specifies three contexts where resources in the Internet are held in common. Then he considers creative production in real space, which does not permit the freedom that the Internet does—the space where films are made, books are written, and discs are recorded. He demonstrates that the constraints of intellectual property that affect real-space creativity have been removed by the original architecture—legal and technical—of the Internet, although now, he argues, following the paradigm of film, new legal barriers are being introduced that will endanger creativity on the Internet. He suggests, "How a system is designed will affect the freedoms and control the system enables" (Lessig 2001, 35). The architecture of

cyberspace and, more generally, the control of telecommunications worldwide are thus vital development questions for both developed and developing countries. In other words, as Mitch Kapor indicates, "Architecture
is politics" (cited in Lessig, 35).

Applying the notion of the commons to the Internet, borrowing from
network communication theorist Yochai Benkler, a New York University
law professor, Lessig defines it as a communication system comprising
different layers: first, the "physical" layer made up of computers and
wires linking computers to the Internet; second, a "logical" or "code"
layer that makes the hardware operational, including the protocols that
define the Internet and the software on which they run; and third, the
"content" layer, that is, the material that gets transmitted across the Internet, including the digital images, texts, and sounds. In principle, each of
these layers could be controlled or free: "Each, that is, could be owned or
each could be organized in a commons" (23). He goes on to argue,

> The Internet was born on a controlled physical layer; the code layer, consti-
> tuted by the TCP/IP, was nonetheless free. These protocols expressed an
> end-to-end principle, and that principle effectively opened the space created
> by the computers linked to the Net for innovation and change. This open
> space was an important freedom, built upon a platform that was controlled.
> The freedom built an innovation commons. That commons, as do other com-
> mons, makes controlled space more valuable. (48)

We do not have the space to explore further the scope of Lessig's thesis
here. Yet there are several important development lessons to be drawn
from his remarks, both by analogy and direct implication. Development
itself has been described by Amartya Sen (1999) as a form of freedom, and
insofar as the World Bank wants to subscribe to a philosophy of development based on knowledge networks and learning communities, it is important to understand that this process, especially in the digital space of
the Internet, ultimately concerns the higher-order values of freedom and
control.

Peter Cukor and Lee W. McKnight (2001) argue that ICTs are playing a
significant role in economic and political development. The Internet, in
particular, they argue, is "well suited to facilitate and support a new and
increasingly more popular paradigm in development, the so called
Knowledge Networks," which bring people from both the North and the
South into new learning relationships and permits participation by people from developing countries in the global knowledge economy on the
basis of their education alone and despite the fact they do not live in an
industrialized country with access to the latest technology. They draw on
Howard Clark's (1998) typology of four kinds of knowledge networks: informal (casual, ad hoc interactions); information access (university or

government libraries); open (research-based networks with a well-defined structure and governance); and development networks, which

> focus on a well defined theme around which various projects converge. These networks exist not only to create new knowledge but to accelerate its application. Development networks are highly structured, have strong governance and participation is by invitation based on merit.

Clark's (1998) typology is a descriptive one based on the Canadian experience, available on the website of the International Institute for Sustainable Development (www.iisd.org/networks), which references downloadable books and papers on knowledge networks in the service of sustainable development.[12] The notion of sustainable development is another aspect of postmodernization that functions in part as a critique of modernization theory.

Cukor and McKnight (2001) go on to suggest:

> Many believe, among them Nicholas Negroponte, Director of the MIT Media Lab., that the developing world can progress by skipping certain stages of industrial development and leapfrogging into the Information Economy.[13]

The article to which they refer is insubstantial and amounts to nothing more than a brief speculation, although Negroponte does point to the change in development philosophy of the World Bank. Nevertheless, the point is one that we have attempted to argue and develop with reference to the World Bank's changing development philosophy, to Stiglitz's (and other economists') recognition of the different economics required to understand the operation of the knowledge economy, to network economics, to the notion of sustainable development, and finally to the critique of the "progress" assumptions underlying modernization theory. Cukor and McKnight (2001) argue that the flexibility and adaptability of the Internet means that it can serve both e-commerce and knowledge networks for development, and they make the policy suggestion that the establishment of an educational infrastructure is necessary to support sustainable knowledge application. In this connection, they cite the examples of the African Virtual University and the satellite-based education networks in the South Pacific and Caribbean, as well as various corporate alliances (e.g., Grammen Bank, World Tel, Africa ONE); partnerships with the public and nonprofit sectors (e.g., SoftBank, WorldSpace digital audio broadcasting); and NGOs (United Nations Development Programme, Sustainable Development Communications Network) that either act as knowledge networks or aid their development.

Knowledge networks represent a major new development education paradigm that is gaining support both in theory and in application. The notion and practice crucially depends upon education—not in its mass, formal, and industrial mode, that is to say, its modern sense or its place within modernization theory, but, more imaginatively, creatively, and with greater freedom, *after* modernization.

NOTES

1. For a collection of web sites on modernization theory (and dependency and world system theories) see people.uncw.edu/pricej/teaching/socialchange/Theory%20links.htm.

2. On postmodern economics see, for instance, Tweeten and Zulauf (1999), Cullenberg (2001) and Ruccio and Amariglio (2003). The term originated with Barbara Brandt's (1995) *Whole Life Economics*. On postmodern management theory see the site available at: www.business.com/search/rslt_default.asp?r4=t&query=postmodern+economics.

3. The European Round Table of Industrialists (2001) sent a message to the European Council saying that to ensure the future of European competitiveness is to create the conditions necessary to prepare citizens for living and working in a new knowledge-based society. It contains ten recommendations, including:

> Set precise targets for knowledge economy skills and attitudes to be acquired by the minimum school leaving age; Harness the experience of business for the benefit of education; Begin the process of conferring a new status and value on the teaching profession; Create a European online lifelong learning service; Develop local and regional forums of representatives of government, education and business to define the short-, medium- and long-term skills requirements of leading economic sectors; Introduce tax benefits to encourage people to acquire the equipment and skills needed for the knowledge economy; Secure early adoption of the Commission proposal to create a Community Patent; Encourage business and academia to define online European processes for exchange of information leading to collaboration in the development and commercial exploitation of projects; Stimulate risk-taking and bring down the cost of capital in Europe at all levels; Agree that each government will produce a master plan, with targets and timings, to ensure that the knowledge society becomes part of every citizen's daily experience through electronic access to the full range of public services and information.

4. For a more grounded account see Bereiter et al (1997).

5. This is a term introduced by Lundvall and colleagues; see, Datum, Johnson and Lundvall (1992), and Lundvall and Johnson (1994). See also *Flexible Learning for the Information Economy*, Vocational Education and Training (VET) Action Plan at http://flexiblelearning.net.au and *Learning for the Knowledge Society: An Education and Training Action Plan for the Information Economy*, Online Education and Training Section, Department of Education, Science and Training (DETYA), Australia: www.dest.gov.au/edu/edactplan.htm.

6. That I viewed this little vignette in Beijing is also important to the globalization mantra I am about to repeat. Across the road from the hotel was the largest "New World" department store I have ever experienced—larger than the California shopping malls—overflowing with Western goods, including the latest items of consumer and popular culture: CDs, TVs, walkmans, Hi-fi, mobile phones, and

a huge range of consumer items that we now take for granted. Clearly, Beijing had become part of the global circuit of commodity flows of consumer goods that define important aspects of postmodernism as the cultural logic of late capitalism. Indeed, the case has been made for mapping Chinese postmodernity (Dirlik and Zhang, 2000) both as a concept in its own right referring to postrevolutionary and postsocialist China, and also in juxtaposition to Euro-American postmodernity, as a theoretical means for illuminating the conditions of postmodernity more generally. The "spatial fracturing and temporal desynchronization" that characterizes the coexistence of precapitalist ("traditional" and in some places "tribal"), regnant socialist, capitalist, and postsocialist economic and social forms, as Arif Dirlik and Xudong Zhang (2000: 3) argue, "represent a significant departure from the assumptions of a Chinese modernity, embodied above all in the socialist revolutionary project." Dirlik and Zhang (2000), having examined postmodernization, elaborate the grammar of Chinese postmodernity in terms of "decentralization, transnational mobility, economic and cultural diversity, consumerism, and some emerging or renewed sense of location, individuality, and diversity" and "cultural postmodernism" or "the cultural vision developed out of the experience of postmodernity" and as illustrated in "fashion, music, architecture, video, art, literature, and theoretical discourses" (p. 8).

7. The notion of an economy of knowledges lies behind Michael Peters's recent book *After the Disciplines: The Emergence of Cultural Studies* (Peters 1999).

8. The World Bank's "Knowledge Economy Policy Services, Reports, and Consulting" is available at www.worldbank.org/wbi/knowledgefordevelopment/programs.html#Policy%20Studies.

9. There is a growing literature on clustering: see, for example, Cook (2002), Mansell et al. (2002), and Hildreth and Kimble (2004).

10. For introductions to the economics of networks see Hal R. Varian's website available at www.sims.Berkeley.edu/resources/infoecon/.

11. For a detailed history of the Internet, its design, basic and advanced use, key features, and security, see www.isoc.org/internet/history. When contemplating next-generation Internet, it is important to note that, as Rutkowski (2000) writes, "*The Internet itself is not a network at all, but a means for integrating networks and resources.*" He understands that the metadevelopments concerning search, retrieval, understanding, and visualization of large databases; information validation; personal coping with information streams and complex systems; and information protection are among the next grand challenges.

12. Its homepage begins with the following: "Knowledge networks have become important mechanisms for coordinating the efforts of civil society organizations to identify priorities for sustainable development action, to undertake joint research, and to engage other stakeholders in developing workable solutions. By combining their efforts, network members are able to have a greater impact on policy and practice that they would have alone. From the perspective of decision-makers in government and industry, knowledge networks simplify the tasks of seeking reliable information and advice."

13. They give the following reference: "The Third Shall Be First: The Net Leverages Latecomers in the Developing World," available at www.media.mit.edu/people/nicholas/Wired/WIRED6-01.html.

10

Educational Policy Futures

Miranda: "Oh brave new world that has such people in it."

—Shakespeare, *The Tempest*

INTRODUCTION: WHY EDUCATIONAL POLICY FUTURES?

There is always the temptation to think that the point that we occupy historically is a period of transformation and unprecedented change. This prevailing ethos, since Baudelaire, at least in aesthetic terms, is a self-constituting moment of modernity. Yet there are some signs that there are some very powerful forces at work reshaping advanced liberal societies—our normative orientations, our subjectivities, and our institutions. These forces have been encapsulated in handy slogans such as "postmodernity," "globalization," "reflexive modernization," "postindustrialization," "post-modernization," and the like (e.g., Touraine 1974; Lyotard 1984; Beck 1992; Beck et al. 1992; Castells 2000b). Many of these developments focus on the importance of changes in the organization of knowledge, the development of new forms of communication, and the centrality of knowledge institutions to an emerging info-capitalism. Often these epithets are conceptualized in metaphors such as the "information society," the "learning society," or the "knowledge economy," and they often work as official policy metanarratives to both prescribe and describe futures (see Peters 2001d).

What is clear from these various theoretical descriptions of the futures we face is that knowledge and learning are central both to modes of

169

production and to social organization. Knowledge and learning have also undergone certain technical and social transformations as advanced societies have entered the networked global knowledge economy, and the same forces of change have begun to transform traditional knowledge institutions such as universities and schools. This chapter maps the emergent field of educational policy studies. First, it discusses the futures of education in relation to the question of globalization. Second, it comments on the discourses of the knowledge economy as an example of futurology. Third, it discusses futurology in terms of scenario planning and foresight before finally examining two examples of futures research in education.

GLOBALIZATION AND THE FUTURES OF EDUCATION

Fundamental to understanding the new global economy has been a rediscovery of the economic importance of education (Papadopoulos 1994, 170). The OECD and the World Bank have stressed the significance of education and training for the development of "human resources," for upskilling and increasing the competencies of workers, and for the production of research and scientific knowledge as keys to participation in the new global economy. Both Peter Drucker (1993) and Michael Porter (1990) emphasize the importance of knowledge—its economics and productivity—as the basis for national competition within the international marketplace. Lester Thurow (1996, 68) suggests that "a technological shift to an era dominated by man-made brainpower industries" is one of five economic tectonic plates that constitute a new game with new rules: "Today knowledge and skills now stand alone as the only source of comparative advantage. They have become the key ingredient in the late twentieth century's location of economic activity."

Equipped with this central understanding and guided by theories of human capital, public choice, and new public management, Western governments have begun the process of restructuring universities and obliterating the distinction between education and training in the development of a massified system of education designed for the twenty-first century. Today the traditional liberal ideal of education is undergoing radical change. In short, as the knowledge functions have become even more important economically, external pressures and forces have seriously impinged upon its structural protections and traditional freedoms. Increasingly, the emphasis in reforming educational institutions has fallen upon two main issues: on the one hand, the resourcing of research and teaching, with a demand from central government to reduce unit costs while accommodating further expansion of the system, and on the other, changes in the nature of governance and enhanced accountability.

In the postwar period, especially since the 1980s, national education systems have experienced a huge growth in both participation and demand, leading to the phenomenon of "massification." This growth is, in part, the result of demographic changes, but also of deliberate policies designed to recognize and harness the economic and social importance of "second-chance" education and "lifelong" education. In a competitive global economy, the accent has fallen on the development of human capital. Educational institutions have become more market oriented and consumer driven as a consequence of funding policies designed to encourage access at the same time as containing government expenditure. As a result, the costs of education in many countries has been transferred to the students themselves or to their parents, and governments have moved away from the premises of universal provision to favor targeting as a means of addressing questions of equity of access.

In some OECD countries, there have been strong moves to change both the size and the composition of governing bodies, from a fully representative stakeholders or "democratic" model to one based on a board of directors and modeled on the private corporation. Enhanced accountability arrangements, influenced by managerialism, have followed the principles of new public management, which are designed not only to improve allocational and productive efficiency but to create incentives to pass costs on to government and consumers.

National education systems in the Western world have had to face the external pressures that come with increased access, lifelong learning, continued reductions in the level of state resourcing (on a per capita basis), and greater competition both nationally and internationally. Both tertiary and secondary education systems in some OECD countries have been incrementally privatized: a regime of competitive neutrality has increasingly blurred the distinction between public and private ownership; the introduction of user-pays policies has created a consumer-driven system; and recourse has been made to various forms of contracting, including "contracting out" and performance contracting. Privatization has involved reductions in state subsidies (and a parallel move to private subsidies), state provision, and state regulation.

In addition, educational institutions, like other parts of society and the economy, face the challenges inherent in the new communications and information technologies, which, by effecting a shift from knowledge to information and from teaching to learning, threaten to further commercialize and commodify the university, substituting technology-based learning systems for the traditional forms of the lecture, tutorial, and seminar. The introduction of technology-based learning systems is blurring the boundaries between on-site and distance learning. It is transforming the nature of scholarship and research, and brings in its wake many problems for reconceptualizing academic labor. Some policy makers see new communications and information technologies as the means by which the problem of growth and expansion in an age of steadily decreasing state subsidy (and unit costs) can be overcome. The virtual university, the virtual classroom, and the virtual laboratory are heralded as *the* answer by what we shall call the techno-utopians (see Peters and Roberts 1998). Some of the main trends facing education, together with the pressures they bring to bear, are summarized in table 10.1.

Table 10.1.   Main Trends and Pressures Facing Education

1. Globalization and increasing competition
   - Increased globalization (as world economic integration).
   - Increased levels of national and international competition.
   - Increased power and importance of global and multinational corporations.
   - Increased importance of research to global multinationals.
   - Importance of regional and international trade and investment agreements.
   - The growing economic and political importance of the Asian economies, including China.
2. Public-sector changes
   - Declining sociopolitical priority of education as an entirely state-funded activity.
   - Corporatization and privatization of the public sector.
   - Greater interpenetration of public and private enterprises.
   - Growth of managerialism (New Public Management) and new contractualism.
   - Localization and autonomy: decentralization, devolution, and delegation of authority to local communities and government agencies.
   - Demands for increased efficiency and accountability.
3. Increasing importance of knowledge
   - Increasing economic, social, and cultural importance of knowledge.
   - Commodification and mercantilization of knowledge.
   - Increasing role and importance of telecommunications and information technologies.
   - New political, legal, and ethical problems of "information economy" (e.g., intellectual property, copyright, plagiarism).
4. Employment
   - Changing nature of advanced economies to knowledge-based industries.
   - Changing structure of the labor market (e.g., casualization, feminization of the workforce).
   - Demand for highly skilled, technically competent workforce, with an emphasis on generic and transferable "core" skills.
5. Education policy
   - Increasing multicultural and international nature of societies and education institutions.
   - Increased demand from a highly diversified, "massified" student population.
   - Need for lifelong learning and "second-chance" education.
   - The vocationalization of education through partnerships with business and the promotion of entrepreneurial culture.
   - Erosion of state education by nontraditional providers.
   - Individualization and customization of programs for learners.

These trends are, of course, very much interrelated phenomena, and each one by itself represents a significant level of political-economic complexity. Considered together, the whole is both uncertain and unpredictable. Certainly, one can say the future has not been "written upon" or determined. To briefly illustrate the level of complexity, we will schematically review how the UK review of tertiary education—the Dearing Report[1] (named after its chairman, Lord Dearing)—elaborates the implications of globalization for higher education (see table 10.2).

Clearly, the Dearing Report recognizes globalization as a major influence on the United Kingdom's economy and labor market, with strong implications for higher education. Analyzing the Dearing Report, it is possible to talk of the globalization of tertiary or higher education according to three interrelated functions: the *knowledge* function, the *labor* function, and the *institutional* function. We can talk of the primacy of the knowledge function and its globalization, which has a number of dimensions— knowledge, its production, and its transmission or acquisition—is still as primary as it was with the idea of the modern university, but now its value is increasingly legitimated in terms of its attraction to and service of global corporations. The globalization of the labor function is formulated in terms of both the production of technically skilled people to meet the needs of global corporations and the ideology of lifelong learning, where individuals can "reequip themselves for a succession of jobs over a working lifetime." The institutional function is summed up in the phrase "higher education will become a global international service and tradable commodity." The competitive survival of institutions is tied to the globalization of its organizational form (emulating private sector enterprises) and its "services." Clearly, with this function there are possibilities for the emergence of both a closer alliance between global corporations and universities, especially in terms of the funding for research and development, and, in some cases, the university as a global corporation. The latter is a likely development with the world integration and convergence of media, telecommunications, and publishing industries.

The developments described here under the banner of globalization, which accentuate the primacy of knowledge, are further underwritten by recent advances in so-called growth theory. Neoclassical economics does not specify how knowledge accumulation occurs. As a result, there is no mention of human capital, and there is no direct role for education. Further, in the neoclassical model, there is no income "left over" (all output is paid to either capital or labor) to act as a reward or incentive for knowledge accumulation. Accordingly, there are no externalities to knowledge accumulation. By contrast, new growth theory has highlighted the role of education in the creation of human capital and in the production of new knowledge. On this basis, it has explored the possibilities of education-related externalities. In short, while the evidence is far from conclusive at

Table 10.2. Globalization as World Economic Integration

Main Causes
- Technological changes in telecommunications, information, and transport.
- The (political) promotion of free trade and the reduction in trade protection.

Main Elements
- The organization of production on a global scale.
- The acquisition of inputs and services from around the world, which reduces costs.
- The formation of cross-border alliances and ventures, enabling companies to combine assets, share their costs, and penetrate new markets.
- Integration of world capital markets.
- Availability of information on international benchmarking of commercial performance.
- Better consumer knowledge and more spending power, hence more discriminating choices.
- Greater competition from outside the established industrial centers.

Consequences for the Labor Market
- Downward pressure on pay, particularly for unskilled labor.
- Upward pressure on the quality of labor input.
- Competition is increasingly based on quality rather than price.
- People and ideas assume greater significance in economic success because they are less mobile than other investments such as capital, information, and technology.
- Unemployment rates of unskilled workers relative to skilled workers have increased.
- More, probably smaller, companies whose business is knowledge and ways of handling knowledge and information are needed.

Implications for Higher Education
- High-quality, relevant higher education provisions will be a key factor in attracting and anchoring the operations of global corporations.
- Institutions will need to be at the forefront in offering opportunities for lifelong learning.
- Institutions will need to meet the aspirations of individuals to reequip themselves for a succession of jobs over a working lifetime.
- Higher education must continue to provide a steady stream of technically skilled people to meet the needs of global corporations.
- Higher education will become a global international service and tradable commodity.
- Higher-education institutions, organizationally, may need to emulate private-sector enterprises in order to flourish in a fast-changing global economy.
- The new economic order will place a premium on knowledge and institutions and will therefore need to recognize the knowledge, skills, and understanding that individuals can use as a basis to secure further knowledge and skills.
- The development of a research base to provide new knowledge, understanding, and ideas to attract high-technology companies.

Source: Developed from Dearing (1997), "The Wider Context," available at www.leeds.ac.uk/educol/ncihe

this stage, there is a consensus emerging that (1) education is important for successful research activities (e.g., by producing scientists and engineers) that in turn are important for productivity growth and (2) education creates human capital, which directly affects knowledge accumulation and therefore productivity growth (see report 8, "Externalities in Higher Education," Dearing 1997).

THE KNOWLEDGE ECONOMY AND FUTURES DISCOURSE

In an attempt to reposition and structurally adjust their national economies to take advantage of global trends, the British, Australian, and New Zealand governments have begun to recognize the importance of education, especially higher education, as an "industry" of the future. There is an emerging understanding that education is now central to economic (post)modernization and is the key to competing successfully within the global economy. This understanding has emerged from the shifts that are purportedly taking place in the production and consumption of knowledge and that are impacting traditional knowledge institutions like universities (see table 10.3).

Senior managers and policy analysts have begun to develop overarching concepts or visions of the future as a method of picturing these changes. Thus, the terms *information society* (which has been around since

Table 10.3. Shifts in the Production and Legitimation of Knowledge

The role of the university is undergoing a transition in late modernity as a result of structural shifts in the production and legitimation of knowledge. The older goal of the democratization of the university has now been superseded by new challenges arising from the dual processes of the globalization and fragmentation of knowledge cultures. These arise from the following developments:

1. the separation of knowledge (research) from the postsovereign state that no longer exclusively supports big science;
2. the rise of new regulatory regimes that impose an "audit society" on the previously autonomous society;
3. a separation of research from teaching (education);
4. the decoupling of knowledge from society and the replacement of the public by target constituencies;
5. the functional contradiction between science and economy in the increasing specialization of knowledge and the decline in occupational opportunities;
6. the deterritorialization of knowledge as a result of new communication technologies and knowledge flows; and
7. the crisis of scientific rationality under conditions of the "risk society," reflexivity, and the new demands for the legitimation of knowledge.

Source: Delanty (1998).

the late 1960s) and *global information economy* abound in policy documents. More recently, the terms *knowledge* and *learning* have been moved to center stage by those reviewing higher education. Thus the Dearing Report uses the central concept of the "learning society" to interpret the likely impact of imminent global trends on the national economy and to reform higher education accordingly. The discourses of the knowledge economy and other futurist discourses are often given a certain shape in relation to education, science, and technology planning and policy through the development of what is called "futurology."

SCENARIO PLANNING AND FORESIGHT

Futurology is a relatively new constellation of fields and disciplines that address the impact of world trends and develop visions of the future with the idea of bridging business, science, and technology to government. This new area has had a strong impact recently on policy in its two predominant forms: scenario planning and foresight. Much of the policy impetus in this area has come from business experts rather than from educational futurists (e.g., Hicks and Slaughter 1998), who, we would argue, are better informed, more critical, and also more sensitive to educational issues. Slaughter's (2002) approach to futures studies as a discipline provides important foundations and a critical orientation based, for instance, on the understandings that neither discourse nor technologies are neutral, that progress is a contestable term, that meaning is negotiated, that futures studies must adopt a reflexive posture, and that narratives are "powerful explanatory devices" that require interpretation.

Scenario planning has emerged during the past forty to fifty years as a generic technique to stimulate thinking about the future in the context of strategic planning (Cowan 1998). It was initially used in military planning and was subsequently adapted for use in business environments (Wack 1985a, 1985b; Schwartz 1991; van der Heijden 1996) and, most recently, for planning political futures in such countries as postapartheid South Africa, Colombia, Japan, Canada, and Cyprus (Cowan 1998).

Scenarios are succinct narratives that describe possible futures and alternative paths toward the future based on plausible hypotheses and assumptions. The idea behind scenarios is to start thinking about the future now in order to be better prepared for what comes later. Proponents of scenario planning make it very clear that scenarios are not predictions. Rather, they aim to perceive futures in the present, to rehearse possible futures, and to ask "what-if" questions. In this sense, scenario planning is based on an imaginative kind of learning.

Scenario planning is very much about challenging the kinds of mindsets that underwrite certainty and assuredness, and therefore it is about reperceiving the world and promoting more open, flexible, and proactive stances toward the future. As Cowan and colleagues put it, the process and activity of scenario planning is designed to facilitate conversation about what is going on and what might occur in the world around us so that we might "make better decisions about what we ought to do or avoid doing." Developing scenarios that perceive possible futures in the present can help us "avoid situations in which events take us by surprise." They encourage us to question "conventional predictions of the future," help us to recognize "signs of change" when they occur, and establish standards for evaluating "continued use of different strategies under different conditions" (Cowan 1998, 8). Most important, they provide a means of organizing our knowledge and understanding of future environments within which the decisions we make today will be played out.

Within typical approaches to scenario planning, a key goal is to aim for making policies and decisions *now* that are likely to prove sufficiently robust when they are played out across several possible futures. Rather than predicting the future, a range of possible futures is entertained, and policies and decisions in the now are framed that will optimize (most approximately) options and outcomes no matter which of the anticipated futures eventually pans out.

Hence, scenarios must narrate particular and credible worlds given the forces and influences currently evident and known to us that are likely to steer the future in one direction or another. A popular way of doing this is to bring participants together for a present policy-making or decision-making exercise and have them frame a focusing question or theme within the area with which they are concerned. If, for instance, our concern is with designing current courses in literacy education and technology for in-service teachers in training, we might frame the question of what learning and teaching of literacy and technology might look like in educational settings for elementary school–age children fifteen years hence.

Once the question is framed, participants try to identify what driving forces they see as operating and important in terms of their question or theme. When these have been thought through, participants identify those forces or influences that seem more-or-less predetermined, that are expected to play out in more-or-less known ways. Participants then identify less predictable influences, or uncertainties—those key variables in shaping the future that could play out in quite different ways and for which we can't be genuinely confident one way or another about how they will play out. From this latter set, one or two variables are selected as "critical uncertainties" (Rowan and Bigum 1997, 81). These are forces or influences that seem especially important in terms of the focusing question or theme but that are genuinely up for grabs and unpredictable. The critical uncertainties are then dimensionalized by plotting credible poles:

between possibilities that at one pole are not too bland and at the other are not too off the wall. These become the raw materials for building scenarios: accessible and catchy, but fruitful, stories about which we can think so as to suggest decisions and policy directions *now*.

Foresight planning is often conceived of as a future-oriented public discussion designed to encourage a consensus among various groups concerning a desirable future. The exercise is based on a notion of foresight, which is neither a form of prediction nor of planning but is rather an analysis of global trends, how they will affect us, and how (given our resources) we might take advantage of them. Foresight planning typically tends to link government investment with the rise of the knowledge economy. Typically, the path by which this will be achieved is seen as an active process that recognizes four key imperatives. We draw an example from New Zealand's Foresight Project (Ministry of Research, Science and Technology 1998) merely to illustrate the approach, although its success has been questioned:

- The focus on the future must not be constrained by what we have been doing in the past.
- Technology (in its broadest sense) is a key driver for the knowledge revolution. It will have wide-ranging implications for the structure of society and the way in which we deal with environmental issues.
- A globalized economy requires us to be internationally competitive.
- The government's strategic investment in public-good science and technology must be used effectively to underpin development as a knowledge society.

Foresight planning is used to underpin a comprehensive review of the priorities for public-good science and technology. It is claimed that while the future is not entirely predictable, there are trends that are presently unfolding that must be taken into account in the foresight process. The Foresight Project in New Zealand specifies seven such trends: the knowledge revolution, globalization, global science and technology trends, changing consumer behaviors and preferences, industry convergence, environmental issues, and social organization. We are informed that the knowledge revolution constitutes a significant global paradigm shift, which is changing the structure of New Zealand's economy and society. Knowledge is the key to the future because it, rather than capital or labor, drives productivity and economic growth, and, unlike either capital or labor, it cannot lose its value, which may even increase with future applications. Knowledge, we are informed, "includes information in any form, but also includes know-how and know-why, and involves the way we interact as individuals and as a community" (Ministry of Research, Science and Technology 1998, 8).

The New Zealand program has not really gone anywhere and has been substantially critiqued (see Peters and Roberts 1999, 66–73). A better example of the foresight *process*, although not a national commission, is the Australian Foresight Institute (AFI) located at Swinburne University of Technology in Melbourne, Australia. Established in 1999, AFI offers postgraduate programs and research in the area of applied foresight. Its main stated aims are as follows:

- to provide a global resource center for strategic foresight,
- to create and deliver world-class professional programs,
- to carry out original research into the nature and uses of foresight,
- to focus on the implementation of foresight in organizations, and
- to work toward the emergence of social foresight in Australia (www .swin.edu.au/afi).

The UK Foresight program was launched in 1994 (www.foresight.gov .uk). It states,

> The UK's Government-led Foresight programme brings people, knowledge and ideas together to look ahead and prepare for the future. Business, the science base, Government, the voluntary sector and others work through thirteen Foresight panels to think about what might happen in the future and what we can do about it now to increase prosperity and enhance the quality of life for all.
>
> Education, Training and Skills is one of two underpinning themes which all the Panels have been asked to consider. It is vital that people are given every chance through education, training and work to realise their full potential and thus build an inclusive and fair society and a competitive economy.

The Foresight Education, Training and Skills Strategy Group (FETS) is the primary interface between Foresight panels and the Department for

Table 10.4.   The Foresight Education and Training Strategy Group Terms of Reference

- Establish a network of education, skills, and training experts on Foresight panels.
- Coordinate briefings for government and Foresight participants on areas of common interest, both to assist the induction of panels and on a continuing basis as the Foresight program evolves.
- Establish and coordinate education, skills, and training activities across Foresight panels so that they build on, are informed by, and inform developments in government policy.
- Periodically convene a forum of education and training experts from the Foresight program to discuss progress and maintain a common agenda.
- Contribute to the development of Foresight findings in education, skills, and training and promote their implementation; and
- Monitor and evaluate the impact of Foresights on education, skills, and training.

Education and Skills (DfES) and their counterparts in Scotland, Wales, and Northern Ireland. Its terms of reference are described in table 10.4.

Various national commissions on the future have been convened with wide-ranging briefs (see, e.g., Tiihonen 2000) with varying degrees of success. They tend to identify global trends and challenges that impact locally, and they also often help to suggest policy options for best coping with these impacts in terms of local resources.[2]

FUTURES RESEARCH IN EDUCATION: TWO EXAMPLES

In this section, we discuss two recent examples of futures research in education. The first comes from the National Educational Research Forum (NERF) and springs from its recent "Research and Development Strategy for Education: Developing Quality and Diversity," and the second comes from the think tank Scottish Council Foundation.

The NERF document describes the steps required to implement its strategy, and the first aspect mentioned is a foresight exercise dedicated to education. The Office of Science and Technology's current foresight program includes education as an underlying theme to other panels, but NERF's proposed foresight is the first dedicated to education. The document, then, describes the three components of foresight as (1) extrapolating from existing trends, (2) speculating, and (3) envisioning. The report goes on to suggest,

> There are two main implications of a dedicated foresight exercise in education for a research and development strategy. First, research will be called upon to inform the foresight process by accurately identifying current trends and by systematically exploring the implications of hypothetical courses of action. Second, we expect that the outcomes of a foresight process will begin to map out a context within which important themes for future research can be identified. (NERF 2001, 8–9)

The strategy document suggests that such an exercise must be wide ranging and able to reflect the changing context of education, that it will require specialists' skills, and that it must also include the broader involvement of different stakeholders. The "Proposal for Foresight in Education," which appears in the paper as annex 2 (17–19), states the aims of the exercise in the following terms:

- Identify areas for action by different sectors to increase national wealth and quality of life, opportunities and reduce barriers to participation;
- Identify emerging capacity to meet future needs;
- Highlight areas where government and others' action would deliver widespread benefits. (17)

The stated aims appear to be an overly technical and managerial conception of foresight that is related to the government's priorities, rather than a wider and more critical foresight process able to canvass "blue sky" research; encourage creative and original thinking; and, above all, foster the need to experiment. The rest of the proposal sets out the membership composition of a panel (of ten) to guide the exercise, methods of consultation, outputs, and timescale.

The Scottish Council Foundation was launched in 1997, on the eve of the establishment of the Scottish Parliament, as an independent nonprofit organization to promote original thinking in public policy, focusing on the themes of health, learning, economy, and governance. The foundation states the aim of its project in the following terms:

> At a time of great change in the world, Scotland is perhaps uniquely blessed. Scotland is of a size—5 million people—that experience suggests is ideally suited to making the most of the digital revolution and the new economy. It has a history of invention and creativity second to none. It has a strong sense of identity and a wealth of networks around the world that can be mobilised to get things done. And, since May 1999, it has a set of new political institutions—the Scottish Parliament and Executive—free from the legacy of the past that so many other government machines around the world are struggling to shake off.
>
> It is the project of the Scottish Council Foundation to help make the most of these advantages, to make sure that as the world changes Scotland changes with it—leading rather than following, and to instil in all those we touch a greater sense of what is possible in Scotland. (www.scottishpolicynet .org.uk/scf/about/frameset.shtml)

The Foundation has produced a bevy of reports on new governance (e.g., e-governance, devolution, building better communities); public health (e.g., social inclusion, food policy); skills and employability (e.g., welfare-to-work); children, families, and learning (e.g., family learning); and the economy (digital Scotland, the intelligent economy).

We want to briefly focus on two reports that are related to education. The first is called *Changing Schools: Education in a Knowledge Economy* by Keir Bloomer (2000), followed by an online discussion and a follow-up report by Bloomer (2001) entitled *Learning to Change: Scottish Education in the Early 21st Century*. The rise of the knowledge economy looms large in both publications. Something of the tenor of the discussion can be gauged by the core strategic questions, which, if answered, are deemed to make a difference to the quality of education in Scotland. The questions are as follows:

Purpose and Values

Can we have a system without a purpose?

How do we decide the purpose of the system? And create agreement about values?

Can we share a picture of the nature of the human being?

Responsible Support

Who in society is responsible for education?
How to devise a system for 5m learners deciding and getting what they
     need?

Learning Direct

What is the appropriate balance between content and processes?
What needs disintermediating and why? What needs to change?

Education in Continuous Change

Who are the drivers of change?
How to develop an education system for uncertainty and risk?

Moving on from Now

How much longer can the status quo remain an option?
How do we devise first steps to move on from the current system?

Learning to Change, which is available online,[3] follows through on the
main line of argument based on an analysis of the rise of the knowledge
economy. It identifies the main forces for change (Scottish Executive's
aims and objective for education, the impact of educational technology,
brain compatible learning, social inclusion, etc.) and the changes that are
necessary in the curriculum (citizenship, work experience, the school as a
brokerage, etc.).

The second report, *Children, Families and Learning: A New Agenda for Education* (Jones 1999), emphasizes shifting the focus in school policy toward
a more holistic concept of learning based on a consideration of when and
where we learn, the role of parents and the family, family learning initiatives, new community schools, the impact of technology, and children's
participation. Both reports are innovative and attempt to think outside the
traditional circle. They are laudable in their attempt to prepare Scotland
for the future and to engage in a consciousness-raising public discussion
about the future of education. Yet along with NERF's foresight exercise,
the reports suffer many of the difficulties of much literature in this newly
emerging field. They lack methodological refinement and sophistication.
They are mainstream and narrowly technicist, managerialist, or economistic—that is, driven by perceived needs of a changing economy (see Peters 2001d). They are not properly scoped or identified in terms of a

medium or long-range horizon. Perhaps most importantly, they foreclose on the future rather than opening up the possibilities.

In a collection entitled *Global Futures*, Jan Pieterse (2000) contrasts the mainstream managerial approach to futures, based on forecasting and risk analysis, with critical approaches to futures that criticize those dominant futures reflecting institutional vested interests, and with the alternative futures approach, which seeks to be inclusive without being alarmist. He asserts that there have been many critiques but few constructive proposals, which reflects the political and ideological malaise that has existed since the 1980s. He states,

> It would be exciting to see an ensemble of forward-looking and affirmative programmes for futures of social policy, gender, culture, human rights, cities, in a context of proposals for transformation of the world economy, global politics, development politics, international financial institutions and ecological economics. (xvii)

We agree with Pieterse, yet it is strange to see no mention of education or knowledge in the various proposals and approaches in his collection. Arguably, transformations of education and the organization of knowledge are at the center of global futures for many of the reasons mentioned above. Hicks and Slaughter (1998), Hicks (2002), and Inayatullah (2002) adopt critical approaches to educational futures that proceed with a clear awareness of Pieterse's political and philosophical agenda.

The challenge for futures theorists of education is to develop their own theoretical and methodological sophistication, to anchor their views in what we call "the prophets of postmodernity"—that group of philosophers, including Nietzsche, Wittgenstein, Heidegger, Marcuse, Foucault, Lyotard, Arendt, Rorty, and others, who sought to establish new value in what they saw as an impending age of nihilism. In futures studies, there are a number of scholars who have devoted themselves to educational questions emphasizing postmodernity, including Richard Slaughter (1992, 1996) and Sohail Inayatullah (2002). Slaughter (2002), for instance, much to our delight, addresses futures studies in critical terms, drawing on a range of related fields in critical theory, sociology of science and technology, semiotics, environmental planning, and the like. Inayatullah (2002) has recently focused on pedagogy and multiculturalism in futures studies. In addition, David Hicks (1998, 2002), along with a number of others, has focused on postmodern education in terms of a futures perspective.

In a range of books published over the last decade and drawing principally on the works of Nietzsche, Wittgenstein, Heidegger, and the French poststructuralist thinkers, we have attempted to provide an introduction in philosophy for what might be called "educational postmodernity."[4] In postmodernity, and in the age of the knowledge economy (one of the aspects of globalization), education becomes reprofiled in the technical-managerialist discourse, as Heidegger warned us, as a "resource" to be used as part of the standing reserve in the game of national economic competition. In this discourse, advances in educational technology, and indeed in learning and teaching, are advances in the efficiency of resource use. It is against this instrumentalist and technical mainstream vision that critical futures of education in postmodernity must be defined.[5]

NOTES

1. See www.leeds.ac.uk/educol/ncihe.

2. For a full list of governmental sites concerned with futures and national commissions, see the OECD futures website, which also contains think tanks, academic research, associations, and journals, at www.oecd.org/department/0,2688,en_2649_33707_1_1_1_1_1,00.html.

3. www.scottishpolicynet.org.uk/scf/publications/paper18/frameset_wide .shtml.

4. See, e.g., Peters (1995, 1996, 2001d, 2002b); Peters and Ghiraldelli (2001); Peters and Marshall (1999); Peters and Roberts (1998, 1999).

5. See the new international online-only journal *Policy Futures in Education* that Michael Peters established with this in mind: www.wwwords.co.uk/PFIE/.

Postscript: Freedom and Knowledge Cultures

> When the past speaks it always speaks as an oracle: only if you are an
> architect of the future and know the present will you understand it.
>
> Friedrich Nietzsche (1873), "On the Use and Abuse of History for Life"[1]

The "prophets of postmodernity" uniformly take a dim view of what
lies before us as technical rationality and information and communications technologies coalesce, mesh with and help to constitute new social systems, and shape the design and form of education and media, in
general. They see the cultural problem of nihilism on the horizon and the
specter of technological order of the system for its own sake. Yet this is
not just a cybernetic, information, communication, or networked global
society but also one in its gestation period where battles are being fought
over the lines of its development: trade in symbolic goods and intellectual properties; the convergence of technologies and their patterns of
ownership; the protocols and governance of the next generation Internet;
the relations between "third wave" modernization, symbolic economy,
and the emergence of regional trading blocs based on ethnicity, language,
and politics.

In this milieu consumer info-communicational practices have asymmetries of power to the state and the corporation, especially as cross-border
communicational flows upset traditional territories and the maintenance
of traditional borders. And yet even the single individual can use the system against itself with disproportionately and sometimes catastrophic results. The age is signified in terms of the shift from identity politics to ID
politics with a consequent mathematization of identity and an emerging

185

congruence of biology and information in new forms of biopower. As the state and the corporation build their databases in order to individualize the citizen-consumer, the individual also learns to elude and resist the most individualizing biometrics based on finger printing and eye/face recognition. Even active consumerism promises an agency once easily denied, as the idiosyncratic talents and preferences of consumers reprofile, assemble, and "rip, burn and mix" in an active co-production of "services" and in "subversions" undreamed of by their designers or innovators.

Clearly, there has been a shift from an underlying metaphysics of production—a "productionist" metaphysics—to a metaphysics of consumption and we must now come to understand the new logics and different patterns of cultural consumption in the areas of new media where symbolic analysis becomes a habitual and daily activity. Here the interlocking sets of enhanced mobility of capital, services, and ideas, and the new logics of consumption become all important. These new communicational practices and cross-border flows cannot be effectively policed. More provocatively, we might argue, the global informational commons is an emerging infrastructure for the emergence of a civil society still yet unborn.

Global civil society will not conform to Kant's dream of "Perpetual Peace." The war of information and the struggle for new forms of freedom in the electronic domain warrant consideration against the planned "information society," the policed "knowledge economy," and futures studies scenarios of postindustrialism. Information is the vital element in a "new" politics and economy that links space, knowledge, and capital in networked practices. Freedom is an essential ingredient in this equation if these network practices develop or transform themselves into knowledge cultures. The specific politics and eco-cybernetic rationalities that accompany an informational global capitalism comprised of new multinational edutainment agglomerations are clearly capable of colonizing the emergent ecology of info-social networks and preventing the development of knowledge cultures based on non-proprietary modes of knowledge production and exchange.

Castells (2004), the theorist of the networked society, identifies society through the "networks powered by microelectronics and software based information and communication technologies" (222). For him "the network society expands on a global scale" without borders where "networked organizations outcompete all other forms of organization" (222) in business, bureaucracy, and education. Furthermore, he argues "the networking of political institutions is the de facto response to the management crisis suffered by nation states in a supranational world" (223) and "civil society is reconstructed at the local and global level through networks of activists, often organized and debated over the internet, which form and reconfigure depending on issues, on events, on moods, on cultures" (223). Thus for Castells, "sociability is transformed in the new historical context, with networked individualism emerging as the synthesis between the affirmation of an individual-centered culture, and the need and desire for sharing and co-experiencing" (223). He concludes, "in this network society, power continues to be the fundamental structuring force of its shape and direction" (234).

In Nietzsche's terms, we are trying to determine the true hierarchy of values in relation to knowledge cultures, and we want to assert the value of *freedom* in relation to the future of knowledge. "Freedom," as many scholars have pointed out, has always been strongly associated with knowledge and with knowledge institutions. The Enlightenment metanarrative conceives of knowledge as the means of emancipation and moral progress. "Freedom" has received its standard liberal account and definition as freedom from the dependence on the will of others first by Locke; then elaborated by Mill, Bentham, Green, and others; and later adopted in the twentieth century by Hayek in his influential *The Constitution of Liberty*. This notion of liberty, which is at the heart of liberalism in both its Protestant and Catholic forms, is also historically tied to democracy and to free intellectual inquiry. Academic freedoms, stemming from freedom of speech, refer to alleged rights of students, teachers, and institutions to pursue the truth or persuade, without political suppression. The U.S. Supreme Court in *Regents of the University of California v. Bakke*, (438 U.S. 265, 312; 1978) states that academic freedom means a university can "determine for itself on academic grounds: who may teach; what may be taught; how it should be taught; and who may be admitted to study." This is not the place to pursue the full genealogy of academic freedom in all its forms; suffice it to say:

- that today its value in relation to the access to and distribution of knowledge (and, therefore, to students, teachers, and universities) is under threat;
- that the study of education should concern itself in a critical way with the historical forms of freedom and how they became established: freedom of thought, freedom to learn, and freedom to publish; and,
- that the assertion and establishment of these freedoms take different historical forms and pose different problems for knowledge cultures.

Nowhere is this more apparent than with the convergence between open source/free software, open access, and free science.

OPEN SOURCE/FREE SOFTWARE

Richard Stallman is the founder of the GNU project launched in 1984 to develop associated free software.[2] Stallman defines the underlying issues as fundamentally political involving the value of freedom:

> Free software is a matter of freedom: people should be free to use software in all the ways that are socially useful. Software differs from material objects—such as chairs, sandwiches, and gasoline—in that it can be copied and changed much more easily. These possibilities make software as useful as it is; we believe software users should be able to make use of them.[3]

He develops this concept in relation to four kinds of freedom;

> Free software is a matter of the users' freedom to run, copy, distribute, study, change and improve the software. More precisely, it refers to four kinds of freedom, for the users of the software:
> - The freedom to run the program, for any purpose (freedom 0).
> - The freedom to study how the program works, and adapt it to your needs (freedom 1). Access to the source code is a precondition for this.
> - The freedom to redistribute copies so you can help your neighbor (freedom 2).
> - The freedom to improve the program, and release your improvements to the public, so that the whole community benefits (freedom 3). Access to the source code is a precondition for this.

The Free Software movement works to make all software free of intellectual property restrictions, which it believes hamper technical improvement and work against the community good. The Open Source movement works toward most of the same goals but takes a more "pragmatic" approach to them, preferring to base its arguments on the economic and technical merits of making source code freely available, rather than on the moral and ethical principles.

GNU stands for "GNU's Not Unix" and dates from 1983 when Stallman announced the GNU project and wrote the GNU Manifesto.[4] Stallman was interested in rejuvenating non-propriety forms of software that emphasized the cooperative spirit characterizing the early days of computing. With the help of the Foundation he started writing a whole operating system and in 1990 combined Linux, developed by Linus Torvalds, with GNU to make a complete operating system—the GNU/Linux system—that is now used by millions across the world. The GNU General Public License (*GNU, GPL,* or *GPL*) is the most widely used free software licence in the world. Through this licensing system, Stallman helped to pioneer the concept of the copyleft.[5]

When Bruce Perens wrote the first draft of "The Debian Free Software Guidelines" in June 1997 he emphasized that open source does not just mean access to the source code but also includes a set of criteria governing distribution of open-source software, including free redistribution of the source code and the allowance of derived work. In addition, the original and standing definition refers to non-discrimination clauses (against persons and fields of endeavor) and the license must not be product specific or restrict other software. Finally, the license must be technology-neutral.[6] As the Open Source Initiative (OSI) explains:

> The *basic idea behind open source* is very simple: When programmers can read, redistribute, and modify the source code for a piece of software, the software evolves. People improve it, people adapt it, people fix bugs. And this can happen at a speed that, if one is used to the slow pace of conventional software development, seems astonishing.[7]

The history of OSI is given on the host site as originating in the response by a small group[8] to Netscape's announcement in 1998 that it intended to make the source code for the next generation of its Netscape Communicator available for free licensing on the Internet. Jim Barksdale, Netscape's president, advanced the argument, "By giving away the source code for future versions, we can ignite the creative energies of the entire Net community and fuel unprecedented levels of innovation in the browser market." OSI also jettisoned the "confrontation attitude" associated with "free software" to embrace a more pragmatic approach based on business grounds.

OPEN ACCESS

Open access has become a fully fledged movement with a burgeoning literature of its own directories and newsletters. For instance, Open Access News[9] advertises the movement as

> Putting peer-reviewed scientific and scholarly literature on the internet. Making it available free of charge and free of most copyright and licensing restrictions. Removing the barriers to serious research.

The newsletter is edited by a philosopher Peter Suber, who also provides an excellent Overview of Open Access,[10] which he defines in the following terms: "Open-access (OA) literature is digital, online, free of charge, and free of most copyright and licensing restrictions." Significantly, he charts the open access movement from 1966 with the launch of ERIC by the U.S. Office of Educational Research and Improvement and the National Library of Education. In his timeline he mentions a number of important precursors prior to 1990 including ARPANET, Project Gutenberg, the Stanford Linear Accelerator Center (SLAC) and the Stanford

Physics Information Retrieval System, Syracuse's *New Horizons in Adult Education*—an early online journal, and *Psycoloquy,* an early free online journal launched by Stevan Harnad that became peer-reviewed in 1990.[11] It is important also to note the early launch of the *Electronic Journal of Communication, Postmodern Culture,* and *Bryn Mawr Classical Review,* all established in 1990.[12] Suber's timeline, then, year by year lists all the significant technological and literary developments from databases, launch of WWW, electronic networks, journals, digital libraries, symposiums, encyclopedias, archives, online bibliographies, and other digital and associated political initiatives. The interface here between library-based initiatives, education, and publishing emerges as a critical one in the development of a self-conscious political movement.[13] Today the Directory of Open Access Journals houses 1,551 journals in the directory with 390 that are searchable at article level and some 72,839 articles in the DOAJ service.[14] This includes 114 education journals, which is by far the largest in any category or subcategory.

Early statements and declarations on open access began as early as 1991 with the Bromley Principles regarding full and open access to global change data.[15] At the Second Symposium on the Electronic Networks in 1992, Anne Okerson, one of the early and most astute commentators, wrote that the symposium series was

> aimed for the not-for-profit scholarly and research publishing community, and its objective is to promote information sharing and discussion among people interested in developing the potentials of electronic publishing and particularly of networked distribution.[16]

And James J. O'Donnell, in his introduction to the collection of papers presented, wrote:

> First, it is reasonable to think that in the change of outward forms and techniques of information preparation, storage, distribution, and retrieval there can and will lie great change in the way users structure the information and thus implicitly structure the world they live in. To consider the power of the media to shape us is to think in almost determinist ways.
>
> Second, at the same time, the intellectual trajectory of the culture that is making and shaping these instruments is one that has a life of its own. If we look to electronic information technology to make non-linear data more accessible and more useful, we should remember that we are continuing here an intellectual enterprise that is many centuries old. Even as the electronic environment transforms the culture, the cultural impulses that seek to shape that environment are profoundly, and in some ways reassuringly, conservative. To think in these terms is to restore a sense of freedom and control to the enterprise at hand.[17]

The major statement on Open Access dates from 2002, beginning with the Budapest Open Access Initiative in 2002. Other Open Access statements soon followed.

Major OA statements
Budapest Open Access Initiative and its FAQ, February 14, 2002
Bethesda Statement on Open Access Publishing, June 20, 2003
ACRL Principles and Strategies for the Reform of Scholarly Communication, August 28, 2003
Wellcome Trust position statement on open access, October 1, 2003
Berlin Declaration on Open Access to Knowledge in the Sciences and Humanities, October 22, 2003
UN World Summit on the Information Society Declaration of Principles and Plan of Action, December 12, 2003
OECD Declaration on Access to Research Data From Public Funding, January 30, 2004
IFLA Statement on Open Access to Scholarly Literature and Research Documentation, February 24, 2004
Australian Group of Eight Statement on open access to scholarly information, May 25, 2004
(Source: Peter Suber, www.earlham.edu/~peters/fos/overview.htm)

The Budapest Initiative begins:

> An old tradition and a new technology have converged to make possible an unprecedented public good. The old tradition is the willingness of scientists and scholars to publish the fruits of their research in scholarly journals without payment, for the sake of inquiry and knowledge. The new technology is the internet. The public good they make possible is the world-wide electronic distribution of the peer-reviewed journal literature and completely free and unrestricted access to it by all scientists, scholars, teachers, students, and other curious minds. Removing access barriers to this literature will accelerate research, enrich education, share the learning of the rich with the poor and the poor with the rich, make this literature as useful as it can be, and lay the foundation for uniting humanity in a common intellectual conversation and quest for knowledge.

The Initiative recommends self-archiving and open-access journals as the means to achieve open access to scholarly journal literature. The Berlin Declaration on Open Access to Knowledge in the Sciences and Humanities, a largely German and European initiative, states

> The Internet has fundamentally changed the practical and economic realities of distributing scientific knowledge and cultural heritage. For the first time

ever, the Internet now offers the chance to constitute a global and interactive representation of human knowledge, including cultural heritage and the guarantee of worldwide access. We, the undersigned, feel obliged to address the challenges of the Internet as an emerging functional medium for distributing knowledge.

It provides a definition of open access and then lists a set of strategies for making the move to the Electronic Open Access Paradigm. Most recently in 2004, both the OECD and the Australian Group of Eight have declared themselves committed to principles of open access, including values such as openness, transparency, legal conformity, formal responsibility, professionalism, protection of intellectual property, interoperability, quality and security, efficiency, and accountability. In 2004 the UK Science and Technology Committee published its report *Scientific Publications: Free for all?*[18] It is useful to quote from the summary as it sums up a line of argument supported by many organizations which is central to this growing movement:

> Academic libraries are struggling to purchase subscriptions to all the journal titles needed by their users. This is due both to the high and increasing journal prices imposed by commercial publishers and the inadequacy of library budgets to meet the demands placed upon them by a system supporting an ever increasing volume of research. Whilst there are a number of measures that can be taken by publishers, libraries and academics to improve the provision of scientific publications, a Government strategy is urgently needed.
>
> This Report recommends that all UK higher education institutions establish institutional repositories on which their published output can be stored and from which it can be read, free of charge, online. It also recommends that Research Councils and other Government funders mandate their funded researchers to deposit a copy of all of their articles in this way. The Government will need to appoint a central body to oversee the implementation of the repositories; to help with networking; and to ensure compliance with the technical standards needed to provide maximum functionality. Set-up and running costs are relatively low, making institutional repositories a cost-effective way of improving access to scientific publications.

The document then indicates that in the long term a more radical solution will be needed and gives an early recommendation to the author-pays publishing model. The report recommends that the government formulate a coherent strategy for future action on scientific publishing as a matter of urgency. It recommends funded work on the preservation of digital material and work on new regulations for the legal deposit of non-print publications to prevent "a substantial breach in the intellectual record of the UK." It also recommends that the UK government act as a proponent for change on the international stage. The report indicates that "Whilst the volume of research output and the price of scientific journals has been steadily increasing—one respected source cites average journal price increases of 58 percent between 1998 and 2003—library budgets have seen funding decreases." And it indicates that "whilst libraries are struggling to purchase journals, scientific, technical and medical publishers" profit margins remain exceptionally high compared with the rest of the publishing industry—as much as 34 percent at the operating level in the case of Reed Elsevier, the market leader. The report then details several publishing models based around the central concept of free online access, indicating that collectively their proponents form the "Open Access" movement and concludes: "The future of the scientific publishing industry has yet to be determined in the light of these new developments."[19]

Clearly, the Open Access movement is still in its infancy, but it is quickly picking up political momentum and global support.

FREE SCIENCE

If the movement of Open Access is still in its infancy then Open and Free Science movement is still in the womb. At this stage the movement for Free Science seems to piggy-back on Open Access. For example, Free Science is interpreted as free access to science, as the website records,

> The *Washington DC Principles for Free Access to Science* outlines the commitment of not-for-profit publishers to work in partnership with scholarly communities such as libraries to "ensure that these communities are sustained, science is advanced, research meets the highest standards and patient care is enhanced with accurate and timely information."

The statement is signed by 49 major science not-for-profit organizations that between them represent over 110 major U.S. science journals. The background statement accompanying the statement of principles makes interesting reading for anyone who has doubts about the direction of scholarly publishing or of the growing significance of online journals:

> Since 1995, more than 100 society and university not-for-profit publishers have been working with Stanford University's HighWire Press to transform traditional print journals into enduring and dynamic online journals. These publishers have invested millions of dollars in online technology for information presentation, distribution, and management; created unique and powerful online services for the education and convenience of scientists; initiated some of the largest and most influential experiments in online-only publishing; led the charge in making information free to people who cannot afford to pay for it; and developed state-of-the-art software to support authors, reviewers, and editors. By effectively harnessing new technologies, these not-for-profit society and university publishers have promoted the

wider dissemination of scientific information as well as free and unfettered access to journal content for both the scientific community and the public. In so doing, these not-for-profit publishers have become leaders in the online revolution for scientific publishing. Through these not-for-profit publishers, the scientific community and the public have easy online access to over 1.6 million articles of which more than 600,000 full-text articles are free. In addition, access is provided to the abstracts of more than 12.6 million articles in more than 4,500 Medline journals, as well as useful alerting and information management tools. The experiments that have been conducted since 1995 and that are ongoing have only been possible because these not-for-profit publishers have been successfully adapting their proven business models to the online environment. As a result, these society and university press journals remain high impact and well-respected custodians of the scientific literature. Through numerous organizations that serve the entire scholarly publishing community, not-for-profit publishers have freely shared their ideas and innovations, with the common goal of improving the dissemination of vital scientific and medical information throughout the world.

Let us mention just two further initiatives that signal futures directions. First, an example called the Public Library of Science.[20]

The Public Library of Science (PLoS) is a nonprofit organization of scientists and physicians committed to making the world's scientific and medical literature a public resource.
Our goals are to:
- Open the doors to the world's library of scientific knowledge by giving any scientist, physician, patient, or student—anywhere in the world—unlimited access to the latest scientific research.
- Facilitate research, informed medical practice, and education by making it possible to freely search the full text of every published article to locate specific ideas, methods, experimental results, and observations.
- Enable scientists, librarians, publishers, and entrepreneurs to develop innovative ways to explore and use the world's treasury of scientific ideas and discoveries.

PloS provides also a statement of principles and a timeline of international policy on open access beginning in 2002. HighWire Press, self-advertised as the earth's largest full-text science archives, is also an impressive venture.[21]

The other example we want to mention is MIT's OpenCourseWare,[22] which is described as:

a free and open educational resource for faculty, students, and self-learners around the world. OCW supports MIT's mission to advance knowledge and education, and serve the world in the twenty-first century. It is true to MIT's values of excellence, innovation, and leadership.

MIT's OpenCourseWare is not restricted to "science" but rather encompasses the full curriculum in HE.

Free science could easily be construed also as "*public* knowledge." This would require an argument to show the intimate relationship between "free" and "public" in both a philosophical and legal sense. The link here may well depend upon the notion of the "commons." This is certainly the way in which some organizations interpret it—such as the Creative Commons,[23] which offers protections and freedoms for authors and artists, and Public Knowledge,[24] which advertises itself as "a group of lawyers, technologists, lobbyists, academics, volunteers and activists dedicated to defending and fortifying a vibrant information commons." In this account "public knowledge" is a catalyst and wellspring for creativity and innovation and a source of economic value. In this case the choices confronting us about knowledge futures are choices about the framework for intellectual property determining scientific development, artistic production, and scientific research.

Free science and public knowledge are not exhausted by the concepts of open source or open access, although such movements might enhance them. The notion of freedom here needs much more careful treatment in philosophical, economic, legal, and political terms. Ultimately, "free science" does not simply refer to copyright or intellectual property rights but indirectly refers to the tangled history of the concept as it developed in relation to the freedom of thought and speech, and to the modern concept which entails the rights of speech and petition (especially in governing bodies), the right to relate and publish, freedom of public meetings, and the freedom of correspondence, teaching, and publishing. Conversely, it also refers to the abuses of freedom of speech, including libel, slander, obscenity, blasphemy, and sedition. These freedoms and rights are the necessary (but not sufficient) condition for the development of knowledge cultures that might prevent the movement toward the individualization, ownership, and privatization of knowledge in the twenty-first century.

REFERENCES

Castells, M. 2004. Afterword: Why networks matter. In McCarthy et al. (2004), 221–25.

NOTES

1. See www.mala.bc.ca/~johnstoi/Nietzsche/history.htm (accessed December 13, 2005).

2. See the GNU project at www.gnu.org/gnu/thegnuproject.html and Stallman's homepage at www.stallman.org/.

3. For statements relating to GNU philosophy see www.gnu.org/philosophy/.

4. See www.gnu.org/gnu/manifesto.html.

5. Wikipedia provides the following explantion and set of links: "*Copyleft* describes a group of licenses applied to works such as software, documents, and art. Where copyright law is seen by the original proponents of copyleft as a way to restrict the right to make and redistribute copies of a particular work, a copyleft license uses copyright law in order to ensure that every person who receives a copy or derived version of a work can use, modify, and also redistribute both the work, and derived versions of the work. Thus, in a non-legal sense, copyleft is the opposite of copyright." See en.wikipedia.org/wiki/Copyleft. For a useful account of Stallman see Sam Williams' (2002) *Richard Stallman's Crusade for Free Software* at www.oreilly.com/openbook/freedom/.

6. See www.opensource.org/docs/definition.php.

7. See www.opensource.org/index.php.

8. The following are listed: "Todd Anderson, Chris Peterson (of the Foresight Institute), John 'maddog' Hall and Larry Augustin (both of Linux International), Sam Ockman (of the Silicon Valley Linux User's Group), and Eric Raymond."

9. See www.earlham.edu/~peters/fos/fosblog.html.

10. See www.earlham.edu/~peters/fos/overview.htm.

11. See www.nova.edu/~aed/newhorizons.html and psycprints.ecs.soton .ac.uk/.

12. See www.cios.org/www/ejcmain.htm, jefferson.village.virginia.edu/ pmc/contents.all.html and ccat.sas.upenn.edu/bmcr/.

13. Let me mention in particular Education Policy Analysis Archives at epaa.asu.edu/ established in 1993 by Gene Glass.

14. See www.doaj.org/.

15. www.worldagroforestry.org/sites/rsu/datamanagement/documents/ Session7/BromleyPrinciples.asp.

16. See www.arl.org/scomm/symp2/Foreword.html.

17. See www.arl.org/scomm/symp2/ODonnell.html.

18. See www.publications.parliament.uk/pa/cm200304/cmselect/cmsctech/ 399/39902.htm.

19. This report is best read in conjunction with other reports issued by the committee, including: *Strategic Science Provision in English Universities, The Work of Research Councils UK, The Use of Science in UK International Development Policy.* In the government's response to the report it is clear that DTI sought to neutralize views put forward in the report and decided against the author-pays model.

20. See www.plos.org/.

21. See highwire.stanford.edu/lists/largest.dtl.

22. See ocw.mit.edu/OcwWeb/.

23. See creativecommons.org/.

24. See www.publicknowledge.org/about.

Appendix 1

Two Contrasting Systems: Characterization of Major Processes

Nature of	Organicist	Mechanist
Capitalism	cyclical	crisis ridden
	progressive	destructive
	wealth enhancing	dysfunctional
	inequality generating	inequality generating
	poverty reducing	poverty enhancing
	competitive	monopolistic/oligopolistic
Society	self-organizing	planned, designed
	spontaneous order (Hayek)	controllable
	dialectical (Marx)	equilibrating
State	external	internal
	redundant	essential
	interfering	enabling
	superstructural	pivotal
Market	search/signaling	resource allocation
	dynamic uncertainty	efficient (Chicago) vs. prone to failure (Harvard/MIT)/static
	innovation/discovery	equilibrium/stationary

Source: Desai (2002).

197

References

Abramowitz, M. 1956. Resource and Output Trends in the United States since 1870. *American Economic Review* 46(2): 5–23.

Abramowitz, M., and P. David. 1996. Technological change and the rise of intangible investments: The US economy's growth path in the twentieth century. In *Employment and Growth in the Knowledge-based Economy*. Paris: OECD.

Aghion, P., and P. Howitt. 1998. *Endogenous growth theory*. Cambridge, MA: MIT Press.

Allen, B. 2004. *Knowledge and civilization*. Foreword by Richard Rorty. Boulder, CO: Westview Press.

Allen, J. 2002. Symbolic economies: The "culturalization" of economic knowledge. In *Cultural economy: Cultural analysis and commercial life*, ed. P. du Gay and M. Pryke, 30–58. London: Sage.

Amin, S. 1996. *Capitalism in the age of globalization: The management of contemporary society*. Atlantic Highlands, NJ: Zed Books.

Appadurai, A., ed. 2001. *Globalization*. Durham, NC: Duke University Press.

Argyris, C. 1999. *On organizational learning*. Malden, MA: Blackwell Business.

Argyris, C., and D. A. Schön. 1974. *Theory in practice : Increasing professional effectiveness*. San Francisco: Jossey-Bass.

———. 1978. *Organizational learning: A theory of action perspective*. Reading, MA: Addison-Wesley Publishing Company.

———. 1996. *Organizational learning*. Reading, MA: Addison-Wesley. (Orig. pub. 1978.)

Aristotle. 2000. *Nicomachean ethics*. Trans. and ed. Roger Crisp. Cambridge: Cambridge University Press.

Arrow, K. J. 1952. Mathematical models in the social sciences. Cowles Foundation Paper 48. Repr. from *The Policy Sciences*.

Austin, J. L. 1962. *How to Do Things with Words*. Ed. J. O. Urmson and Marina Sbisá. 2nd ed. Cambridge, Mass.: Harvard University Press.

Baeyer, H. C. von. 2004. *Information: The new language of science*. Cambridge, MA: Harvard University Press.

Barnes, B. 1977. *Interests and the growth of knowledge*. London: Routledge.

——. 1995. *The elements of social theory*. London: UCI Press.

Barro, R. J., and X. Sala-i-Martin. 1995. *Economic growth*. New York: McGraw-Hill.

Beck, U. 1992. *Risk society: Towards a new modernity*. London: Sage.

Beck, U., A. Giddens and S. Lash. 1994. *Reflexive Modernization: Politics, Tradition and Aesthetics in the Modern Social Order*. Cambridge: Polity Press.

Becker, G. S. 1964. *Human capital: A theoretical and empirical analysis, with special reference to education*. New York: National Bureau of Economic Research.

——. 1997. Interview with Prof. Gary Becker, Nobel Prize winner, Economics, 1992. Interview by Dr. E. C. Wit on Friday, October 3. galton.uchicago.edu/~wit/becker.txt (accessed November 10, 2005).

Bell, D. 1973. *The coming of post-industrial society: A venture in social forecasting*. New York: Basic Books.

Bello, W. 2001. *Future in the balance: Essays on globalization and resistance*. Oakland, CA: Food First Books.

Benhabib, J., and M. Spiegel. 1994. The role of human capital in economic development: Evidence from aggregate cross-country data. *Journal of Monetary Economics* 34 (2): 143–73.

Bereiter, C., M. Scardamalia, C. Cassells, and J. Hewitt. 1997. Postmodernism, knowledge building, and elementary science. *The Elementary School Journal* 97 (4): 329–41.

Berger, P. L., and T. Luckmann. 1966. *The social construction of reality: A treatise in the sociology of knowledge*. Garden City, NY: Anchor Books.

Blake, N., and P. Standish. 2000. *Enquiries at the interface: Philosophical problems of online education*. Oxford: Blackwell.

Bloomer, K. 2001 *Learning to Change: Scottish education in the early 21st century*, Scottish Council Foundation, at www.scottishcouncilfoundation.org/pg_learning.php

Bloor, D. 1976. *Knowledge and social imagery*. London: Routledge.

——. 2001. Wittgenstein and the priority of practice. In *The practice turn in contemporary theory*, ed. T. Schatzki, K. K. Cetiona, and E. von Savigny, 95–106. London: Routledge.

Bourdieu, P. 1977. *Outline of a theory of practice*. Trans. R. Nice. Cambridge: Cambridge University Press.

——. 1990. *The logic of practice*. Trans. R. Nice. Cambridge, UK: Polity.

——. 1998. *Practical reason: On the theory of action*. Stanford, CA: Stanford University Press.

Braun, H., and W. Klooss, eds. 1995. *Postmodernization? A comparative view of Canada and Europe*. Kiel: Verlag.

Braverman, H. 1974. *Labor and monopoly capital: The degradation of work in the twentieth century*. London: Monthly Review Press.

Brown, J. S., and P. Duguid. 1991. Organizational learning and communities-of-practice: Toward a unified view of working, learning, and innovation. www2.parc.com/ops/members/brown/papers/orglearning.html (accessed November 10, 2005).

——. 2002. *The social life of information*. Boston, MA: Harvard Business School Press.

Bruner, J. 1973. *Going beyond the information given*. New York: Norton.

———. 1990. *Acts of meaning*. Cambridge, MA: Harvard University Press.

———. 1996. The culture of education. Cambridge, MA: Harvard University Press.

Buchanan, J., and G. Tullock. 1962. *The calculus of consent? Logical foundations of constitutional democracy*. Ann Arbor: University of Michigan Press.

Burbules, N., and C. Torres, eds. 2000. *Globalization and education: Critical perspectives*. New York: Routledge.

Burton-Jones, A. 1999. *Knowledge capitalism: Business, work, and learning in the new economy*. Oxford: Oxford University Press.

Butler, J. 1990. *Gender trouble: Feminism and the subversion of identity*. New York: Routledge.

———. 1993. *Bodies that matter: On the discursive limits of "sex."* New York: Routledge.

Card, D., and A. Krueger. 1992. Does school quality matter? Returns to education and the characteristics of public schools in the United States. *Journal of Political Economy* 100:1–40.

Carlson, M. 1996. *Performance: A critical introduction*. London: Routledge.

Carnoy, M. 2000. *Globalization and educational restructuring*. Paris: International Institute of Educational Planning.

Carnoy, M. and D. Rhoten. 2002. What Does Globalization Mean for Education Change? A Comparative Approach. *Comparative Education Review* 46 (1): 1–9.

Castells, M. 1997. *The power of identity*. Oxford: Blackwell.

———. 1998. *End of millennium*. Oxford: Blackwell.

———. 2000a. Information technology and global capitalism. In *On the edge: Living with global capitalism*, ed. W. Hutton and A. Giddens, 52–74. London: Jonathan Cape.

———. 2000b. *The rise of the network society*. Oxford: Blackwell.

———. 2004 Afterword: Why networks matter. In *Network Logic Who governs in an interconnected world?* eds. H. McCarthy, P. Miller, P. Skidmore, Demos, at www.demos.co.uk/catalogue/networks/

Cavell, S. 1976. *Must we mean what we say? A book of essays*. Cambridge: Cambridge University Press.

———. 1979. *Claim of reason: Wittgenstein, skepticism, morality, and tragedy*. New York: Oxford University Press.

Chisholm, L. 1999. The transition to a knowledge society and its implications for the European social model. Discussion Paper 17, European Symposium on Science and Culture, Bruges, Belgium, September 30–October 1.

Clark, H. C. 1998. *Formal Knowledge Networks—A Study of the Canadian Experience*. International Institute for Sustainable Development.

Coffield, F. 1999. Breaking the consensus: Lifelong learning as social control. Inaugural lecture, University of Newcastle, Newcastle, UK.

———, ed. 1995. *Higher education in a learning society*. Durham, UK: University of Durham, School of Education.

———, ed. 2000. *Differing visions of a learning society: Research findings*. 2 vols. Bristol, UK: Economic and Social Resource Council.

Collins, H. 1990. *Artificial experts: Social knowledge and intelligent machines*. Cambridge, MA: MIT Press.

Cook, P. 2002. *Knowledge economies: Clusters, learning and cooperative advantage*. London: Routledge.

Cowan, J. 1998. Destino Colombia: A scenario planning process for the new millennium. *Deeper News* 9 (1): 7–31.

Cox, R. W. 1997. The global political economy and social choice. In *Approaches to world order*. Cambridge: Cambridge University Press.

Cox, T. 1993. *Cultural diversity in organizations.* San Francisco, CA: Berrett-Koehler.

Coyle, D., and D. Quah. 2002. *Getting the measure of the new economy.* London: Work Foundation.

Crary, A., and R. Read, eds. 2000. *The new Wittgenstein.* London: Routledge.

Crook, S., J. Pakulski, and M. Waters. 1992. *Postmodernization: Change in advanced society.* London: Sage.

Cross, K. F., J. J. Feather, and R. L. Lynch. 1994. *Corporate renaissance: The art of reengineering.* Oxford: Blackwell.

Cukor, P., and L. W. McKnight. 2001. Knowledge networks, the internet, and development. *Fletcher Forum of World Affairs* 25 (1): 43–58.

Cullen, J., K. Hadjivassiliou, E. Hamilton, J. Keheller, E. Sommerlad, and E. Stern. 2002. *Review of current pedagogic research and practice in the fields of post-compulsory education and lifelong learning.* British Economic and Social Research Council, Teaching and Learning Research Programme, Phase III—Emerging Themes. www.tlrp.org/pub/acadpub/Tavistockreport.pdf (accessed November 10, 2005).

Cullenberg, S., J. Amariglio and D. Ruccio, eds. 2001. *Postmodernism, Economics and Knowledge.* London: Routledge.

Cunningham, S., Y. Ryan, L. Stedman, S. Tapsall, K. Bagdan, T. Flew, and P. Coaldrake. 2000. *The business of borderless education.* Evaluations and Investigations Programme, Higher Education Division, Department of Education, Training and Youth Affairs, Commonwealth of Australia. www.dest.gov.au/archive/highered/eippubs/eip00_3/bbe.pdf (accessed November 10, 2005).

Dahlman, C., and J.-E. Aubert. 2001. *China and the knowledge economy: Seizing the 21st century.* Washington, DC: World Bank.

Dalum B., B. Johnson and B. A. Lundvall. 1992 Public Policy in the Learning Economy. In *National Systems of Innovation*, Lundval B. A. Pinter, London.

Dearing, R. 1997 The National Committee of Inquiry into Higher Education (known as the Dearing Report), at http://www.leeds.ac.uk/educol/ncihe/

Delanty, G. 1998. *Challenging knowledge: The university in the knowledge society.* Buckingham, UK: Open University Press.

Department of Trade and Industry, UK. 1998a. *Our competitive future: Building the knowledge-driven economy.* London: Cm4176. www.dti.gov.uk/comp/competitive/wh_int1.htm (accessed November 10, 2005).

———. 1998b. *Our competitive future: Building the knowledge-driven economy: Analytical background.* www.dti.gov.uk/comp/competitive/an_reprt.htm (accessed November 10, 2005).

Derrida, J. 1977. Signature event context. *Glyph* 1:172–97.

———. 1998. *Limited Inc.* Ed. Graff, trans. Weber. Evanston, IL: Northwestern University Press.

Desai, M. 2002. *Marx's revenge: The resurgence of capitalism and the death of statist socialism.* London: Verso.

Dirlik and Zhang, eds., 2000. *Postmodernism and China.* Durham: Duke University Press.

DiZerega, G. 1989. Democracy as spontaneous order. *Critical Review*, Spring, 206–40.

Dreyfus, H. 1993. Heidegger on the connection between nihilism, art, technology, and politics. In *The Cambridge companion to Heidegger*, ed. C. Guignon, 289–316. Cambridge: Cambridge University Press.

Drucker, P. 1969. *The Age of Discontinuity: Guidelines to Our Changing Society*. New York: Harper & Row.

———. 1993. *Post-capitalist society*. New York: Harper.

———. 1998. From capitalism to knowledge society. In *The knowledge economy*, ed. D. Neef. Woburn, MA: Butterworth.

Dunne, J. 2001. *Back to the rough ground: "Phronesis" and "techne" in modern philosophy and in Aristotle*. South Bend, IN: University of Notre Dame Press.

Economist. Fast publishing: A book in a day. December 20, 2003: 116–17.

Ernest, P. 1998. *Social constructivism as a philosophy of mathematics*. Albany, NY: SUNY Press.

———. 1999. Social constructivism as a philosophy of mathematics: Radical constructivism rehabilitated? www.ex.ac.uk/~PErnest/soccon.htm (November 10, 2005).

———. 2000. Why teach mathematics? In *Why learn maths?* ed. J. White and S. Bramall. London: London University Institute of Education. www.ex.ac.uk/~PErnest/why.htm (accessed November 10, 2005).

Escobar, A. 1995. *Encountering development: The making and unmaking of the third world*. Princeton, NJ: Princeton University Press.

———. 2003. Other worlds are (already) possible: Cyber internationalism and post-capitalist cultures. Draft notes for the Cyberspace Panel, Life after Capitalism Programme, World Social Forum, Porto Alegre, January 23–28, 2003. www.zmag.org/escobarcyner.htm (accessed November 10, 2005).

European Commission. 1995. *Teaching and learning: Towards the learning society*. http://europa.eu.int/en/record/white/edu9511 (accessed November 10, 2005).

———. 1999. The European House of Education—Education and Economy, a New Partnership. Working Document, SEC 796, May 21.

European Round Table of Industrialists. www.ert.be/ert_milestones_and_its_chairmen.html

Ferré, F. 1998. *Knowing and value: Toward a constructive postmodern epistemology*. New York: State University of New York.

Florida, R. 2002. *The rise of the creative class*. New York: Basic Books.

Foray, D., and B. Lundvall. 1996. The knowledge-based economy: From the economics of knowledge to the learning economy. In *Employment and growth in the knowledge-based economy*. Paris: OECD.

Foucault, M. 1978. La Philosophie analytique de la politique. In *Dits et écrits 1954–1988*, ed. Daniel Defert and François Ewart with Jacques Lagiange, 4 vols., 540–41. Paris.

———. 1991. *Remarks on Marx: Conversations with Duccio Trombadori*. Trans. R. J. Goldstein and J. Cascaito. New York: Semiotext(e).

Frank, A. G. 1969. *Capitalism and underdevelopment in Latin America*. New York: Monthly Review Press.

Freire, P. 1972. *Pedagogy of the oppressed*. Trans. Myra Bergman Ramos. Harmondsworth, UK: Penguin.

Friedman, M. 1962. *Capitalism and freedom*. Chicago: University of Chicago Press.

Gates, Bill. 2000. *Business @ the speed of thought: Succeeding in the digital economy*. New York: Time-Warner.

Gay, P. du, and M. Pryke, eds. 2002. *Cultural economy: Cultural analysis and commercial life*. London: Sage.

Gee, J. P., G. Hull, and C. Lankshear. 1996. *The new work order: Behind the language of the new capitalism*. St. Leonards, New South Wales: Allen & Unwin.

Gergen, K. 1985. The social constructionist movement in modern psychology. *American Psychologist* 40:266–75.

———. 1991. *The saturated self: Dilemmas of identity in contemporary life*. New York: Basic Books.

———. 2001. *Social construction in context*. London: Sage.

Gergen, K., and L. Warhus. 2001. Social construction and pedagogical practice. In *Social construction in context*, ed. K. Gergen. London: Sage.

Gibbons, M., et al. 1994. *The new production of knowledge: The dynamics of science and research in contemporary societies*. London: Sage.

Giddens, A. 1991. *Modernity and self-identity: Self and society in the late modern age*. Cambridge, UK: Polity Press.

———. 2000. *The third way and its critics*. Cambridge, UK: Polity Press.

Glasersfeld, E. von. 1989. Constructivism in education. In *International encyclopedia of education*, ed. T. Husen and N. Postlethwaite, supp. vol., 162–63. Oxford: Pergamon.

Goodman, N. 1978. *Ways of worldmaking*. Indianapolis, IN: Hackett.

Gorz, A. 1999. *Reclaiming work: Beyond the wage-based society*. Trans. C. Turner. Cambridge, UK: Polity.

Gregersen, B., and B. Johnson. 1997. Learning economies, innovation systems and European integration. *Regional Studies* 31 (5): 467–79.

Gross, P., and N. Levitt. 1998. *Higher superstition: The academic left and its quarrels with science*. Baltimore, MD: Johns Hopkins University Press.

Guardian. 2001. Prime minister's speech on public service reform. October 16. society.guardian.co.uk/futureforpublicservices/story/0,8150,575220,00.html.

Habermas, J. 1987. *The philosophical discourse of modernity: Twelve lectures*. Cambridge: MA: MIT Press.

Hacking, I. 1999. *Social construction of what?* Cambridge, MA: Harvard University Press.

Hall, H. 1993. Intentionality and world: Division I of *Being and Time*. In *The Cambridge companion to Heidegger*, ed. C. Guignon, 122–40. Cambridge: Cambridge University Press.

Handy, C. 1984. *The future of work: A guide to a changing society*. Oxford: Blackwell.

Hanley, S. 1994. On constructivism. Maryland Collaborative for Teacher Preparation, University of Maryland. www.inform.umd.edu/UMS+State/UMDProjects/MCTP/Essays/Constructivism.txt (accessed November 10, 2005).

Hardt, M., and A. Negri. 2001. *Empire*. Cambridge, MA: Harvard University Press. excess4all.com/empire/empire_original.pdf (accessed November 10, 2005).

Hargreaves, D. 2000. *Knowledge management in the learning society*. Centre for Educational Research and Innovation, OECD. Paris: OECD.

Harré, R. 1983. *Personal being: A theory of individual psychology*. Oxford: Blackwell.

———. 1986. The step to social constructionism. In *Children of social worlds*, ed. M. Richards and P. Light. Cambridge, MA: Polity Press.

Harré, R., and G. Gillet. 1994. *The discursive mind*. London: Sage.

Harrison, L. E., and S. P. Huntington. 2000. *Culture matters: How values shape human progress*. New York: Basic Books.

Harvey, D. 1989. *The condition of postmodernity*. Oxford: Blackwell.

Hayek, F. 1937. Economics and knowledge. *Economica* 4. www.virtualschool .edu/mon/Economics/HayekEconomicsAndKnowledge.html (accessed November 10, 2005).

———. 1945. The use of knowledge in society. *American Economic Review* 35 (4): 519–30. www.virtualschool.edu/mon/Economics/HayekUseOfKnowledge .html (accessed November 10, 2005).

Heidegger, M. 1991. *Nietzsche*. Trans. D. Krell. 4 vols. San Francisco: Harper.

Heims, S. J. 1991. *The cybernetic group*. Cambridge, MA: MIT Press.

Held, D. 1995. *Democracy and the global order: From the modern state to cosmopolitan governance*. Cambridge, UK: Polity Press.

Henderson, D. 1999. *The changing fortunes of economic liberalism: Yesterday, today and tomorrow*. Melbourne: Institute of Public Affairs.

Hicks, D. 1994. *Educating for the Future: A Practical Classroom Guide*. Worldwide Fund for Nature, UK: Godalming.

———. 2002. Postmodern education: A futures perspective. In *Advancing futures: Future studies in higher education*, ed. J. A. Dator, 321–30. Westport, CT: Praeger.

Hicks, D., and R. Slaughter. 1998. *Futures education: World yearbook of education 1998*. London: Kogan Page.

Hildreth, P., and C. Kimble. 2004. *Knowledge networks: Innovation through communities of practice*. London: Idea Group Publishing.

Houghton, J., and P. Sheehan. 2000. *A primer on the knowledge economy*. Centre for Strategic Economic Studies, Victoria University. www.enterweb.org/know.htm (accessed November 10, 2005).

Howie, D., and M. A. Peters. 1996. Positioning theory: Vygotsky, Wittgenstein, and social constructionist psychology. *Journal for the Theory of Social Behaviour* 26 (1): 51–64.

Inayatullah, S. 2002. Pedagogy, culture, and future studies. In *Advancing futures: Future studies in higher education*, ed. J. A. Dator, 109–22. Westport, CT: Praeger.

Information Technology Advisory Group, New Zealand. 1999. *The knowledge economy*. Ministry of Economic Development. www.med.govt.nz/pbt/infotech/ knowledge_economy (accessed November 10, 2005).

Inglehart, R. 1997. *Modernization and postmodernization: Cultural, economic, and political change in 43 societies*. Princeton, NJ: Princeton University Press.

Jameson, F. 1981. *The Political Unconscious*. New York: Cornell University Press.

Janik, A., and S. Toulmin. 1973. *Wittgenstein's Vienna*. New York: Simon & Schuster.

Jefferson, T. 1861. Letter to Isaac McPherson, August 13, 1813. In *The Writings of Thomas Jefferson*, ed. H. A. Washington. New York: H. W. Derby.

Jones, P. 1991. *Children, Families and Learning: A New Agenda for Education*. Scottish Council Foundation, at www.scottishcouncilfoundation.org/pubs_more .php?p=32

Kao, J. 1998. *Jamming: The art and discipline of business creativity*. New York: Harper-Business.

Krogh, G. von, K. Ichijo, and I. Nonaka. 2000. *Enabling knowledge creation: How to unlock the mystery of tacit knowledge and release the power of innovation*. Oxford: Oxford University Press.

Krugman, P. 1995. *Peddling prosperity: Economic sense and nonsense in an age of diminished expectations*. New York: Norton.

———. 2004. The fall and rise of development economics. www.wws .princeton.edu/~pkrugman/dishpan.html (accessed November 10, 2005).

Kuhn, T. 1962 *The structure of scientific revolutions*. Chicago: University of Chicago Press.

Lane, R. E. 1966. The decline of politics and ideology in a knowledgeable society. *American Sociological Review* 31 (5): 649–62.

Lash, S., and J. Urry. 1994. *Economies of signs and space*. London: Sage.

Lave, J., and E. Wenger. 1991. *Situated learning: Legitimate peripheral participation*. Cambridge: Cambridge University Press.

Leighton, D. 2003. Happy days? Freedom and security in a consumer society. *Renewal: A Journal of Labour Politics* 11 (2). www.renewal.org.uk/issues/2003 _Volume_11/Summer%202003%20Volume_11_2/Editorial.htm (accessed November 10, 2005).

Lessig, L. 2001. *The future of ideas: The fate of the commons in a connected world*. New York: Random House.

Lucas, R. E., Jr. 1988. On the mechanics of economic development. *Journal of Monetary Economics* 22 (1): 3–42.

Lundvall, B.-Å., and D. Foray. 1996. The knowledge-based economy: From the economics of knowledge to the learning economy. In *Employment and growth in the knowledge-based economy*. Paris: OECD.

Lundvall, B.-Å and B. Johnson. 1994. The learning economy. *Journal of Industry Studies* 1, no. 2:23–42.

Lyotard, J.-F. 1984. *The postmodern condition: A report on knowledge*. Trans. G. Bennington and B. Massumi. Minneapolis: University of Minnesota.

———. 1992. *The postmodern explained to children*. Sydney: Poir Press.

Machlup, F. 1962. *The production and distribution of knowledge in the United States*. Princeton, NJ: Princeton University Press.

———. 1970. *Education and economic growth*. Lincoln: University of Nebraska Press.

———. 1980. *Knowledge and knowledge production*. Princeton, NJ: Princeton University Press.

Mandle, J. 2003. *Globalization and the poor*. Cambridge: Cambridge University Press.

Mankiw, N. G., D. Romer, and D. N. Weil. 1992. A contribution to the empirics of economic growth. *Quarterly Journal of Economics* 107 (1992): 407–37.

Mannheim, K. 1952. *Essays in the sociology of knowledge*. London: Routledge and Kegan Paul.

Mansell, R., R. Samarajiva, and A. Mahan. 2002. *Networking knowledge for information societies: Institutions and intervention*. Delft, the Netherlands: Delft University Press.

Marginson, S. 1993. *Education and public policy in Australia*. Cambridge: Cambridge University Press.

Marschak, J. 1960. Remarks on the economics of information. Cowles Foundation Paper 146. Repr. from *Contributions to scientific research in management*. Berkeley: University of California.

Marx, K. 1963. The eighteenth Brumaire of Louis Bonaparte. In *Marx and Engels: Basic writings on politics and philosophy*, ed. L. S. Feuer. New York: Anchor.

———. 1969. Theses on Feuerbach. In *Marx and Engels: Basic writings on politics and philosophy*, ed L. S. Feuer. New York: Anchor.

———. 1974. *The German ideology*, ed. C. J. Arthur. London: Lawrence & Wishart.

Masuda, Y. 1981. *Information society as post-industrial society*. Bethesda, MD: World Future Society.

Mattessich, R. 1993. On the nature of information and knowledge and the interpretation in the economic sciences. *Library Trends* 41 (4): 567–74.

Matthews, M. 2003. Teaching science. In *A companion to the philosophy of education*, ed. R. Curren, 342–53. Oxford: Blackwell.

McCarthy, E. D. 1996. *Knowledge as culture: The new sociology of knowledge*. London: Routledge.

McCarthy, H., P. Miller and P. Skidmore, eds. 2004. *Network Logic Who governs in an interconnected world?* Demos, at http://www.demos.co.uk/catalogue/networks/

McKenzie, J. 2001a. Performance and global transference. *Drama Review* 45 (3): 5–7.

———. 2001b. *Perform or else: From discipline to performance*. London: Routledge.

———. 2003. Soft wares and hard truths: Performance, globalization and affective networks. *Dokkyo International Review* 16:7–26. Abstract at www.dokkyo.ac.jp/kokuse/symposium/performance2002/English-abstract-jon_mckenzie (accessed November 10, 2005).

McSherry, C. 2001. *Who owns academic work? Battling for control of intellectual property*. Cambridge, MA: Harvard University Press.

Miller, G. A., and P. N. Johnson-Laird. 1976. *Language and perception*. Cambridge, MA: Harvard University Press.

Ministry of Research, Science and Technology (MoRST), New Zealand. 1998. *Building tomorrow's success: Guidelines for thinking beyond today*. The Foresight Project, MoRST, Wellington. www.morst.govt.nz/uploadedfiles/Documents/Publications/policy%20discussions/success.pdf (accessed November 10, 2005).

Mishra, R. 1999. *Globalization and the welfare state*. Cheltenham, UK: Edward Elgar.

Morss, J. 1996. *Growing critically: Alternatives to developmental psychology*. London: Routledge.

Needham, C. 2003. *Citizen-consumers: New labour's marketplace democracy*. London: Catalyst.

NERF. 2001. *A Research and Development Strategy for Education: Developing Quality and Diversity*. London: NERF

Nietzsche, F. 1974. *The gay science*. Trans. W. Kaufmann. New York: Vintage.

Noble, D. 2001. *Digital diploma mills: The automation of higher education*. New York: Monthly Review Press.

Nyiri, J. C. 1982. Wittgenstein's later work in relation to conservatism. In *Wittgenstein and his times*, ed. B. McGuinness, 44–68. Oxford: Blackwell.

OECD. 1996a. *Employment and growth in the knowledge-based economy*. Paris: OECD.

———. 1996b. *The knowledge-based economy*. Paris: OECD.

———. 1996c. *Measuring what people know: Human capital accounting for the knowledge economy*. Paris: OECD.

———. 1997. *Industrial competitiveness in the knowledge-based economy: The new role of governments*. OECD Conference Proceedings. Paris: OECD.

———. 1999. *The knowledge-based economy: A set of facts and figures*. Paris: OECD.

———. 2001. *The New Economy: Beyond the Hype*. Paris: OECD.

Papadopoulos, G. 1994. *Education 1960–1990: The OECD perspective*. Paris: OECD.

Parker, M. A., and D. Jary. 1995. The McUniversity: Organization, management and academic subjectivity. *Organization* 2:319–37.

Peters, M. A., ed. 1995. *Education and the postmodern condition*. Westport, CT: Bergin and Garvey.

———. 1996. *Poststructuralism, politics and education*. Westport, CT: Bergin and Garvey.

———, ed. 1999. *After the disciplines: The emergence of cultural studies*. Westport, CT: Bergin & Garvey.

———. 2000a. Orthos logos, recta ratio: Pope John Paul II, nihilism and postmodern philosophy. *Journal for Christian Theological Research* 5. http://home.apu .edu/~CTRF/jctr.html.

———. 2000b. *Pós-estruturalismo e filosofia da diferença Uma introdução* [Poststructuralism and the Philosophy of Difference: An Introduction]. Trans. into Portuguese by Tomaz Tadeu da Silva. Belo Horizonte, Brazil: Autêntica Editora.

———. 2001a. Lyotard and philosophy of education. *Encyclopaedia of Philosophy of Education*. www.vusst.hr/ENCYCLOPAEDIA/lyotard.htm (accessed November 10, 2005).

———. 2001b. National education policy constructions of the "knowledge economy": Towards a critique. *Journal of Educational Enquiry* 2 (1): 58–71. www.literacy .unisa.edu.au/jee/Papers/JEEVol2No2/200144.pdf (accessed November 10, 2005).

———. 2001c. *Poststructuralism, Marxism and neoliberalism: Between politics and theory*. Lanham, MD: Rowman & Littlefield.

———. 2001d. Wittgensteinian pedagogics: Cavell on the figure of the child in the Investigations. *Studies in Philosophy and Education* 20:125–38.

———. 2001e. Humanism, Derrida, and the new humanities. In *Derrida and Education*, ed. G. Biesta and D. Egea-Kuehne, 209–31. London: Routledge.

———. 2001f. Politics and deconstruction: Derrida, neo-liberalism and democracy to come. In *Derrida Downunder*, ed. L. Simons and H. Worth, 145–63. Palmerston North: Dunmore Press.

———. 2002a. Anti-globalization and Guattari's *The Three Ecologies*. *Globalization* 2 (1). globalization.icaap.org/content/v2.1/02_peters.html (accessed November 10, 2005).

———. 2002b. Education policy in the age of knowledge capitalism. Keynote address to the World Comparative Education Forum, Economic Globalization and Education Reforms, Beijing Normal University, October 14–16. *Policy Futures in Education* 1 (2): 361–80.

———. 2002c. Globalisation and the knowledge economy: Implications for education policy. *Common Ground*. MichaelPeters.Author-Site.com (accessed November 10, 2005).

———, ed. 2002d. *Heidegger, education and modernity*. Lanham, MD: Rowman & Littlefield.

———. 2002e. New Zealand as the "Knowledge Society": Universities, the Foresight Project and the Tertiary White Paper. *Leading and Managing* 6 (2): 16–32.

———. 2002f. Universities, globalisation and the knowledge economy. *Southern Review* 35 (2): 16–36.

———. 2002g. The university in the knowledge economy. In *Scholars and entrepreneurs: The universities in crisis*, ed. S. Cooper, J. Hinkson, and G. Sharp, 137–52. Melbourne: Arena Publications.

———. 2002h. Wittgenstein, education and the philosophy of mathematics. *Theory and Science* 3 (3). theoryandscience.icaap.org/content/vol003.002/peters.html (accessed November 10, 2005).

———. 2003a. *Building knowledge cultures: Education in an age of knowledge capitalism.* Lanham, MD: Rowman & Littlefield.

———. 2003b. Education and ideologies of the knowledge economy: Europe and the politics of emulation. Paper presented at the University of Leuven. Social Work & Society 2 (2): 160–72. www.socwork.de/Peters2004.pdf (accessed November 10, 2005).

———. 2003c. Poststructuralism and Marxism: Education as knowledge capitalism. *Journal of Education Policy* 18 (2): 115–30.

———. 2003d. Theorising educational practices: The politico-ethical choices. In *Beyond empiricism: On criteria for educational research*, ed. P. Smeyers and M. Depaepe. Leuven, Belgium: University Press.

Peters, M. A., and S. Appel. 1996. Positioning theory: Discourse, the subject and the problem of desire. *Social Analysis* 40 (September): 120–45.

Peters, M. A., and N. Burbules. 2002. Wittgenstein/styles/pedagogy. *Theory & Science* 3 (1). theoryandscience.icaap.org/content/vol003.001/peters.html (accessed November 10, 2005).

Peters, M. A., and J. D. Marshall. 1999. *Wittgenstein: Philosophy, postmodernism, pedagogy.* Westport, CT: Bergin & Garvey.

———. 2002. Reading Wittgenstein: The rehearsal of prejudice. *Studies in Philosophy and Education* 21 (3): 263–71.

Peters, M. A., J. D. Marshall, and P. Smeyers, eds. 2000. *Nietzsche's legacy for education: Past and present values.* Westport, CT: Bergin & Garvey.

———, eds. 2001. *Past and present values: Nietzsche's Legacy for Education.* Westport, CT: Bergin & Garvey.

Peters, M. A. and P. J. Ghiraldelli, eds. 2001. *Richard Rorty: Education, Philosophy and Politics.* Lanham, MD: Rowman & Littlefield.

Peters, M. A., and P. Roberts, eds. 1998. *Virtual technologies and tertiary education.* Palmerston North, New Zealand: Dunmore Press.

———. 1999. *University futures and the politics of reform.* Palmerston North, New Zealand: Dunmore Press.

Phillips, D. C. 1995. The Good, the Bad and the Ugly: The Many Faces of Constructivism. *Educational Researcher* 24 (7): 5–12.

———, ed. 2000. Constructivism in education: Opinions and second opinions on controversial issues. In *99th Yearbook of the National Society for the Study of Education.* Chicago: University of Chicago Press.

———. 2003. Theories of teaching and learning. In *A companion to the philosophy of education*, ed. R. Curren, 232–45. Oxford: Blackwell.

Pieterse, J., ed. 2000. *Global futures: Shaping globalization.* London: Zed Books.

Pinch, T. 1986. *Confronting nature: The sociology of solar-neutrino detection.* Dordrecht, the Netherlands: Reidel.

Polanyi, M. 1958. *Personal knowledge: Towards a post-critical philosophy.* London: Routledge & Kegan Paul.

———. 1967. *The tacit dimension*. London: Routledge and Kegan Paul.

Popper, K. 1968. *The logic of scientific discovery*. London: Hutchinson.

Porter, M. 1990. *The competitive advantage of nations*. New York: Free Press.

Probert, S. K. 2003 Knowledge management: A critical investigation, *Electronic Journal of Business Research Methods*, http://www.ejbrm.com/vol2/v2-i1/issue 1-art6-probert.pdf

Putnam, H. 2002. *The collapse of the fact/value distinction and other essays*. Cambridge, MA: Harvard University Press.

Quah, D. T. 1998. A weightless economy: The knowledge economy; When ideas are capital. *UNESCO Courier*, December: 18–21.

———. 2001. Demand-driven knowledge clusters in a weightless economy. econ.lse.ac.uk/staff/dquah/p/0104dkc.pdf (accessed November 10, 2005).

———. 2003a. Digital goods and the new economy. CEP Discussion Paper 563, March 2003, Technology and Growth. In *New Economy Handbook*, ed. Derek Jones, 289–321. San Diego: Academic Press. econ.lse.ac.uk/staff/dquah/dp-0212hbne.html (accessed November 10, 2005).

———. 2003b. The weightless economy: Can people eat 1s and 0s? econ.lse.ac.uk/staff/dquah/tweirl0.html (accessed November 10, 2005).

Rifkin, J. 1998. A civil education for the twenty-first century: Preparing students for a three-sector society. *National Civic Review* 87 (2): 177–82.

Ritzer, G. 1994. McDonaldization is not an all-or-nothing process: A response to the critics. *Sociale Wetenschappen*, 4:75–76.

———. 1999. Assessing the resistance. In *Resisting McDonaldization*, ed. Barry Smart. London: Sage.

———. 2000. *The McDonaldization of society*. New century edition. Thousand Oaks, CA: Pine Forge Press.

Romer, P. M. 1986. Increasing returns and long-run growth. *Journal of Political Economy* 94 (5): 1002–37.

———. 1990. Endogenous technological change. *Journal of Political Economy* 98 (5): 71–102.

———. 1991. Increasing returns and new development in the theory of growth. In *Equilibrium Theory and Applications: Proceedings of the Sixth International Symposium in Economic Theory and Econometrics*, ed. W. Barnett et al. Cambridge: Cambridge University Press.

———. 1994. The origins of endogamous growth. *The Journal of Economic Perspectives* 8:3–22.

Rorty, R., ed. 1967. *The linguistic turn*. 2nd, enlarged ed. Chicago: University of Chicago Press, 1992.

———. 1993. Wittgenstein, Heidegger, and the reification of language. In *The Cambridge companion to Heidegger*, ed. C. Guignon, 337–57. Cambridge: Cambridge University Press.

———. 1999. Phony science wars. *Atlantic Monthly Online*, November.

Rostow, W. W. 1960. *The stages of economic growth: A non-communist manifesto*. Cambridge: Cambridge University Press.

Rowan, L., and C. Bigum. 1997. The future of technology and literacy teaching in primary learning situations and contexts. In *Digital rhetorics: Literacies and technologies in education—current practices and future directions*, ed. C. Lankshear, C. Bigum, C. Durrant, B. Green, E. Honan, J. Murray, W. Morgan, I. Snyder, and M.

Wild, vol. 3. Canberra, Australia: Department of Education, Training and Youth Affairs.

Ruccio, D. and J. Amariglio. 2003. *Postmodern Moments in Modern Economics.* Princeton: Princeton University Press.

Rutkowski, A. 2000. Understanding the next generation Internet: An overview of developments. *Telecommunications Policy Online.* www.tpeditor.com/contents/2000/rutkowski.htm.

Sartre, J.-P. 1946. *Existentialism and humanism.* Trans. Philip Mairet. Repr., Brooklyn, NY: Haskell House, 1977. www.marxists.org/reference/archive/sartre/works/exist/sartre.htm (accessed November 10, 2005).

Schatzki, T. 2001. Introduction: Practice theory. In *The practice turn in contemporary theory,* ed. T. Schatzki, K. K. Cetiona, and E. von Savigny, 1–14. London: Routledge.

Schectner, R. 2000. Performance as a "formation of power and knowledge." *The Drama Review* 44 (4): 5–7.

Schlosser, E. 2002. *Fast food nation.* New York: Perennial.

Schön, D. A. 1987. *Educating the reflective practitioner: Toward a new design for teaching and learning in the professions.* San Francisco: Jossey-Bass.

——. 1983. *The Reflective Practitioner.* New York: Basic Books

——. 1995. *The reflective practitioner: How professionals think in action.* Aldershot, England: Arena. (Orig. pub. New York: Basic Books, 1983.)

Schultz, Theodore. 1963. *The Economic Value of Education.* New York: Columbia University Press.

Schütz, A. 1972. *The phenomenology of the social world.* Trans. G. Walsh and F. Lehnert. London: Heinemann Educational.

Schwartz, P. 1991. *The art of the long view.* New York: Doubleday.

Scottish Office. 1999. *Targeting excellence: Modernising Scotland's schools.* www.scotland.gov.uk/library/documents-w6/edsp-00.htm (accessed November 10, 2005).

Sen, A. 1999. *Development as freedom.* Oxford: Oxford University Press.

Sharp, J. 1997. Communities of practice: A review of the literature. www.tfriend.com/cop-lit.htm (accessed November 10, 2005).

Sheenan, T. 1993. Reading a life: Heidegger and hard times. In *The Cambridge companion to Heidegger,* ed. C. Guignon, 70–96. Cambridge: Cambridge University Press.

Shotter, J. 1993. Harré, Vygotsky, Bakhtin, Vico, Wittgenstein: Academic discourses and conversational realities. *Journal for the Theory of Social Behaviour* 23:459–82.

Slaughter, R. 1992. Futures studies and higher education. Special issue, *Futures Research Quarterly* 8 (4).

——. 1996. *The knowledge bases of futures studies.* 3 vols. Hawthorn, Australia: DDM Media Group.

——. 2002. Futures studies as an intellectual and applied discipline. In *Advancing futures: Future studies in higher education,* ed. J. A. Dator, 91–108. Westport, CT: Praeger.

Slezak, P. 2000. A critique of radical social constructivism. In *Constructivism in education: Opinions and second opinions on controversial issues,* ed. D. C. Phillips, 91–126. hps.arts.unsw.edu.au/hps_content/staff_homepages/p_slezak_site/Article%20Links/2000/Slezak_SocCon_2000.pdf (accessed November 10, 2005).

Smeyers, P., and M. Depaepe, eds. 2003. *Beyond empiricism: On criteria of educational research*. Leuven: University of Leuven Press.

Smith, K. 2002. What is the "knowledge economy"? Knowledge intensity and distributed knowledge bases. United Nations University, Institute for New Technologies. www.intech.unu.edu/publications/discussion-papers/2002-6.pdf (accessed November 10, 2005).

Sokal, A., and J. Bricmont. 1998. *Intellectual impostures: Postmodern philosophers' abuse of science*. London: Profile Books.

Solow, R. 1956. A contribution to the theory of economic growth. *Quarterly Journal of Economics* 70:65–94.

——. 1994. Perspectives on growth theory. *Journal of Economic Perspectives* 8:45–54.

——. 2000. *Growth theory: An exposition*. Oxford: Oxford University Press.

Stehr, N. 1994. *Knowledge societies*. London: Sage.

Stern, D. 2000. Practices, practical holism and background practices. In *Heidegger, coping and cognitive science: Essays in honor of Hubert L. Dreyfus*, ed. M. Wrathall and J. Malpas, vol. 2. Cambridge, MA: MIT Press.

Stigler, G. 1961. The economics of information. *Journal of Political Economy* 59 (3): 213–25.

Stiglitz, J. 1998a. Knowledge for development: Economic science, economic policy and economic advice. Address to the World Bank's Tenth Annual Bank Conference on Development Economics (ABCDE), Washington, DC, April 20. www.worldbank.org/html/rad/abcde/stiglitz.pdf (accessed November 10, 2005).

——. 1998b. Towards a new paradigm for development: Strategies, policies, and processes. Prebisch Lecture at UNCTAD. www.worldbank.org/html/extdr/extme/prebisch98.pdf (accessed November 10, 2005).

——. 1999a. Knowledge as a global public good. World Bank. www.world bank.org/knowledge/chiefecon/articles/undpk2/index.htm (accessed November 10, 2005).

——. 1999b. On liberty, the right to know, and public discourse: The role of transparency in public life. Oxford Amnesty Lecture, Oxford, UK, January 27. www2.gsb.columbia.edu/faculty/jstiglitz/download/2001_On_Liberty_the_Right_to_Know_and_Public.pdf (accessed November 10, 2005).

——. 1999c. Public policy for a knowledge economy. Remarks at the Department for Trade and Industry and Center for Economic Policy Research, London, January 27. www.worldbank.org/html/extdr/extme/knowledge-economy.pdf (accessed November 10, 2005).

 ——. 2002. *Globalization and its discontents*. London: Allen Lane.

Thompson, P. 1989. *The nature of work*. 2nd ed. London: Macmillan.

Thrift, N. 2002. Performing cultures in the new economy. In *Cultural economy: Cultural analysis and commercial life*, ed. P. du Gay and M. Pryke, 201–34. London: Sage.

Thurow, L. 1996. *The future of capitalism: How today's economic forces shape tomorrow's world*. London: Nicholas Breasley.

Tiihonen, P. 2000. Committee for the future: Action plan for the years 1999–2003. *International Journal of Futures Studies*, 4.

Toffler, A. 1972. *The futurists*. New York: Random House.

Touraine, A. 1974. *The post-industrial society: Tomorrow's social history, classes, conflicts and culture in the programmed society.* Trans. L. Mayhew. London: Wildwood House.

Trifonas, P., and M. A. Peters. 2003. *Derrida and education.* Oxford: Blackwell.

Turner, S. 1994. *The social theory of practices: Tradition, tacit knowledge, and presuppositions.* Chicago: University of Chicago Press.

Tweeten, L. and C. Zulauf. 1999 The Challenge of Postmodernism to Applied Economics, *American Journal of Agricultural Economics* 81 (5):116–22.

Vaidhyanathan, S. 2001. *Copyrights and copywrongs: The rise of intellectual property and how it threatens creativity.* New York: New York University Press.

van der Heijden, K. 1996. *Scenarios: The art of strategic conversation.* Chichester, UK: Wiley.

Van Manen, M. 1995. On the epistemology of reflective practice. *Teachers and Teaching: Theory and Practice* 1 (1): 33–50.

———. 1999. The practice of practice. In *Changing schools/changing practices: Perspectives on educational reform and teacher professionalism,* ed. M. Lange, J. Olson, H. Hansen, and W. Bünder. Luvain, Belgium: Garant.

Vattimo, G. 1991. *The end of modernity: Nihilism and hermeneutics in post-modern culture.* Trans. Jon Snyder. Cambridge, UK: Polity Press.

Virilio, P. 1985. *Speed and politics.* New York: Semiotexte Foreign Agent Series.

Wack, P. 1985a. The gentle art of reperceiving. *Harvard Business Review,* September–October, 73–89.

———. 1985b. Scenarios: Shooting the rapids. *Harvard Business Review,* November–December, 139–50.

Walberg, H. J., and S. J. Paik. 2000. *Effective educational practices.* Geneva: IBE/UNESCO.

Walkerdine, V. 1984. Developmental psychology and child-centered pedagogy. In *Changing the subject: Psychology, social regulation and subjectivity,* ed. J. Henriques, W. Hollway, C. Urwin, C. Venn, and V. Walkerdine. London: Methuen.

Wallerstein, I. 1979. *The capitalist world economy.* Cambridge: Cambridge University Press.

Walsh, V. 1996. *Rationality, Allocation and Reproduction.* Oxford: Oxford University Press.

Wardell, M., T. Steiger, and P. Meiksens. 1999. *Rethinking the labor process.* Albany: State University of New York Press.

Weber, M. 1930. *The Protestant ethic and the spirit of capitalism.* London: Routledge, 2001.

Wenger, E. 1998. *Communities of practice: Learning, meaning, and identity.* Cambridge: Cambridge University Press.

White, J. 1997. *Education and the end of work.* London: Cassell.

Wiener, N. 1948. *Cybernetics, or control and communication in the animal and the machine.* New York: Wiley & Sons. 2nd ed., Cambridge, MA: MIT Press, 1961.

Williams, K. 2001. Business as Usual, *Economy and Society* 30 (4):399–411.

Wilson, W. 1980. *The declining significance of race.* Chicago: University of Chicago Press.

———. 1987. *The truly disadvantaged.* Chicago: University of Chicago Press.

Winch, C. 2000. *Education, work and social capital: Towards a new conception of vocation education.* London: Routledge.

Wittgenstein, L. 1953. *Philosophical investigations*. Trans. G. E. M. Anscombe. New York: Macmillan.

World Bank. 1994. Higher education: The lessons of experience. www-wds.world bank.org/servlet/WDSContentServer/WDSP/IB/2000/07/19/000009265_397 0128113653/Rendered/PDF/multi_page.pdf (accessed November 10, 2005).

———. 1998. *World development report: Knowledge for development*. Oxford: Oxford University Press.

———. 2002. *Constructing knowledge societies: New challenges for tertiary education*. Washington, DC: The International Bank for Reconstruction and Development, World Bank. www1.worldbank.org/education/pdf/Constructing%20Knowledge %20Societies.pdf (accessed November 10, 2005).

Zappia, C. 1999. The economics of information, market socialism and Hayek's legacy. *History of Economic Ideas* 7 (1–2): 105–38. www.econ-pol.unisi.it/ pubdocenti/HEI99.pdf (accessed November 10, 2005).

Zysman, J. 1999. The digital economy in international perspective: Common construction or regional rivalry. e-conomy.berkeley.edu/events/deip/summary .html#John%20Zysman.

Index

About the Authors

Michael A. Peters is professor of education at the University of Illinois at Urbana-Champaign. He held a chair as research professor and professor of education at the University of Glasgow (2000–2005), as well as positions as adjunct professor at the University of Auckland and the Auckland University of Technology (New Zealand). He is the author or editor of more than thirty books and the editor of the international journals *Educational Philosophy and Theory, Policy Futures in Education*, and *eLearning*. His research interests include educational philosophy, education and public policy, and social and political theory. His most recent books include *Deconstructing Derrida* (2005), *Education, Globalization and the State in an Age of Terrorism* (2005); *Poststructuralism and Educational Research* (2004); *Critical Theory and the Human Condition* (2004), and *Futures of Critical Theory* (2004).

A.C. (Tina) Besley is currently a visiting research associate in the Department of Educational Policy Studies, University of Illinois, Urbana-Champaign. Formerly, following four years as a research fellow, she was lecturer in the Department of Educational Studies at the University of Glasgow, Scotland, UK. Tina is a New Zealander with degrees in counseling and education and has been a secondary school teacher and a school counselor. Tina's research interests include youth issues, in particular, notions of self and identity and contemporary problems; school counseling; education policy; education philosophy; and the work of Michel Foucault and poststructuralism. She is on the editorial boards of six academic journals,